us GO AHEAD!

Kate

Thomas

Jessica

Ravi

Holidays on the farm

Rocky Ricky Ralfi

Cindy Justin

and, in CALIFORNIA …

GO AHEAD

Go Ahead 6

für die Jahrgangsstufe 6 an sechsstufigen bayerischen Realschulen

erarbeitet von	John Eastwood, Street, Somerset
	Klaus Berold, Kulmbach
	Elke Zahn, Bayreuth
unter beratender Mitarbeit von	Werner Epp, Kempten
	Renate Grieshaber, Kempten
	Renate Heidemeier, Eichstätt
	Jürgen Hempel, Regensburg
	Jürgen Kanhäuser, Rain
Verlagsredaktion	Helga Holtkamp, Stefanie Oberhellmann
redaktionelle Mitarbeit	Tom Parkinson, Fritz Preuss, Barbara Swayne
Design und Layout	David Graham, London (*Units*)
	James Abram (*Anhänge*)

Bestellnummer 25080

zum Schülerbuch sind erhältlich **Workbook** 25098 **CDs** 25110

Hinweise zu weiteren Bestandteilen im Lehrerhandbuch.
Bild-, Text- und Musikquellen auf Seite 167.

1. Auflage ✔

5.   4.   3.   2.   1.
04   03   02   01   00

© 2000 Cornelsen & Oxford University Press GmbH & Co., Berlin

Das Werk und seine Teile sind urheberrechtlich geschützt.
Jede Verwertung in anderen als den gesetzlich zugelassenen Fällen
bedarf deshalb der vorherigen schriftlichen Einwilligung des Verlags.

Druck und Weiterverarbeitung	Freiburger Graphische Betriebe
Vertrieb	Cornelsen Verlag, Berlin

ISBN 3-8109-2508-X

Um die Wiederverwendbarkeit zu gewährleisten, darf in dieses Buch nicht hineingeschrieben werden.
Gedruckt auf chlorfrei gebleichtem Papier ohne Dioxinbelastung der Gewässer.

CONTENTS / INHALT

Page Unit   What we learn in this unit

LIVING IN LONDON

4	W & P	A–B, Song
6	Intro 1	Sit 1–2, Ex 1–4
8	Text 1	**The Circle Line**, Ex 5–8
9	Com	**Saying what you want**, Ex 9
10	Act 1	
11	Intro 2	Sit 3–5, Ex 10–17
14	Text 2	**They look very real**, Ex 18–20, List Ex 21
16	Act 2	

Comparison of adjectives: *fast – faster – fastest, interesting – more interesting – most interesting*

Irregular comparison: *good – better – best, bad – worse – worst*
Comparison with *than, as … as*

2 IN THE COUNTRY

18	W & P	A–B, Song
20	Intro 1	Sit 1–3, Ex 1–4
22	Text 1	**Easy to ride**, Ex 5–7
23	Com	**Saying how you liked something**, Ex 8
24	Act 1	
25	Intro 2	Sit 4–5, Ex 9–14
28	Text 2	**Ring 999**, Ex 15–17, List Ex 18
30	Act 2	
32	PYE	1–7, List 8

Simple past: *be – was/were*
Regular, irregular verbs: *ask – asked, drive – drove*

Simple past: *I didn't … , Did you … ?* (negative, questions)

FINDING OUT

34	W & P	A–E
36	Intro 1	Sit 1, Ex 1–4
38	Text 1	**The baseball project**, Ex 5–7, List Ex 8
40	Act 1	
42	Intro 2	Sit 2–3, Ex 9–11
44	Text 2	**Remember me?** Ex 12–15
45	Com	**Asking for information**, Ex 16
46	Act 2	

Future with 'going to': *I'm going to leave*
(positive, negative, questions)

Possessive pronouns: *mine, yours, …*

CONTENTS / INHALT

| Page | Unit | | What we learn in this unit |

 SPECIAL DAYS

Page	Unit		
48	W & P	A–D	
50	Intro 1	Sit 1–2, Ex 1–4	Present perfect: *I've walked* (positive, negative, questions)
52	Text 1	**The gunpowder plot**, Ex 5–7	Irregular verbs: *write – wrote – written*
54	Com	**Asking what the matter is**, Ex 8	
55	Act 1		
56	Intro 2	Sit 3–4, Ex 9–13	Present perfect with *already/just/yet*
58	Text 2	**The one o'clock gun**, Ex 14–16, List Ex 17, Ex 18	*Some, any* (positive, negative, questions)
60	Act 2		
62	PYE	1–5, List 6	

 HAVE YOU GOT A JOB?

Page	Unit		
64	W & P	A–D	
66	Intro 1	Sit 1–2, Ex 1–4	Future with 'will': *It will rain tomorrow.* (positive, negative, questions)
68	Text 1	**Bad news**, Ex 5–7	
69	Com	**Reacting to news**, Ex 8	
70	Act 1		
71	Intro 2	Sit 3–4, Ex 9–13	Present perfect – simple past
74	Text 2	**The garage sale**, Ex 14–16, List Ex 17	Present perfect with *ever/never*
76	Act 2		

 WHAT'S ON TELEVISION?

Page	Unit		
78	W & P	A–D	
80	Intro 1	Sit 1, Ex 1–3	Past progressive: *was dancing* (positive, negative, questions)
82	Text 1	**Holiday Monday**, Ex 4–6	
83	Com	**Describing people**, Ex 7	
84	Act 1		
86	Intro 2	Sit 2–3, Ex 8–10	Adverbs of manner: *nervously*
88	Text 2	**Can you do me a favour?** Ex 11–14, List Ex 15	Special forms
90	Act 2		
92	PYE	1–6, List 7	

CONTENTS / INHALT

Page   Unit   What we learn in this unit

THE GOLDEN STATE

94	W & P	A–B, Song
96	Intro 1	Sit 1–2, Ex 1–3
98	Text 1	**Welcome to California**, Ex 4–6, List Ex 7
100	Act 1	
102	Intro 2	Sit 3–4, Ex 8–12
104	Text 2	**Kirsty's diary**, Ex 13–17
106	Com	**Explaining words**, Ex 18–19
107	Act 2	
108	Poems	

Much, many, a lot of / lots of (positive, negative, questions)

Relative clauses

110	British and American English	Britisches und amerikanisches Englisch
111	Grammatical terms	Grammatikalische Fachausdrücke
113	Classroom phrases	Redewendungen für den Unterricht
114	Grammar	Grammatikanhang
131	Using the vocabulary list	Erklärung des Wörterverzeichnisses
132	English sounds	Erklärung der Lautschriftzeichen
133	Unit vocabulary list	Wörterverzeichnis
152	Irregular verbs	Unregelmäßige Verben
154	List of names	Liste der Namen
172	Index	Alphabetisches Wörterverzeichnis

W & P = Words and pictures   Intro = Introduction
Act   = Activities   Com   = Communication
Ex   = Exercise   Sit   = Situation
List = Listening   PYE   = Practise your English

UNIT 1
LIVING IN LONDON

WORDS AND PICTURES

Covent Garden has some interesting shops and cafés. And you can often see fire-eaters or jugglers there.

A 001 London is a very big city. It's a lively and exciting place. Most of the famous sights are in the centre. You can take a bus tour of the sights. When you see something interesting, you can leave the bus and visit it. Later on you can get on the bus again.

The Houses of Parliament are by the River Thames. The bell in the tower is called Big Ben.

The Tower of London is an old palace and prison. And not far away is the famous Tower Bridge.

In Hyde Park you can take a boat on a lake called the Serpentine. You can do in-line skating, too.

WORDS AND PICTURES

Buckingham Palace is where the Queen lives when she's in London.

The Millennium Dome is by the river, too. It's in Greenwich, in south-east London.

B When you're in London, you can also get around on the Underground ('the tube'). This is a tube map of central London with the names of the different lines.

Which tube lines do you use for these journeys?

➡ Paddington to Victoria?
  The Circle Line.

➡ Queensway to Regent's Park?
  The Central Line and the Bakerloo Line.

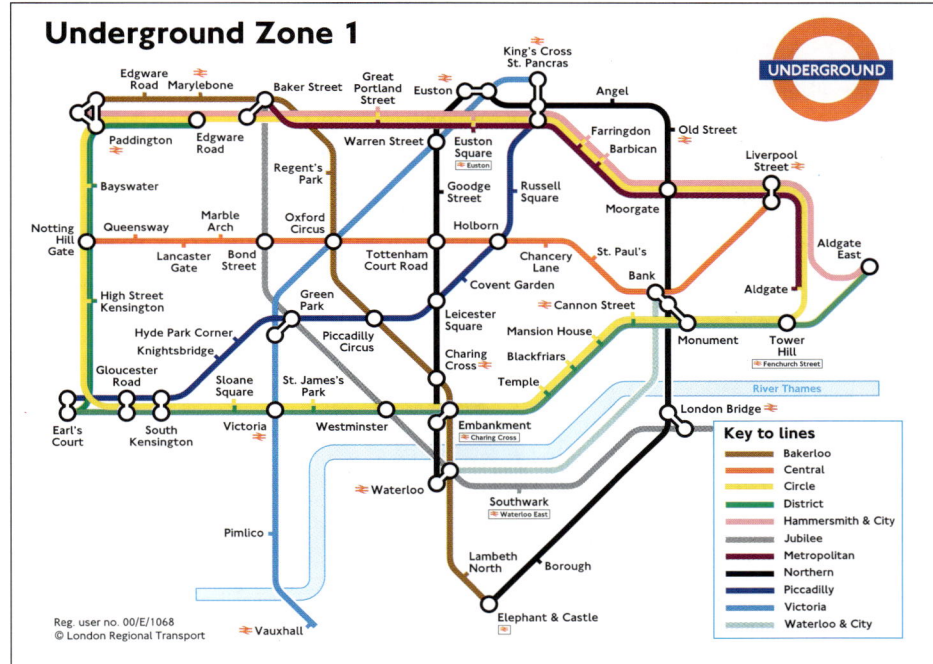

Then ask a partner about tube journeys in London.

1 Green Park to Baker Street?
2 King's Cross to Victoria?
3 Bond Street to Bank?
4 Covent Garden to South Kensington?
5 Blackfriars to Piccadilly Circus?
6 Tower Hill to Marble Arch?
7 Oxford Circus to Westminster?
8 Aldgate to Paddington?
9 Waterloo to Leicester Square?

SONG London Bridge is falling down

London Bridge is falling down,
Falling down, falling down.
London Bridge is falling down,
My fair lady.

2 We must build it up again, ...
3 Build it up with wood and clay, ...
4 Wood and clay can wash away, ...
5 Build it up with bricks and stones, ...

five 5

Unit 1   **INTRODUCTION 1**

004

SITUATION 1

the Fosters

Do you remember the Foster family? There's Alison Foster and her husband Richard. Mr and Mrs Foster have got two daughters, Emily and Sophie, and a son, Adam. And there's the dog Rusty, of course. They all live in Wimbledon in south-west London. Emily, Sophie and Adam have got an Uncle Steve and an Aunt Monika. Steve Mitchell is Mrs Foster's brother. Uncle Steve and Aunt Monika have got a son called Thomas. He's the Foster children's cousin. Steve's wife is German, and the family live near Augsburg in Bavaria. At the moment they are on holiday. They are staying with the Fosters in Wimbledon.

the Mitchells

EXERCISE 1

Look at this family tree and make sentences about the Fosters and the Mitchells.

Richard Foster   Alison (Mitchell) Foster   Steve Mitchell   Monika (Haas) Mitchell

Emily   Sophie   Adam   **Thomas**

➡ Sophie / Thomas
  Sophie is Thomas's cousin.
➡ Thomas / Steve and
  Monika Mitchell
  Thomas is Steve and
  Monika Mitchell's son.
1 Emily / Adam

2 Steve Mitchell / Thomas
3 Monika Mitchell / Emily
4 Sophie / Richard and
  Alison Foster
5 Richard Foster / Thomas
6 Alison Foster / Sophie
7 Thomas / Adam
8 Steve Mitchell / Alison Foster

EXERCISE 2

Ben and Kirsty are asking Adam about his cousin Thomas. Complete their questions.

Ben   How old is your cousin?
Adam He's twelve.
Ben   … speak English?
Adam Yes, his English is really good. His dad is English.
Kirsty … staying at your house?
Adam Yes, he's here with his parents.
Ben   … like football?
Adam Yes, he does. He's a good footballer.

Kirsty … like Thomas?
Adam   Yes, I do. He's great.
Kirsty … got a girlfriend?
Adam   Questions, questions. I don't know. But he's coming now, so we can ask him. Thomas, … got a girlfriend?
Thomas Er –
Kirsty Well, I must go now. See you!

INTRODUCTION 1

SITUATION 2

I've got the nicest shoes.

Be careful with the spelling.

London is the biggest, liveliest and most exciting city in England. A lot of tourists visit London and see the sights. One of the most popular places for tourists is Madame Tussaud's, a museum of waxworks of famous people.

Madame Tussaud's isn't cheap. It's one of the most expensive sights in London. It also has the longest queues – you usually wait 45 minutes. It's quickest if you go late in the day. The latest time you can go in is half past five.

late → latest	quick → quickest
big → biggest	expensive → most expensive
lively → liveliest	
	→ page 114-115

EXERCISE 3

Look again at Situation 2. Find words with *est* on the end and words with *most* in front of them. Write them in two groups like this.

> 1 biggest   2 most exciting
> ...   ...

Look at the words with *est* on the end. Are they long or short?

EXERCISE 4

Complete these sentences about London. Use the correct form of the word.

▶▶ London is the (large) city in England.
   London is the largest city in England.
▶▶ Most people also think it's the (interesting).
   Most people also think it's the most interesting.
1 The (popular) sights are in the centre.
2 If you want to see all the sights, a bus tour is the (quick) way.
3 The Millennium Dome is London's (new) sight.
4 But maybe the Tower is the (famous).
5 The Tower and Madame Tussaud's are two of the (expensive) sights in London.
6 Baker Street is the (near) tube station to Madame Tussaud's.

Now complete these sentences in the same way. Say what you think.

7 I think … is the (interesting) thing on television.
8 … is the (famous) person in Germany.
9 The (nice) place for a holiday is … .
10 I think … is the (difficult) school subject, and … is the (easy).

Unit 1   TEXT 1

The Circle Line

006

Sophie and Adam are going to Madame Tussaud's with their cousin Thomas. Mrs Foster is driving them.

5 **Mum**   I'm taking you to South Kensington tube station. Take a Circle Line train to Baker Street.
Adam   Yes, mum. We know.
10 **Mum**   Have you got the money for the tickets, Sophie?
Sophie   Yes, mum. Don't worry. I am thirteen, you know. I can look after two little boys.
15 **Adam**   You aren't looking after us. We aren't babies. Don't listen to her, Thomas.
Mum   Come on. No arguments.
Thomas   Do you think there are waxworks of famous Germans? If there are,
20   I'd like to see them.
Mum   Of course there are German people in there.
Sophie   I want to see the Chamber of Horrors. That's the most interesting part.
25 **Adam**   Look at all these cars. It's very busy today.
Mum   Friday is the busiest day of the week.

Twenty minutes later they are at the station.

Mum   Well, here we are – South Kensington.
30   Have a good time.
Sophie   Thanks, mum. Bye!
Mum   Circle Line, don't forget.

Sophie, Adam and Thomas are in the tube train.

Sophie   Have you got your ticket, Thomas?
Thomas   Yes, it's in my pocket.   35
Adam   Sophie, you're doing what mum does. Don't worry. We've all got our tickets.
Thomas   No arguments, remember.
Adam   OK, sorry.
Sophie   How far is it to Baker Street?   40
Adam   Where are we now?
Thomas   This is Victoria.
Sophie   We can see on the map. ... Oh, no! We're going the wrong way.
Thomas   But this is the Circle Line.   45
Sophie   Yes, but we're going the wrong way. We're going this way, look. Baker Street is the other way.
Thomas   Yes, but the train goes round in a circle. We can go round   50 this way to Baker Street.
Sophie   But that's too far. Quick, let's get out, we must go the other way.
Adam   How old are you, Sophie? Thirteen? You're hopeless. You're the most   55 hopeless sister in the world.

EXERCISE 5

Look again at the text and put in the right form of the verb.

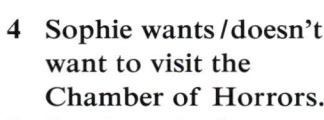

➡ Thomas is / isn't with his cousins.
   Thomas **is** with his cousins.
1 They are / aren't going on the bus.
2 Sophie has / hasn't got the money for the tickets.
3 Thomas is / isn't looking forward to the waxworks. 
4 Sophie wants / doesn't want to visit the Chamber of Horrors.
5 On the train they have / haven't all got their tickets.
6 Sophie says they can / can't get a train back the other way.

EXERCISE 6

Can you say it in English?
The sentences are all in the text.

⇒ Hab keine Angst.
  Don't worry.
1 Keine Streitereien.
2 Heute ist viel los.
3 Hast du deine Fahrkarte?
4 Wo sind wir jetzt?
5 Wir fahren in die falsche Richtung.
6 Schnell! Steigen wir aus.

EXERCISE 8

What's the opposite? Put in the missing words.

⇒ Sophie hasn't got a big brother, but she's got a little brother.
1 Remember your ticket. Don't … it.
2 We aren't going the right way. We're on the … train.
3 Don't go that way. It's … way.
4 You must be quick. You're too … .
5 Madame Tussaud's isn't far. It's very … the tube station.

EXERCISE 7

Put in these words: *looking after, looking at, looking for, looking forward to*.

1 Thomas is … the map.
2 Adam and Ben are … their football.
3 Kirsty is … the basketball game.
4 Royston is … his neighbour's dog.
5 Amy is … her pen.
6 Mrs Lester is … her watch.

Saying what you want

Sagen, was man will

I want a new bike for my birthday.
I'd like an orange juice, please.
I want to play this computer game.
I'd like to look around the Tower.

Want and would like mean the same thing, but would like is usually more polite.
I like and I'd like do not mean the same thing.

I like pizza. = Ich esse gern Pizza.
I'd like a pizza. = Ich hätte gern eine Pizza.

EXERCISE 9

007

COMMUNICATION

What are they saying? Use *I want to* and *I'd like to* and these words: *buy this magazine, play table tennis, take your photo, watch MTV*.   ⇒ I'd like to watch MTV.

TEXT 1

nine 9

Unit 1   **ACTIVITIES 1**

1 SIGHTSEEING TOUR

008

The Fosters and Thomas are on a sightseeing tour of London. Listen to them and find the places they are visiting. In your group make a list and write the name of the place.

➡ The Rock Circus
1 … 2 … 3 … 4 … 5 …
Which place is the most interesting? Which sight would you like to visit?

2 AROUND THE WORLD

Now think of a place you would like to visit. It can be in Britain or in Germany or in America or in … . In your group write about the place but don't use the name. Give the piece of paper to your teacher. He or she gives it to another group. Can they find the place?

➡ It's a big tower. It's in a city in France. You can walk up, but there are also lifts. There is a nice view from the top.
– Is it The Eiffel Tower?
– Yes, it is.

3 WHO IS IT?

Think of a girl or a boy from your class and tell us three things about her or him. Can the other pupils say who it is?

➡ It's a boy. His sweater is red and blue and he comes from Memmingen.

➡ It's a girl. Her shirt is green and she likes The Bill Cosby Show.

INTRODUCTION 2

SITUATION 3

Thomas I like London. It's a great place.
Sophie Is it nicer than Augsburg?
Thomas It's different. Augsburg is much smaller. London is bigger and busier and more exciting.
Sophie Let's cross the road here. Thomas! Wait!
Thomas Oh, dear. London is more dangerous, too.

small → smaller
nice → nicer
exciting → more exciting
big → bigger
busy → busier

→ page 114-115

Remember the spelling.

EXERCISE 10

Some words have *er* on the end (*small* → *smaller*), and some have *more* in front of them (*exciting* → *more exciting*). Do you think there is a rule about which words can have *more* in front of them?

EXERCISE 11

Make sentences with *than*. Use these words: *big, dangerous, exciting, expensive, hot, hungry.*

➡ The tea is hotter than the coffee.
➡ A go-kart race is more exciting than a maths lesson.

EXERCISE 12

Make sentences about the sights of London.

➡ the Tower of London / Madame Tussaud's / big
The Tower of London is bigger than Madame Tussaud's.
➡ the Houses of Parliament / the British Museum / popular
The British Museum is more popular than the Houses of Parliament.

	big	expensive	popular	nice
Buckingham Palace	♦♦	♦♦♦	♦♦	♦♦
Madame Tussaud's	♦	♦♦♦	♦♦♦	♦♦
The British Museum	♦♦	♦	♦♦	♦♦♦
Covent Garden	♦	♦	♦♦	♦♦♦
The Tower of London	♦♦	♦♦♦	♦♦♦	♦♦♦
The Houses of Parliament	♦♦	♦	♦	♦♦
Hyde Park	♦♦♦	♦	♦♦	♦♦♦

Can you make more sentences?

I'm bigger than you!

Unit 1   **INTRODUCTION 2**

SITUATION 4

010
Outside Baker Street tube station they can walk to Madame Tussaud's.

Adam   What's your favourite football team, Thomas?
Thomas Bayern München, of course. They're the best team in Europe.
Adam   Maybe in Germany but not in Europe. Manchester United are better than Bayern Munich.
Thomas What? How can you say that?
Adam   Well, I support United. I say they're the best.
Thomas So you don't support Wimbledon?
Adam   Wimbledon? They're a joke. They must be the worst team in the world. I can't think of a worse team.

EXERCISE 13

Amy and Kirsty are talking about the weather. Complete the dialogue. Put in these words: *better, best, worse, worst*.

good → better → best
bad → worse → worst
→ page 115

Amy   Look at the rain.
Kirsty It's … than before.
Amy   It's Saturday, and this is the … weather of the week. The … day was Wednesday, a school day – that was really nice. And now it's raining.
Kirsty Maybe there's … weather on the way. Then we can go out on Sunday.

EXERCISE 14

Look at the advertisements. Which slogans go with which pictures?

▶ Our T-shirts are nicer than all the others. ▶ F
1 Food is cheaper if you come to us.
2 Our watches are the most popular in the world.
3 You can take better photos.
4 Our coffee is the best.
5 We give you a more interesting time.
6 It's the fastest on the road.

Think of two more slogans. Draw pictures in your exercise book and write a sentence for each picture.

INTRODUCTION 2

SITUATION 5

Adam   This queue is very long.
Sophie   It isn't as long as the last time I was here. And the weather isn't as bad today.
Thomas   No, and that's good because my parents are looking around Kew Gardens.
Adam   Gardens are boring. They aren't as interesting as waxworks.

EXERCISE 15

Look at the pictures and make sentences with *as … as*. Use these words: *expensive, far, fast, long, old, tired*.

➡ The car is as long as the bus.
1   The boy is … the girl.
2   Number 3 is … number 7.
3   The girl … the boy.
4   The hospital … the swimming-pool.
5   The map … .

EXERCISE 16

Make five sentences.

April		long		Mr Bean.
Augsburg		expensive		an hour.
A school day	isn't as	funny	as	a computer.
Baywatch		hot		a holiday.
A minute		nice		July.
A bike		big		Munich.

A raven isn't as fast as a plane.

➡ **page 115**

➡ April isn't as hot as July.

Can you think of more sentences with *isn't as … as*?

EXERCISE 17

Complete the dialogue. Put in these words: *as, best, more, most, than* (2x).

Ben   It's Adam's birthday on the 10th.
Mum   And it's your birthday on the 17th. Adam is a week older … you.
Ben   Yes, but what can I buy him?
Mum   Oh, I don't know. A book?
Ben   No, something … exciting – like a computer game. But that's too expensive.
Jade   I know. A Manchester United shirt. Adam supports Manchester United.
Ben   Don't be silly. That's more expensive … a computer game.
Mum   What about a CD? That isn't as expensive … a football shirt.
Jade   What about a pet rabbit?
Ben   Yes, good. That's the … idea. I can give him our rabbit. He can have Softy.
Jade   No, he can't. Ben, you're the … awful brother in England.

Unit 1 **TEXT 2**

They look very real

Sophie, Adam and Thomas are at Madame Tussaud's.

Sophie   Oh, here's Brad Pitt. I like him.
Thomas   They all look very real, these waxworks.
Sophie   Yes, they do.
5 *Thomas*   Oh, here's Thomas Gottschalk.
Adam   Who's he?
Thomas   He's a television presenter. He's famous. He's the biggest star on German television.
Sophie   I can take a photo of you with him.
10 *Thomas*   Good idea. Come on, Adam. You stand there.
Sophie   That's good. Smile! Say 'cheese'.

In the next rooms there are some sports people. Then there are film stars and singers.

Thomas   Look at these here.
15 *Adam*   Oh, yes. There's Marilyn Monroe.
Sophie   And Elvis Presley with his guitar.

There's a room full of kings, queens and presidents.

Adam   Here's the royal family.
Thomas   They don't look very happy.
20 *Adam*   The Queen is the worst. She looks really fed up.
Sophie   Where's Princess Diana?
Thomas   She's over there, look. Why is she on her own?
Sophie   Poor Diana.
Adam   Never mind about her. I can see the Beatles. They're more interesting than Diana.
25

Now there's the Chamber of Horrors. There are waxworks of famous criminals and some scenes of torture.

Sophie   Well, what do you think?
Adam   I think, it was boring.
30 *Thomas*   Boring? It was horrible. Those torture scenes.
Sophie   Of course it was horrible. That's why it's called the Chamber of Horrors.
Adam   Where are we going now?
Sophie   I think that's the end. What time is it?
35 *Adam*   I don't know. Four o'clock?
Sophie   It must be later than that.
Thomas   We can ask that woman behind the desk … Excuse me, can you tell me the time, please? … Excuse me, …
40 *Adam*   Thomas, you idiot.
Sophie   It's a waxwork, Thomas.
Thomas   Oh dear! They look very real, you know.

EXERCISE 18

That's wrong! What are the correct sentences?

➡ The three kids are looking at pictures.
  The three kids are looking at waxworks.
1 Thomas Gottschalk plays football for Germany.
2 Adam, Thomas and Sean Connery are in Sophie's photo.
3 Sophie says 'Say crisps.'
4 Elvis Presley has got his piano.
5 The Queen looks very happy.
6 Princess Diana is with the Queen.
7 In the Chamber of Horrors there are some very nice scenes.
8 The woman behind the desk is real.

EXERCISE 20

Make sentences from the table about famous people.

| Michael Owen
Brad Pitt
Thomas Gottschalk
Diana
John F. Kennedy
Marilyn Monroe
Elvis Presley
Jürgen Klinsmann
Naomi Campbell | is
was | a
an | American
English
German | president.
model.
footballer.
singer.
TV presenter.
film star.
princess. |

➡ Michael Owen is an English footballer.

Can you talk about other famous people? Work with a partner. One of you says a name, and the other says who the person is.

➡ *Frank* Leo DiCaprio.
  Ute He's an American film star.

EXERCISE 19

Listen and repeat. [p]   [b]

pig   big

Listen to the words. Are the missing letters 'p' or 'b'? Write the words in your exercise books with the correct letters.

*ell • stu*id • chea* •
*o*ular • grou* • *u*il •
*eo*le • *ig • *a*y •
*ro*lem • *ig

Now read the words and check.

You can play 'Who am I?' Imagine you are a famous person. The other kids ask questions and find out who you are.

Ingo Who am I?
Karin Are you German?
Ingo No, I'm not.
Markus Are you English?
Ingo Yes, I am.
Markus Do you play football?
Ingo No, I don't.
Tanja Do you sing in a band?
Ingo Yes, I do.
Heike Are you one of the Rolling Stones?
Ingo Yes, I am.
Heike Are you Mick Jagger?
Ingo Yes, I am.

EXERCISE 21

Listening

Adam and Thomas are in town together. Which picture shows what they can see?

Unit 1   **ACTIVITIES 2**

1 THAT WAS ME!

Make a poster about yourself. Don't put your name on. Use a baby photo or one where you were a little child. Number the posters and put them up in the classroom. Now make lists and find as many names as possible. You can walk round the class and ask the other pupils questions:

➡ Who is your favourite pop group?
– All Saints.
Is your poster number 5?
– No, it isn't. Football isn't my favourite hobby.

favourite hobby: football
favourite film star: Will Smith
favourite pop group: All Saints
favourite food: chicken and chips

2 POEMS

Crocodile ~ Anon.

If you see a crocodile,
don't you try to hurt him;
don't think how he can smile,
be careful when you tease him.

'cause as he sleeps there on the Nile,
he thinner gets and thinner;
and when you see a crocodile,
he's ready for his dinner.

My dog ~ by C. Norton

I have a dog,
his name is Jack,
his coat is white
with spots of black.

I take him out
'most every day,
such fun we have,
we run and play.

3 I SPY WITH MY LITTLE EYE …

Find something blue, green, white, … in your classroom and just tell us its colour:

'I spy with my little eye something red.'
The other pupils must find out what it is:
'Is it Dominik's sweater?'
'No, it isn't.'
'Are you thinking of
    Mrs Berghammer's bag?'
'Yes, that's it.'

ACTIVITIES 2

🔴 SONG 4 **BUDDY HOLLY**
015

Do you know Buddy Holly? No? He was a famous singer, who died in a plane accident in 1959. Now there is a musical about him in London. Listen to the song and sing it if you like.

Everyday ~ by Buddy Holly

*Everyday, it's a-getting closer,
going faster than a roller coaster,
love like yours will surely come my way,
hey hey hey ...*

*Everyday, it's a-getting faster,
everyone says go ahead and ask her,
love like yours will surely come my way,
hey hey hey ...*

*Everyday seems a little longer,
every way love's a little stronger,
come what may, do you ever long for
true love from me?*

seventeen **17**

UNIT 2
IN THE COUNTRY

WORDS AND PICTURES

A Mr and Mrs Jewell have got four children – Carl, Lauren, Kirsty and Sam. In the summer holidays the family sometimes stay on a farm in the country. Their favourite place is Midway Farm. They stay in a cottage on the farm. They all like it there. But this year Carl and Lauren are staying in London. They are at their grandparents' house.

There are cows and sheep on the farm. The farmer's daughter has got a pony called Mopsy. The family have also got two dogs and three cats. Kirsty likes the farm animals and the pets. She thinks life on the farm is wonderful, much better than life in Wimbledon.

cow

sheep

horse

hen

18 eighteen

WORDS AND PICTURES

SONG Old MacDonald
017

Old MacDonald had a farm, e i e i o
And on his farm he had some cows, e i e i o
With a moo-moo here and a moo-moo there
Here a moo, there a moo, everywhere a moo-moo
Old MacDonald had a farm, e i e i o

2 ... some sheep (baa-baa)
3 ... a dog (bow-wow)
4 ... a pig (oink-oink)
5 ... some hens (cluck-cluck)
6 ... a car (rattle-rattle)

B
018

Kirsty and Amy are back at school.
Kirsty is showing Amy some photos.

Kirsty Look, this is a lovely view. It's from the tree house in one of the old apple trees.
Amy Yes, it's lovely. Who is this young man?
Kirsty Oh, he's a neighbour. He's riding one of the farmer's horses. And this is his dog. It's lying on the ground.
Amy Oh yes, it looks like a nice dog. And that, is that a deer?
Kirsty Yes, it's drinking from the stream. And can you see the birds in the air?
Amy Yes, they look like swallows. There aren't any swallows in Wimbledon. And where is this?
Kirsty It's in the farm garden. There are so many flowers. I don't know all their names.

What can you see in these photos?
Say what there is in these pictures.

Unit 2   **INTRODUCTION 1**

SITUATION 1

Oliver Where were you yesterday afternoon? You weren't at home.
Ben I was at the swimming-pool with Adam. Kirsty and Amy were there, too. It was great.
Oliver Was Adam with his cousin Thomas?
Ben No, he wasn't. Thomas is back in Germany now. Adam was on his own.

| I he she it | was | you we they | were |

→ page 116

EXERCISE 1

Complete the dialogue.
Put in *was, wasn't, were* or *weren't*.

Amy You **weren't** at home yesterday afternoon.
Kirsty No, I … . I … at school. It's basketball on Wednesdays.
Amy Oh, of course. … Lehka there?
Kirsty No, she … . She doesn't play basketball. Only six people … there yesterday. Some people … there because they … ill. But there … a new girl called Holly. She's very good.
Amy Do you know where Lehka … yesterday?
Kirsty No, I don't. Two of her friends … in that new hamburger place after school, but Lehka … with them.

SITUATION 2

Lehka writes her diary every day. This is her diary for last Sunday.

Sunday
I stayed at home all day. I worked on my English project. I wanted to go out, but it rained all afternoon. When at last it stopped, it was too late. I tidied my room and moved my bed and my desk. The room looks better now. I washed my hair and then I listened to some music. I was in a day-dream. In my day-dream Leo DiCaprio phoned and asked me out to a disco. We danced and everyone watched us. Then someone really phoned, but it wasn't Leo – it was Kirsty with a question about the English project.
I'm looking forward to tomorrow when I can see all my friends again.

Be careful with the spelling.

stay	ed
work	ed
want	ed
rain	ed

→ page 117

Now you can talk about the past.

move	→ moved
stop	→ stopped
tidy	→ tidied

→ page 117

INTRODUCTION 1

EXERCISE 2

Make sentences from the table. ➡ Yesterday evening we watched television.

Yesterday evening we watched	all day.
It was cold, so I closed	at the post office.
Mr Sharma travelled to India	in the park.
On Thursday it rained	in the country.
Yesterday Adam and Ben played football	from the library.
I borrowed this book	on a plane.
I posted the letter	our cousins in Scotland.
Last summer we visited	television.
When she was a girl, Mrs Jewell lived	the window.

EXERCISE 3

Say what happened last Sunday.

➡ Lehka (work) on her English project.
  Lehka **worked** on her English project.
1 Adam and Ben (play) football.
2 Mr Foster (wash) his car.
3 Oliver (walk) to the park.
4 Jessica (listen) to music.
5 Sophie (watch) Star Trek.
6 Amy (visit) her aunt and uncle.
7 Anita (tidy) her room.

SITUATION 3

Amy   We went to Germany in the summer. We stayed in a cottage in a little village in the Black Forest.

Oliver   One weekend we went to Disneyland. We had a great time there.

Royston   We went to Spain. We stayed in a flat by the sea. In the day we played tennis or lay on the beach. Not in the sun of course, because it was really hot.

Adam   We all went to North Wales and stayed in a caravan. We drove around and visited places. And we walked up Snowdon.

Ravi   You're lucky. You all did exciting things. We flew to India and visited our relatives there. That wasn't very exciting.

Not all verbs have 'ed' in the past.

lie → lay
fly → flew
drive → drove
have → had
go → went

→ page 119

EXERCISE 4

Jack is telling Anita about his family's holiday. Put in the verbs in the past.

Jack   We **went** to France. We … in a cottage in the country. It … nice there. And we … to the seaside. We … on the beach. We … mini-golf, too. And we … around in the car and … places. We … a good time.

Anita   We … to India and … my dad's family. We … there for a month.

Unit 2 TEXT 1

Easy to ride

When she was a little girl, Jessica loved animals. Most of all she loved horses. She wanted to live in the country and ride every day. She read hundreds of stories about horses and ponies. She had her first riding lesson when she was six. Her brother Daniel liked riding, too.

Three years ago, the Hursts were on holiday in the New Forest near the south coast, about 85 miles from London. Jessica was ten, Daniel fourteen. They stayed in a cottage on a farm. There are nice places to walk or ride in the forest, and you can see wild ponies and deer.

Mum and dad took Daniel and Jessica to a riding school. They went on rides through the forest with a group of other young people. Jessica thought it was wonderful, the best part of the holiday.

One evening the Hursts went to a place where you can see badgers. The animals come out of their underground home every evening and look for food. There were about twenty people there. They all waited in a shed with a big window. It was dark, but there was a little light on. There was no noise – everyone was very quiet. When she saw the badgers, Jessica thought they were lovely. They were only about two metres away from her. 'I really enjoyed that,' she said, 'I think badgers are really nice animals.'

On Saturday Jessica and Daniel went on their last ride. There were eight people, and their guide was a young woman called Hayley. Jessica's pony was Lollipop. He was nice and quiet and easy to ride. It was a hot day, but it was cool in the forest.

Hayley was at the front of the group with Daniel and Jessica behind her. They rode along the path for about a mile, and then the path went down to a stream. They walked through the stream and then up again on the other side. Then they came out of the forest into more open country.

'How's your pony?' asked Jessica.
'He's fine,' said Daniel. 'How's Lollipop?'
'He's lovely. I like him.' Jessica felt fine on Lollipop. Today Jessica often thinks back to those last moments before the accident happened.

EXERCISE 5

Put in these verbs: *came, had, loved, saw, started, stayed, thought, took, were*.

➥ When Jessica was little, she **loved** horses.
1 At six years old she … her first riding lesson.
2 The family … on a farm in the New Forest.
3 Their parents … Daniel and Jessica to a riding school.
4 Jessica … it was great.
5 One evening they … some badgers only two metres away from them.
6 Their last pony ride … at three o'clock.
7 Daniel and Jessica … behind the guide.
8 After a time they … out of the forest.

TEXT 1

EXERCISE 6

What's the right answer?

➡ Jessica loved a) animals
  b) cars c) computers d) sport.
  Jessica loved animals.
1 Her favourite activity was a) dancing
  b) riding c) running d) walking.
2 The Hursts stayed in a a) caravan
  b) cottage c) flat d) hotel.
3 After dark one evening the family watched some a) badgers b) deer
  c) sheep d) wild ponies.
4 Jessica thought her pony was a) difficult to ride
  b) easy to ride c) too big d) too small.
5 The ride was on the last day of the holiday.
  It was a) a cold afternoon b) a cold morning
  c) a hot afternoon d) a nice evening.
6 On their way through the forest there was
  a) a cottage b) a farm
  c) a stream d) a petrol station.
7 This part of the story ends before the
  a) accident b) argument
  c) party d) stupid idea.

EXERCISE 7

How many words for animals do you know? Draw a word tree and write in the words. (Some words can be in more than one group.)

You can play the animal game. For your homework you write two or three sentences about an animal. Then you say the sentences in class, and the others must guess what the animal is.

➡ *Max* I'm a wild animal. I've got a black and white head. You don't see me in the day because I only come out at night.
 Evi Are you a badger?
 Max Yes, I am.

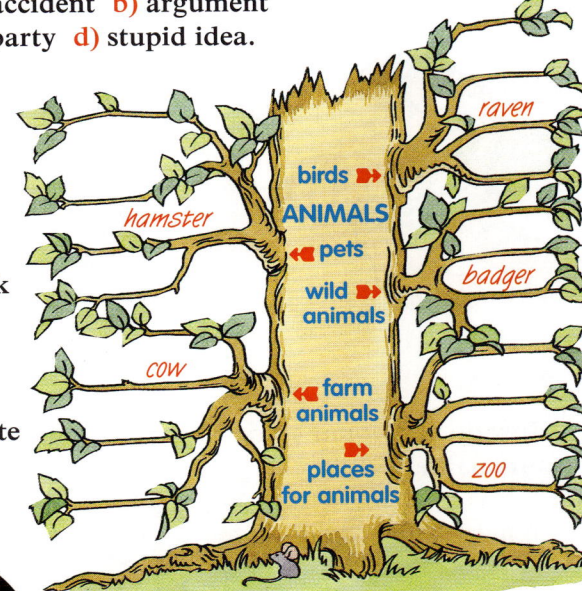

Saying how you liked something

Sagen, wie dir etwas gefiel

Dad How was your riding lesson?
Jessica It was great. I enjoyed it. I had a really nice pony.

Adam How was the film?
Kirsty It was terrible. I hated it. We walked out before the end.

(It was) great / fantastic.
I / We (really) enjoyed it.
I / We had a lovely / wonderful time.

(It was) all right / OK.

(It was) awful / terrible / horrible.
I / We hated it.

COMMUNICATION

EXERCISE 8

Complete the dialogues.

1 *Dad* How was the disco?
  Kirsty It … . I … . They played some … .
2 *Adam* … your flight home?
  Ravi … . I felt … .
3 *Daniel* … the party?
  Jessica … . We had … .
4 *Mum* … the go-kart race?
  Ben …
5 *Royston* … your day at the seaside?
  Lehka … . … rained … .
6 *Mr Foster* … Madame Tussaud's?
  Thomas …

Unit 2 **ACTIVITIES 1**

1 POEMS

At the zoo ~ Clive Sansom

I saw, I saw, I saw
   a lion at the zoo.
I saw, I saw, I saw
   a baby tiger too.
I saw, I saw, I saw
   a great big kangaroo.
I saw, I saw, I saw
   I saw them at the zoo.

Eletelephony ~ Laura Richards

Once there was an elephant,
Who tried to use the telephant –
No! No! I mean an elephone
Who tried to use the telephone –
(Dear me, I am not certain quite
That even now I've got it right.)

Howe'er it was, he got his trunk
Entangled in the telephunk;
The more he tried to get it free,
The louder buzzed the telephee –
(I fear I'd better drop this song
Of elephop and telephong!)

2 RIDDLES

How do you count cows?
With a cowculator.

What do mice do after breakfast?
Mousework.

What time is it when an elephant sits on your car?
Time for a new car.

Why do some cows jump up and down?
Because little cows like milkshakes.

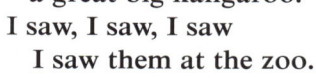

3 CARTOON

Excuse me, Dr Woof, it's Mrs Miller. She's got a problem with her budgie.

Good morning, Dr Woof.

INTRODUCTION 2

SITUATION 4
024

Oliver You look tired.
Ben I feel tired. I didn't sleep last night.
Oliver Oh? Why was that?
Ben I watched a Dracula film before I went to bed.
Oliver So you felt afraid and you didn't sleep. You are an idiot, Ben.
Ben Maybe I slept for an hour or two. I didn't want to get up this morning.
Oliver Are you OK now?
Ben No, I'm hungry. I didn't have breakfast.

I didn't bring my umbrella.

Ben		sleep last night.
The badgers	didn't	see Jessica.
Ravi		enjoy the flight.

→ page 118

EXERCISE 9

Say what people did and didn't do yesterday. Use *ate/didn't eat, went/didn't go, played/didn't play, rode/didn't ride, watched/didn't watch, wore/didn't wear.*

▶ Ravi **ate** a banana. He **didn't eat** an apple.
1 Sophie and Emily …
2 Ben and Adam …
3 Amy …
4 Royston and Lehka …
5 Daniel …

You can play this alphabet game. What did you do yesterday?

Regina I **ate** an ice-cream yesterday.
Christian I **didn't eat** an ice-cream yesterday, but I **bought** a magazine.
Karin I **didn't buy** a magazine yesterday, but I **caught** a bus.
Matthias I didn't …

You can use these verbs: *ate, bought, caught, drank, enjoyed, found, got, helped, interviewed, …*

Unit 2 INTRODUCTION 2

EXERCISE 10

Put in the past forms. But be careful. Sometimes you must use *didn't*.

▶ Oliver sometimes plays basketball after school. Yesterday he played with Ben.
▶ Ravi often wins at chess. But he didn't win his game against Oliver on Wednesday.

1 Amy and Kirsty enjoy discos. But they … the disco last week. It wasn't very good.
2 Mr Jewell usually comes home at six, but yesterday he worked late. He … home at eight.
3 Anita takes a lot of photos. Last weekend she … a photo of her parents.
4 Ben usually walks to school. Yesterday the weather was terrible, so he … . His mum took him in the car.
5 Sophie usually watches television when she gets home. Yesterday she … it because she had a lot of homework.
6 The Sharmas visit relatives most summers. They … their relatives in India last summer.
7 Adam rides his bike most weekends. Last Sunday he and Ben … to the park.
8 The Hursts sometimes go to Spain on holiday, but they … there last summer. They had a canal holiday in England.

SITUATION 5

025

Sophie Did you do your maths homework?
Jessica Yes, I did.
Sophie What did you get for number two?
Jessica I can't remember. Here.
Sophie Oh no. We've got different answers. I'm sure I've got it wrong.
Jessica Why? Maybe I've got it wrong.
Sophie Maybe we've both got it wrong.
Jessica Yes, maybe.
Sophie Did Mr Williams say he wants it today?
Jessica No, he didn't. I think he wants it tomorrow.
Sophie Well, we can look at it later then. Let's go and have our lunch now.

EXERCISE 11

What happened to these people last year? Answer the questions.

▶ Did Adam go to a new school? ~ Yes, he did. He started at Brookfield School.
▶ Did Jade catch her hamster? ~ No, she didn't. She caught her rabbit.
1 Did Adam see Ravi's Arsenal poster? ~ … He saw it on the bedroom wall.
2 Did Kirsty have a birthday party? ~ … All her friends were there.
3 Did Royston give Kirsty a CD? ~ … He gave her a computer game.
4 Did Oliver fall down on his in-line skates? ~ … He fell down in the park.
5 Did the kids find a better place to skate? ~ … They found an old car park.
6 Did Ben say something stupid to Sophie? ~ … He said it to Jessica.
7 Did the Fosters go to Scotland on holiday? ~ … They went to Wales.
8 Did Sophie walk up Snowdon? ~ … She walked all the way to the top.

INTRODUCTION 2

EXERCISE 12

The Mitchells have some friends in Scotland. These friends have got a daughter called Laura. When Thomas was at their house, Laura asked him about their visit to London. Ask her questions.

What			see?
Where	did	you	go in London?
What sights		your parents	like best?
			think of London?
			do in London?

			enjoy the visit?
Did		you	take you to some interesting places?
		your cousins	speak English to your cousins?
			see the sights?
			show you the sights?

➡ *Laura*   Did you enjoy the visit?
   Thomas Yes, I had a … time.
➡ *Laura*   What sights did you see?
   Thomas Sophie and Adam took me to …

Write four or five questions and answers.

EXERCISE 13

Ask a partner about his or her last holiday. You can ask these questions.

Where did you go on your last holiday?
Where … you stay?
… did you do when you were there?
… enjoy the holiday? … weather good?

Make notes and then act the conversation.

EXERCISE 14

Complete the conversation. Put in the questions with *did*.

Amy   You weren't here at the weekend.
         Where did you go? (where / you / go)
Kirsty Oh, sorry I didn't tell you before.
         We were on the farm in the country.
Amy   Oh, that's nice. … (you / enjoy / it)?
Kirsty Yes, it was great. I love all the animals.
         And Mopsy, the pony. She's nice.
Amy   … (you / ride / her)?
Kirsty Yes, I did. Sam did, too.
Amy   … (Lauren and Carl / go / with you)?
Kirsty No, they didn't. They stayed in London.
Amy   … (how / you / get / there)?
Kirsty We all went in the car. It's about two hours.
Amy   And … (how long / you / stay / there)?
Kirsty Just for the weekend. We went on Friday evening.
Amy   … (when / you / get / home)?
Kirsty About eight o'clock last night. I didn't phone you because I was really tired.

Unit 2 TEXT 2

🔴 Ring 999

026

It was a hot afternoon. They came out of the forest and into the sun. Jessica and Daniel were together. Now the trees of the forest were behind them, but there were some bushes by the path. Suddenly on Jessica's left a big bird flew up
5 from one of the bushes. It didn't make much noise, but Lollipop didn't like it. He was afraid. He jumped up and lifted his front legs into the air. Jessica fell back. She fell off the pony and landed on the ground on her back. There was a big stone in the path where Jessica
10 landed. It wasn't her first fall from a pony, but it was a shock. She lay there and didn't move.

'I must get up,' Jessica thought. 'I must get back on the pony.' But she didn't get up. She felt very strange. She lay there and looked at the blue sky.
15 She heard voices. 'Jessica, are you all right?'
'What happened?' 'Where did the pony go?'
'Keep back. Give her some air.'
The last voice was their guide, Hayley. 'Can you get up?' she asked.
'No, I can't,' said Jessica. 'I can't move.' Then Daniel was there. She
20 looked at him. 'Don't move her,' said Hayley. 'She must keep still. Hold her head.'

Someone said, 'I can ride back and ring for an ambulance.' 'It's OK,' said Hayley. 'I've got my mobile. I can ring 999.'

She rang 999 and asked for an ambulance. She explained where they were. 'About a mile from the village there's a camp site. The path is by the camp site, on the right. I don't think you can
25 drive an ambulance along the path, but we're only about two hundred metres from the road.'

Jessica lay still. 'It's all right. The ambulance is coming,' said Hayley. They waited for a long time. At last they heard the noise of the ambulance, and then two paramedics came, a man and a woman. 'Did you move her?' the woman asked Hayley. 'No, we didn't. We kept her still.'

The man spoke to Jessica. 'Don't worry,' he said. 'It's OK. We've got you now.' The
30 paramedics carried Jessica to the ambulance on a stretcher. She can't remember the journey to the hospital in Southampton. She was there for six weeks, and all that time she lay on her back and didn't get up. Most of the time her mum or dad or Daniel was there with her. At first she felt nothing, but then her back hurt. It was a terrible time for Jessica. She felt bored and sad, and sometimes she felt angry. 'Why did this happen to me?' she thought.

35 Later they moved Jessica to a hospital in London. A woman called Charlotte came and talked to her. Charlotte was in a wheelchair. She told Jessica, 'At the moment you feel bad because you can't do things. You can't do sport or go out with your friends. But you can learn these things. You can learn to use a wheelchair and move around. That's what I did. It isn't easy, but you can do it. So things aren't as bad as you think they are.'

40 Three months after the accident, Jessica got out of bed for the first time, and in the New Year her parents drove her back to school, and Sophie pushed her into the classroom in her wheelchair. It was great when all her friends said hello to her.

28 twenty-eight

EXERCISE 15

Answer the questions on the text.

1. Why was Lollipop afraid?
2. What did he do?
3. Where did Jessica land?
4. Did she get back on Lollipop?
5. What did Hayley say to Daniel?
6. What number did Hayley ring on her mobile?
7. How far were they from the nearest road?
8. How did the paramedics get Jessica to the ambulance?
9. Where did the ambulance take her?
10. How did Jessica feel when she was in bed in hospital?
11. Who told Jessica that her situation wasn't really so bad?
12. When did Jessica go back to school?

EXERCISE 16

Find the odd word out and explain why.
Use these words: *actions, animals, in the air, in the country, relatives, school subjects, water.*

➤ aunt, cousin, guide, sister, uncle
It's 'guide'. The others are all **relatives**.

1. cinema, cow, farm, forest, hen
2. bird, cloud, path, plane, swallow
3. ambulance, English, French, maths, music
4. badger, deer, horse, sheep, waxwork
5. lake, river, sea, stream, tree
6. fall, jump, leg, lift, move

EXERCISE 17

Listen and repeat.

[t]	[d]	[ɪd]
work**ed**	phon**ed**	want**ed**

Listen to the words and put them in three groups in your exercise book.

closed • danced • hated • helped •
landed • lifted • listened • lived •
looked • moved • played • posted •
rained • started • stayed • stopped •
tidied • visited • waited • walked •
wanted • washed • watched • worked

[t]	[d]	[ɪd]
danc**ed**	clos**ed**	hat**ed**

Now listen and check.

EXERCISE 18

Listening

Your English friend is ringing you and explaining how you get to her parents' cottage. Which map is right?

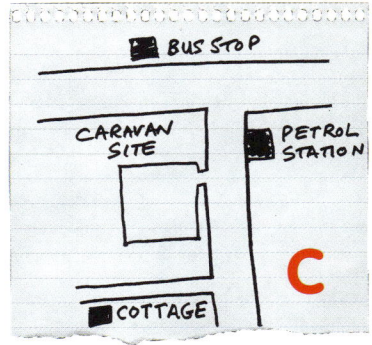

Unit 2 — ACTIVITIES 2 / HALLOWE'EN

1 THE GHOSTS' PARTY

On the night of October 31st, British and American ghosts are free and have a party. Children dress up as ghosts, monsters and witches and when it's dark they go from door to door and ask 'Trick or treat?' So you must give them a 'treat' (apples, oranges, chocolate or money), or they can play a trick on you: put soap on your windows, shout your name, …

Can you think of other tricks?
Which treat would you like to have?

2 HALLOWE'EN LANTERNS

Many people use pumpkin lanterns for Hallowe'en night. Let's make a Hallowe'en lantern!

➤ Take a big, round pumpkin.
➤ Cut off its top.
➤ Spoon out the pumpkin.
➤ Cut a horrible face.
➤ Put a small light in the pumpkin so that it looks like a ghost.

3 HALLOWE'EN PARTY

Have a Hallowe'en party with your friends. First you can give them a card like this:

Would you like some horrible snacks? No problem. Look what we've got:

Come and join us, little witches, monsters and ghosts! Big Hallowe'en party on Friday, 6pm.

4 IT'S TIME FOR A RHYME

This is the night of Hallowe'en,
When all the witches can be seen.
Some are black and some are green.
And some are the colour of a kidney bean.

ACTIVITIES 2

5 MAGIC DRINKS

- For drinks in different, magical colours mix red syrup with different kinds of fruit juice.
- Put it into bottles. You can also make your own labels for the bottles like 'SPIDER'S JUICE' or 'WITCHES' WINE'.
- Put it into glasses with Hallowe'en straws.

6 MINI PUMPKINS

- Cut off the top of an orange in a zig-zag line.
- Spoon out the orange.
- Fill the orange with fruit salad, chocolate or vanilla custard (with blackcurrants).
- Decorate with a Hallowe'en straw.

7 HALLOWE'EN STRAWS

- Take pieces of paper in different colours (black, red, orange, white).
- Fold the paper in half.
- At the fold draw the half outline of a bat, ghost or pumpkin.
- Cut it out: now you've got a bat, ghost or pumpkin.
- Make two holes in the middle and put the straw through.

8 CAKE

- You need two flat cakes. You can buy them or bake them yourself (maybe your teacher or mother can help you to make the cake).
- Spread the first one with red jam.
- Cut triangles out of the second for eyes and nose and a zig-zag mouth.
- Put the second cake onto the first and cut out a zig-zag line above the eyes.

9 DECORATION

A Hallowe'en party is very spooky: decorate the table and room in black and red. You can use plastic animals, spiders (chocolate marshmallows and jelly bananas as legs), red jelly spaghetti, …

thirty-one

Unit 2 **PRACTISE YOUR ENGLISH**

1 Letters and sentences.

uklerc**have**nereyoutygothomerxyourarnuatickettyirik?
husowegetarenukegoingsengthekenrowrongenarywaynzop!
utrothenauwaxworksisgopswatlookreddyoveryfitrealtysis.
tweencansruyoutellerommetgathemorwayottozibakeroastreeteit?

2 Find the words and put them in the right groups in your exercise book.

stoac • tremas • celamanbu • glugerj • scherrett • cogatet • mumuse • toistru • gevilla • esa • gerins • arapicmed • lapace • estorf • repersten

water	country	sights	accident	show
coast				

3 Find word pairs.

aunt • bored • cheap • daughter • everything • interesting • king • last • long • sad • start • tomorrow • worst • young • best • boring • expensive • first • happy • interested • nothing • old • queen • short • son • stop • uncle • yesterday

➡ aunt   uncle

4 Compare Sophie and Oliver. Use these adjectives: *young/old, tall/short, big/small (family), good/bad (at English/maths), cheap/expensive (stereo).*

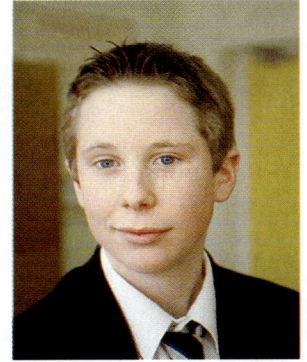

I'm Sophie Foster. I'm 13 and I'm 1.65 metres tall. I've got a brother and a sister. At school I'm terrible at English but I'm good at maths and music. My stereo cost £33.

My name is Oliver Cassidy. I'm 12 years old and I'm 1.59 metres tall. I've got one brother. At school I'm good at English but not very good at maths. I bought a new stereo for £49 last week.

➡ Oliver is younger than Sophie. Sophie is older than Oliver. Oliver isn't as old as Sophie.

5 Find the right past tense forms for these verbs and write them in your exercise book: *bring, buy, catch, eat, fall, ring, speak, wear.*

➡ catch   caught

Then write a sentence with each verb in the past tense.

➡ Our cats caught two mice yesterday.

PRACTISE YOUR ENGLISH

6 What do you think? Answer the questions.

| Who is the oldest? | Which is the nicest? | Which is the most interesting? | Which is the fastest? | Which is the most exciting? |

➡ I think the man is the oldest.

7 Can you talk to your friend? Your partner is your friend.

You

Du triffst deinen Freund/deine Freundin und fragst, wie seine Englisch-Schulaufgabe war.

Du antwortest, dass ihr vor drei Tagen eine furchtbare Mathe-Schulaufgabe hattet.

Du antwortest, dass du es jetzt spielen möchtest und dass du spannende Spiele magst.

Friend

Du antwortest, dass der Text in Ordnung war. Dann fragst du, ob er/sie gestern eine Schulaufgabe geschrieben hat.

Du sagst, dass du gestern ein neues Computerspiel „Verbrecher und Gefängnisse" gespielt hast. Du sagst, dass es toll war.

8 Listen. Where are the animals on the farm?   cows • hens • pony • sheep

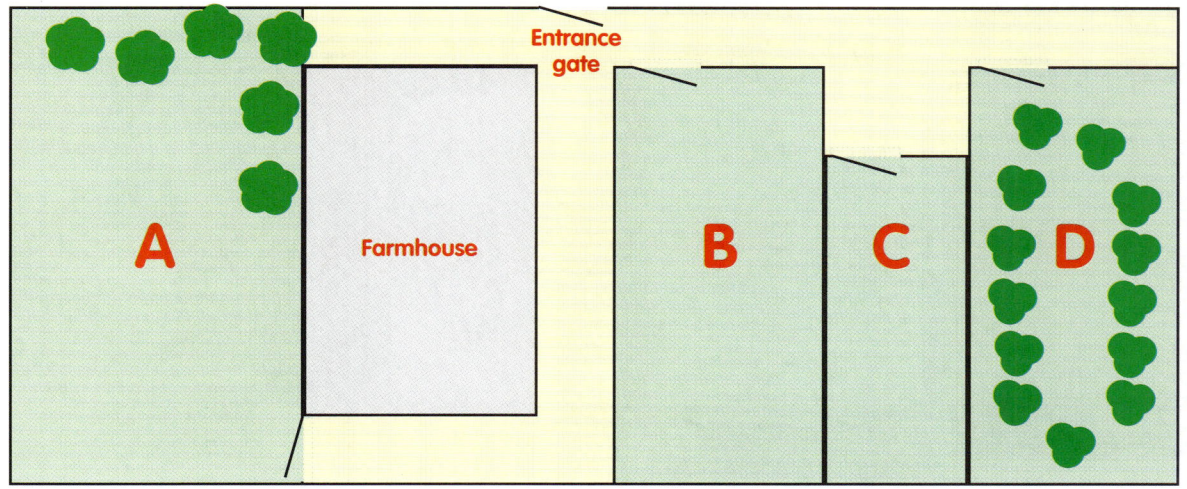

029

UNIT 3
FINDING OUT

WORDS AND PICTURES

A Jessica and Kate are in the computer room at school. They're doing a project about wild animals in Africa. They're finding out about elephants.

B How do you find information with a computer? You can use a CD or a DVD. They have a lot of information on them. You put the disc in the computer and then click on what you want. You can see the information on the screen. You can print out pages, too.

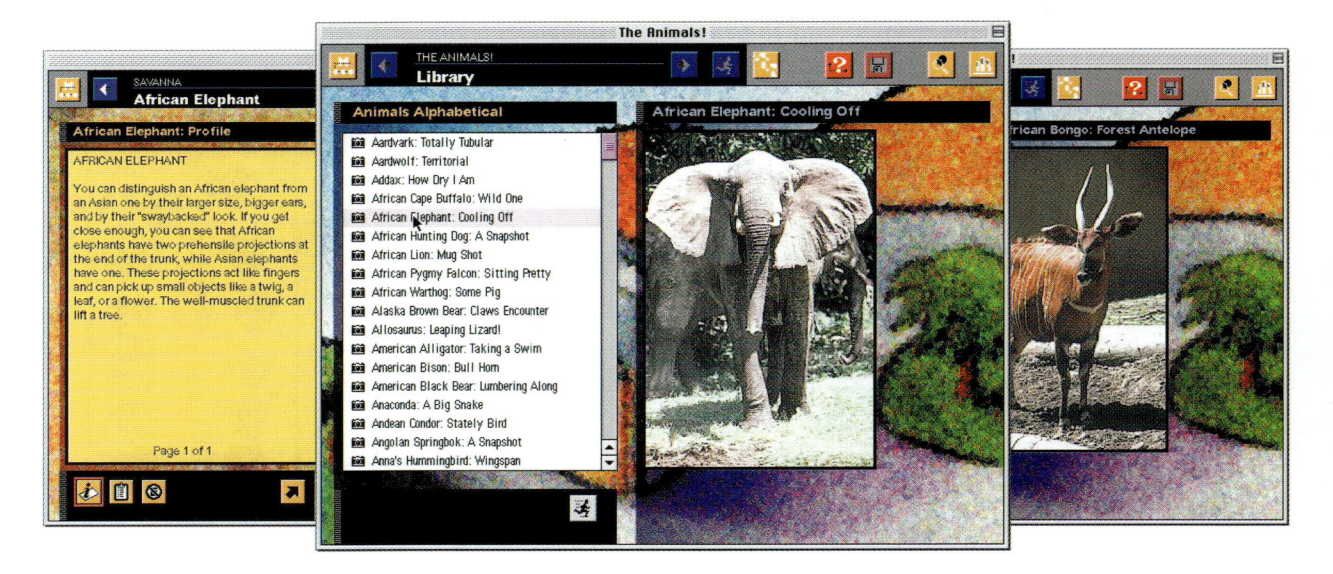

34   thirty-four

WORDS AND PICTURES

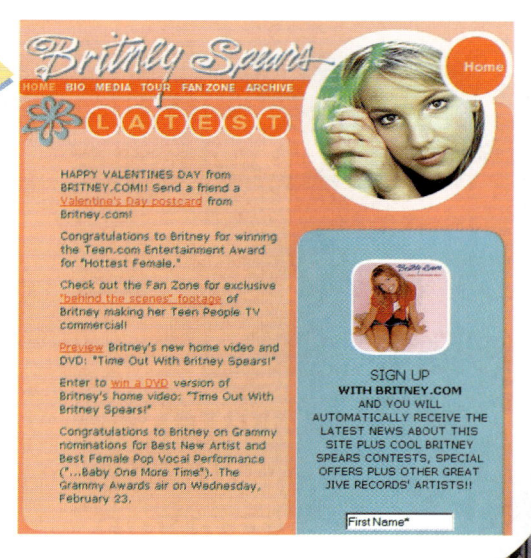

C You can also find information from other computers on the internet. The information comes along the telephone line to your computer. You type in a word or phrase, and the computer searches for websites on your subject. There are a lot of websites – millions of them. You can find out about everything from train times to sports results. You can get the latest news on your favourite film stars. You can also send messages to other computers. These messages are called e-mails.

D You can usually find up-to-date information on the internet. But it isn't the only place where you can look. It's always a good idea to visit your library. You can look at books, magazines and newspapers. Or maybe you can find some interesting information on television or on the radio.

E Where in the library can you find these books?

➡ You can find 'Play the Guitar' under 'Music'.

Unit 3　INTRODUCTION 1

SITUATION 1

035

Sophie is watching the weather forecast.

Sophie Oh no! It's going to rain tomorrow.
Emily It isn't going to rain in the morning. It says 'fine and warm'.
Sophie It is in the afternoon. I wanted to play tennis with my friends.
Emily Well, play in the morning.
Sophie I'm going to look round the shops with Jessica in the morning. She's going to look for a sweater.
Emily Well, go to the shops in the afternoon.
Sophie We can't. Jessica and her parents are going to visit her grandma in the afternoon.
Emily Well, that's life.

FINE AND WARM IN THE MORNING
RAIN IN THE AFTERNOON

EXERCISE 1

Look at the table and write the sentences.

Sophie is writing an e-mail. She's		eat lunch.
Oliver is borrowing a library book. He's		be late.
Emily doesn't like tennis. She isn't		stay in a hotel.
Adam is typing in a word. He's		send it to Thomas.
I'm not hungry today. I'm not		wear them tomorrow.
Take an umbrella. It's	going to	search for a website.
We're travelling to London. We're		watch it.
You're very slow this morning. You're		play with Sophie.
My parents don't like Star Trek. They're not		go to bed in a minute.
These shoes hurt my feet. I'm not		read it at the weekend.
Mr and Mrs Foster are tired. They're		rain.

➡ Sophie is writing an e-mail. She's going to send it to Thomas.

EXERCISE 2

Adam is making some New Year resolutions.

Adam I'm going to tidy my room every week.
　　　　I'm not going to have arguments with Sophie.

And you? Can you make four New Year resolutions?

I'm going to sing.
You're going to be late.
He's going to write a letter.
We're going to make a cake.
They're going to go out.

→ page 119

36　thirty-six

INTRODUCTION 1

EXERCISE 3

Say what they are going to do. Use these words: *buy an ice-cream, eat a banana, fall, feed the tiger, sing a song, take a photo, wash the elephant.*

➡ She's going to **fall**.

EXERCISE 4

Practise this dialogue with a partner.

Tom What are you going to do at the weekend?
Jim I don't know. Why?
Tom My friend from London is going to visit me on Saturday. We're going to play table tennis. Would you like to come?
Jim Oh, sorry, I can't. I'm going to help my mum on Saturday.

Now make new dialogues with a partner. Use these words:

~~London~~ • Munich • Manchester • Texas • New York
~~play table tennis~~ • swim in the pool • have a party • go to the skate park • listen to music
~~help my mum~~ • work on my project • go out with my parents • ride my friend's pony • visit my aunt and uncle

You can play this game. Use picture cards. Look at your card and think what you're going to do. Don't show the card to the other kids. Then answer their questions.

Karin What are you going to do with it?
Markus I'm going to eat it.
Karin Is it a sandwich?
Markus No, it isn't.
Tanja Is it a biscuit?
Markus Yes, it is. Now it's your turn, Tanja.

Unit 3 TEXT 1

🔴 The baseball project

036

This year Ben is in Class 8DP. His class tutor is Mrs Parry. But his favourite teacher is Mr Coleman. He's American and he runs the baseball club. Ben and some of his friends go to the club every Wednesday. Mr Coleman also teaches information technology. Two weeks ago he told the class about their new internet project.

'We're going to do a project on sport,' said Mr Coleman. 'You can do it in groups of two or three. Each group takes a different sport – tennis, golf, hockey, baseball, … .'
'Baseball, sir?' 'Yes, Ben. Baseball. Three of you here are members of the baseball club: you, Kirsty and Royston. You can be the baseball group. Find out everything about baseball. Where is it most popular? How many people watch it? When and where was the first baseball game? What leagues are there? Which are the best teams? What are the rules of the game? And so on. Each person in the group can answer different questions. Search the internet and see what you can find. I'm not going to tell you the answers.'

Ben, Kirsty and Royston went on the internet and searched for baseball.

Royston   There are a lot of websites on baseball: results, news and information, baseball in Japan, the Texas Rangers website, … .
Ben   I've got the Major League Baseball home page here.
Kirsty   Oh, can I see? Look, there's a report on the New York Yankees. Click on that.
Ben   OK. This looks interesting. They won the league, it says. I'm going to print this out.
Kirsty   Oh, it says here you can play a baseball game on your computer.
Royston   Great. Can you download it?
Ben   I can try.
Kirsty   Do girls and women play baseball in America? This is all about men.
Ben   I don't know. Hey! I can ask Cindy!
Royston   Who's Cindy?
Ben   Cindy Scott. She lives in America. Her parents are friends of my mum.  
Kirsty   Where in America do they live?
Ben   California. I can send them an e-mail. Maybe Cindy can tell us the answer. Maybe she plays baseball.
Kirsty   OK, are you going to do that now?
Ben   Well, I don't know their e-mail address, but I can ask my mum and send the message in the next lesson.

EXERCISE 5

Are the sentences right or wrong?
Correct the wrong sentences.

➡ Ben's class tutor this year is Mr Coleman.
   No, that's wrong. His class tutor is Mrs Parry.
➡ The new class project is about sport.
   Yes, that's right.
1 Kirsty, Royston and Ben are doing a baseball project because they are American.
2 There are two or three baseball websites.
3 The New York Yankees are a baseball club.
4 Kirsty is going to download the report.
5 The Scott family are friends of Royston's mum.
6 Cindy lives in California.
7 Ben can't send an e-mail because he can't use the computer.

EXERCISE 6

Can you ask these questions in English?
The questions are all in the text.

➡ Welche Ligen gibt es?
   What leagues are there?
1 Spielen Mädchen und Frauen in Amerika Baseball?
2 Was sind die Spielregeln?
3 Wann und wo war das erste Baseballspiel?
4 Hast du vor, das jetzt zu machen?
5 Wo wohnen sie?
6 Welche sind die besten Mannschaften?

EXERCISE 7

Do you know the computer words? Put in the missing words. They are all in the text.

1 We learn about computers in our … technology lessons.
2 With the computer mouse, you can … on different things.
3 You can find the most up-to-date information on the … .
4 Some schools have their own … with news and information.
5 I can … information from the internet onto my computer.
6 You can also … out interesting information and then look at it later.
7 You can send a letter to someone with a computer. This is called an … .
8 But first you must know the person's … .

EXERCISE 8

Listening

Listen to the teacher. She is telling her class about a new project. Then answer the questions.

1 How much time is there for the project?
   a) one day b) one term
   c) two months d) two weeks
2 What is the best name for the project?
   a) living in the city b) our classroom
   c) spare-time activities d) travelling to school
3 Which two of these questions are right for the project?
   a) How far is your home from the school?
   b) When do you leave home in the morning?
   c) Where do you go in your holidays?
   d) Who is your favourite teacher?
4 How are the pupils going to work?
   a) all together b) each pupil with a partner
   c) in groups d) each pupil on his/her own

Unit 3 **ACTIVITIES 1**

1 WAITING FOR SANTA

Sometimes your computer works well, sometimes everything goes wrong. Do you know why? Well, it has to do with the McByte family. Some members of this family live behind your computer's screen. Here they are:

Daddy McByte reads his websites or sleeps in his mailbox

Mummy McByte repairs the computer when the children nibble at the chips

Punky McByte would like to be a cool rat - and not a nice little mouse

Sugar Baby McByte is a nice girl but she's always hungry

1
Mummy, can I have some chips?

Come on, Sugar, you can't be hungry again!

2
But Mummy, it's not for me! I really need it!

It's Christmas time. The McBytes are busy and are looking forward to their presents and the Christmas party.

3
Show me your mousework for school! I hope you didn't download it from the internet this time!

I'll press the escape key when I'm two!

4
And don't throw your cursors again! It's dangerous!

No, Mummy, I'm a good boy ...

This year I'm going to catch Santa Click, er, Claus! Then all the presents will be mine!

It is a nice and quiet evening but then Daddy reads the news page on his website.

5
Oh my God! They say that Virus the cat will be around at Christmas. He's going to destroy all the food and fun files!

That's awful! What can we do?

Be quick! We must save all files on disk. Put the joystick into the garage and mail a warning to all the other mice outside.

6
Oooops, that was close! Look out! There he is!

40 forty

ACTIVITIES 1

7

Hey, friends! Let's play odd mouse out! Where's my favourite, little Sugar Baby?

Oh dear! He'll eat us all ...

What ab-b-b-bout my cursors? M-m-m-maybe they can help?

WWSSSHHHHH! CRKKKRRKKSS!!!

8

Oh? What's going on here? I can't see Virus any more.

Look, there's a new e-mail in our mailbox!

Don't open it! It's dangerous. Maybe it's Virus and his friends!

9

Now I know what we can do. Virus, we're fed up with you. I'll press escape and send you off to Poodle Island far out on the internet.

Yes, there is a chamber of horrors .... Merry Christmas, Virus! Look! The Virus mail is gone!

10

What's that? Oh, I see. Santa was here already. There are Christmas presents for all of us.

Maybe next year my day will come ...

Read the story again and find all the computer words. Make a list. In a group find German words for all of them. Are they different or the same?

2 ALIBI

Someone broke the screen of the McBytes' computer. The mouse police are trying to find out who was near the computer yesterday evening. What did YOU do between four and six o'clock? Write down your alibi in about 30 words.

Unit 3 **INTRODUCTION 2**

SITUATION 2

038

Kirsty I'm looking forward to my birthday next month.
Amy You're lucky. Yours isn't in the summer. Mine is in August.
Kirsty My sister Lauren and my younger brother have their birthdays in the summer. Hers is on 8th July, and his is on the 9th.
Amy Yes, but that's in the school term. On my birthday everyone is on holiday.
Kirsty Poor Amy. I must remember your birthday postcard next year.

my birthday	→	mine
your dog	→	yours
his bike	→	his
her cake	→	hers
	→	page 120

EXERCISE 9

Whose are these things? Can you guess? Use *his* or *hers* in your answers.

▶ Anita takes photos, so the camera must be hers.
1 Jessica likes horses, so the … must be … .
2 Sophie plays tennis, so … .
3 Jack phones Emily when he's in the garden, … .
4 Ravi supports Arsenal, so the … .
5 Oliver has got a mouse, … .
6 Kirsty plays basketball, … .

EXERCISE 10

Complete the dialogue. Put in *my, mine, your, yours, his* (2x), *her* and *hers*.

Mum Did you and … friends enjoy the school disco?
Amy Yes, it was good. We had a great time. I liked the music. They played all … favourite songs.
Mum That's good.
Amy Oh, something funny happened. Adam Foster didn't have a ticket. He forgot it.
Mum Oh, dear. You remembered … , I hope.
Amy Of course. I didn't forget … , and Kirsty didn't forget … , but silly old Adam left … at home. He rang … mum, and she found it and took it to the disco in … car.

42 forty-two

INTRODUCTION 2

SITUATION 3

Adam   Have the Hursts got a lot of money?
Sophie   I don't know. Why?
Adam   They've got a new car, and it's bigger than ours. And their house is bigger than ours, too.
Sophie   Our garden is bigger than theirs.
Adam   Mm, yes. And our dog is bigger than theirs. That's because they haven't got a dog.

> our car → ours
> their house → theirs
> → page 120

EXERCISE 11

Whose is it? Complete the dialogues.

Ravi   Is that Kirsty's video?
Adam   I think it's **hers**. Yes, it's got her name on it.

1   *Amy*   Is that my … ?
    Lehka   It must be … . It's got … name on it.

2   *Ben*   Are these Royston's … ?
    Kirsty   I think they're … . Yes, here's … name, look.

3   *Ben*   Are these our … ?
    Adam   They must be … . They've got … names on them.

4   *Adam*   Is this Luke and Oliver's … ?
    Ravi   Of course it's … . They've got … names on the door.

5   *Teacher*   Is this your … , Sophie?
    Sophie   I think it's … . Yes, here's … name.

6   *Emily*   Is that Jessica's … ?
    Daniel   I think it's … , but I'm not sure.
    Emily   Oh, yes, it is. It's got … name on it.

forty-three

Remember me?

040

When Ben's mum got home from work, Ben asked her about the Scotts' e-mail address. Later that evening Mrs Preston found a letter from Cindy's mum, and there was an e-mail
5 address on it. In the next IT lesson Ben wrote an e-mail to Cindy.

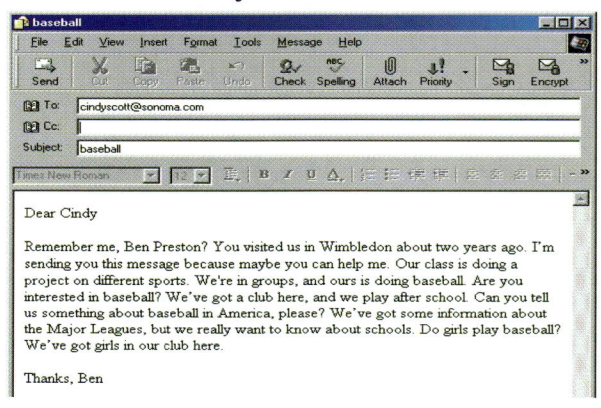

baseball
To: cindyscott@sonoma.com
Subject: baseball

Dear Cindy

Remember me, Ben Preston? You visited us in Wimbledon about two years ago. I'm sending you this message because maybe you can help me. Our class is doing a project on different sports. We're in groups, and ours is doing baseball. Are you interested in baseball? We've got a club here, and we play after school. Can you tell us something about baseball in America, please? We've got some information about the Major Leagues, but we really want to know about schools. Do girls play baseball? We've got girls in our club here.

Thanks, Ben

Three days later, in the next lesson, Ben switched on the computer and found two e-mails from Cindy. This was the first message.

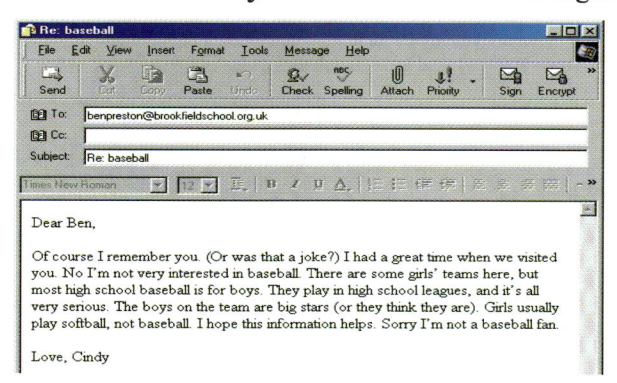

Re: baseball
To: benpreston@brookfieldschool.org.uk
Subject: Re: baseball

Dear Ben,

Of course I remember you. (Or was that a joke?) I had a great time when we visited you. No I'm not very interested in baseball. There are some girls' teams here, but most high school baseball is for boys. They play in high school leagues, and it's all very serious. The boys on the team are big stars (or they think they are). Girls usually play softball, not baseball. I hope this information helps. Sorry I'm not a baseball fan.

Love, Cindy

10 Ben printed out the message and gave it to Kirsty. 'There. That's yours,' he said. 'Thanks,' said Kirsty. She read the message. 'Hey, I think she fancies you,' she said. 'Don't be silly,' said Ben. 'I never see her.'
15 He opened the second e-mail.

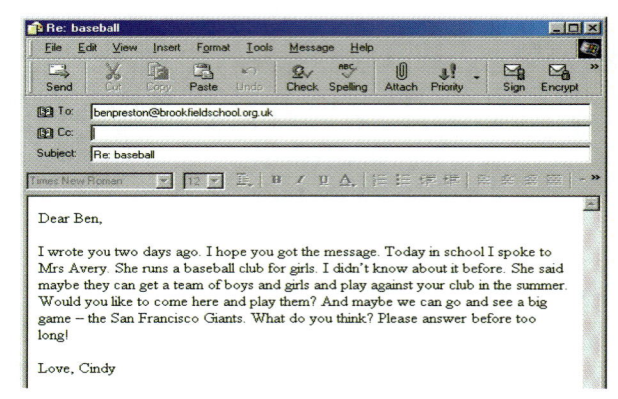

Re: baseball
To: benpreston@brookfieldschool.org.uk
Subject: Re: baseball

Dear Ben,

I wrote you two days ago. I hope you got the message. Today in school I spoke to Mrs Avery. She runs a baseball club for girls. I didn't know about it before. She said maybe they can get a team of boys and girls and play against your club in the summer. Would you like to come here and play them? And maybe we can go and see a big game – the San Francisco Giants. What do you think? Please answer before too long!

Love, Cindy

'Wow!' said Ben. 'That's a great idea.' Kirsty and Royston came and looked at the e-mail on the screen.
'Yes, great,' said Royston. 'But I know what my mum's going to say. It's too expensive.' 20
'Mine too,' said Kirsty. 'But I can tell you one thing, Ben. Now I *know* she fancies you.'

EXERCISE 12

Look at the words and imagine which people in the story said them.

➡ Thanks, mum. Now I can send a message. Ben said it to his mum.
1 Dad, I've got an e-mail from Ben Preston in London.
2 Maybe you and Kirsty can go, but my dad is going to say we haven't got the money.
3 Oh, good. Thanks. That answers my question about girls and baseball.
4 I'm going to look on the computer. Maybe there's an e-mail from Cindy.
5 That's very interesting. Maybe our team can play against these English kids.
6 Maybe the address is on her mum's last letter to me.
7 How is the baseball project going, you three? Is everything OK?

TEXT 2

EXERCISE 13

Make sentences from the table.

After tea Mrs Preston found	not baseball.
Ben told Cindy about	from Cindy.
Ben found two messages	to America.
Cindy isn't really	Ben.
Cindy sent Ben	a baseball fan.
Most girls play softball,	the baseball project.
High school teams play	for girls.
Kirsty thinks Cindy likes	**Cindy's address.**
She runs a baseball club	some information.
Maybe the team can go	in baseball leagues.

➡ After tea Mrs Preston found Cindy's address.

EXERCISE 15

Write the dialogue and then act it with a partner.

Kirsty It's SAT.10 tomorrow. What (you/do)?
Amy I've got a lesson in the morning. Let's ride (we) in the afternoon.
Kirsty I think (it/rain) in the afternoon. That's what it (say) on the at breakfast time.
Amy OK, what about a game of ?
Kirsty Yes, that's a good At (you) or (me)?
Amy At (we), if you like. We've got the up in the dining-room.

We can to Boyzone, too. My brother (buy) (they) new CD last

Kirsty You're lucky. (I) brothers never buy good They're hopeless.

➡ *Kirsty* It's Saturday tomorrow. What are you going to do?

EXERCISE 14

041

Listen and repeat.

[k]   [g]
class glass

Listen to the words and find the odd ones out.

1	magazine	sausage	hamburger
2	bag	rough	pig
3	sugar	page	again
4	juggler	slogan	daughter
5	car	cake	city
6	pocket	fence	hockey
7	lucky	mice	skater

Now listen and check.

COMMUNICATION

EXERCISE 16

042

What are the missing words?

1 *Girl* I'd … how … this … costs.
  Woman Oh, it's cheap. And it's a good computer.
2 *Girl* Excuse … . Do … how … it is to the hospital?
  Boy It's about half a mile from here.
3 *Man* Can … the nearest supermarket is?
  Woman Yes, down there on the left.
4 *Boy* … me. Can … the time?
  Man It's twenty past ten.
5 *Woman* Excuse me. … where I can get a taxi?
  Man Sorry, no, I don't.

Asking for information

Sich erkundigen

Excuse me. Can you tell me the way to the shopping centre, please?
~ Yes, go along here and turn right.

Do you know your e-mail address?
~ I can write it down for you.

I'd like to know when the film starts, please.
~ Quarter to eight.

forty-five **45**

Unit 3 **ACTIVITIES 2**

1 OUR XMAS CARD TO PRINCE HARRY

Christmas in Britain is different from the quiet Christmas in Germany. To us, it looks like a big, funny party. People go out and dance, wear paper hats and sing silly songs about reindeer and snowmen. But nothing happens on December 6th, there is no Adventskranz and not many children have an Adventskalender.

In the weeks before Christmas people in Britain write Christmas cards to their families and friends. So you think, 'Well, that's what I do, too?' OK, but do you write fifty or sixty cards? Do you write cards and give them to your friends when you see them?

Why don't you write a Christmas card to the Royal Family? Let's wish Prince Harry, Prince William or the Queen a Merry Christmas and a Happy New Year. Tell them about your town, your class, what you would like to do at Christmas and don't forget your wishes and your regards to the family.

And maybe, in a few weeks' time ...

2 RUDOLPH THE RED-NOSED REINDEER

SONG 043

Rudolph the red-nosed reindeer
had a very shiny nose,
and if you ever saw it,
you would even say it glows.
And all the other reindeer
used to laugh and call him names.
They never let poor Rudolph
join in any reindeer games.

Then one foggy Christmas Eve,
Santa came to say:
'Rudolph, with your nose so bright,
won't you guide my sleigh tonight?'
Then how the reindeer loved him,
as they shouted out with glee:
'Rudolph the red-nosed reindeer,
You'll go down in history!'

ACTIVITIES 2

3 CHRISTMAS ALL OVER THE WORLD

Let's have a look at Christmas in other countries. Who brings the presents in Sweden? What do people eat in Spain? When do children in Australia get their presents?

Form groups of about five pupils, choose a country and try to collect some information and pictures for your Christmas poster.

Maybe you can use a computer (at school or at home) and go on the internet. Look for the website www.christmas.com and click on the 'worldview' button. You can also look for other websites with more information about 'Christmas dinner', 'Christmas traditions', 'Boxing day', 'Santa Claus', ...

Philippines

Gambia

Australia

Canary Islands

4 TIME FOR A SMILE

What does Adam tell Eve on the evening of December 24th?

It's Christmas Eve.

What is the name of Santa's wife?

Mary Christmas.

forty-seven **47**

UNIT 4
SPECIAL DAYS

WORDS AND PICTURES

A The fifth of November is Bonfire Night in Britain. People light bonfires and have fireworks. You can go to a park and see some fireworks, or you can buy your own and light them in your garden after dark.

Some people make a guy and then burn him on the fire. The word 'guy' comes from a man called Guy Fawkes. About four hundred years ago he tried to blow up the Houses of Parliament and the King.

When do people in Germany light fireworks?

WORDS AND PICTURES

B 045

In autumn there's also a festival called Diwali. It's the Hindu festival of light. The Sharmas are Hindus. At Diwali they light candles, and they go to the temple. Diwali is like Christmas because people give presents and they eat nice food. It's also a bit like 5th November. There are no bonfires at Diwali, but there are fireworks.

C 046

Another special day is Valentine's Day, on the 14th February. If you love someone, you can send him or her a Valentine card. But you don't write your name on the card. If you get a card, you must guess who sent it.

D 047

April Fool's Day is good fun. You can play jokes on people. You can tell someone there's a spider on their head when there isn't really. If this gives them a shock, you can shout 'April Fool!' But be careful that someone doesn't play a joke on you.

Can you remember an April Fool's joke? Did you play a joke on someone, or did they play a joke on you? Tell the class about it.

Valentine
Be mine!

Roses are red,
Violets are blue,
Sugar is sweet,
And so are you.

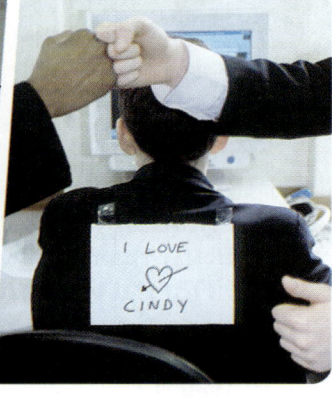

What's your favourite time of the year? And can you say why?

forty-nine 49

Unit 4   **INTRODUCTION 1**

● SITUATION 1
048

Sophie and Emily and their mum have gone to Oxford Street. They're doing some Christmas shopping.

we've walked	= we have walked
we haven't walked	= we have not walked
she's walked	= she has walked
she hasn't walked	= she has not walked

→ page 121

Mum Be careful with your money, Sophie. Don't lose it.
Sophie It's OK, mum.
Emily I'm tired. We've walked miles.
Mum We haven't walked very far, Emily. And you've bought some nice presents.
Sophie I've looked everywhere, but I haven't found a present for dad. He hasn't said what he wants.
Mum Your dad has lost his umbrella.
Sophie Oh, right. I can buy him a new umbrella. Thanks, mum.
Emily Can we have a cup of tea now?

I walk	I walked	I have walked
you find	you found	you have found
we fly	we flew	we have flown

→ page 123

EXERCISE 1

Look at the table and write the sentence pairs.

➡ I can't phone Amy. I've forgotten her number.

I can't phone Amy.	He's bought a hamburger.
Ravi is hungry.	She's finished her homework.
Anita can watch television now.	The rain has stopped.
Ben's room looks all right now.	I've read it.
Sophie's maths book isn't in her bag.	He's tidied it.
We can go out now.	She hasn't brought it to school.
The Dillons are travelling home.	I've forgotten her number.
I don't need this magazine now.	They've been to Disneyland.

EXERCISE 2

Emily has got a new boyfriend called Simon. He's phoning Emily. Put in the correct forms and complete the dialogue.

Simon Hi, Emily. Let's go to the cinema.
Emily When? Tonight? OK. I've done (do) my homework, and I … (finish) my history project. And I … (tidy) my room.
Simon Better than me. I … (do) my homework, but I … (not/tidy) my room. But never mind. My mum … (not/see) it.
Emily I wanted to see 'Big Gun', but it … (finish) now.
Simon Well, I … (look) in the newspaper. What about 'Millennium'? My sister … (see) it, and she says it's good.
Emily But Simon, that's a long film. It starts early.
Simon Yes, in twenty minutes.
Emily I can't get to the cinema in twenty minutes. Look, my mum … (bring) home a video of 'The Spiders'. We can watch that.
Simon But we … (see) 'The Spiders'. We … (not/see) 'Millennium'.
Emily Well, let's see it tomorrow then.
Simon OK, tomorrow.

INTRODUCTION 1

EXERCISE 3

Say what these people have done. Use these words: *drunk the milk, fallen off her bike, fed the fish, hurt his foot, made a cake, washed her hair, won a prize, written an e-mail.*

▶ He's **written** an e-mail.

SITUATION 2

Kirsty Ben, have you answered your e-mail from Cindy?
Ben Yes, of course I have.
Kirsty And has Mr Coleman said we can go to California?
Ben No, he hasn't.
Kirsty Have you asked him?
Ben Yes, and he's thinking about it. He's going to tell us in a few days. Kirsty, have you finished that map with the baseball clubs on it?
Kirsty Oh, no, I haven't.

EXERCISE 4

Put in the missing words: *have, haven't, has* or *hasn't*.

1. ... you lost something? / Yes, I can't find my ruler.
2. Let's watch this video. / Yes, OK. I ... seen it.
3. Why ... the bus stopped? / There's an accident.
4. Rusty ... eaten his food. / He must be ill.
5. ... you read this book? / Well, I've started it, but I ... finished it.

Unit 4 TEXT 1

The gunpowder plot
050

"Come back to England with me, Guy. The Catholics of England need you. It's a bad time for us under King James."

"We're going to blow up the Parliament, and the King with it. Then England can be Catholic again."

"Well, I know all about gunpowder."

Guy Fawkes was a Catholic and a soldier of the King of Spain. One evening in the spring of 1604, his friend Tom Winter visited him.

Guy went back to London with Tom, and Tom's cousin, Robert Catesby, explained the plot to them.

"What's the matter, Guy? What's wrong?"

"I can't dig in this water."

"It's God's work, don't forget."

The plotters bought a house near the Parliament. They wanted to dig a tunnel under it.

Then the plotters found an empty cellar under the Parliament. They brought some gunpowder on a boat across the Thames.

"We've brought in all the barrels now."

"Good. The King is going to be in the Houses of Parliament on Tuesday, 5th November."

"Be careful! Don't drop it in the river!"

They put the gunpowder in the cellar.

52 fifty-two

TEXT 1

"Someone has sent me this letter – I don't know who."

"What does it say?"

"It says, 'Don't go to the Parliament on 5th November. Something terrible is going to happen.'"

One day near the end of October, a Member of Parliament, Lord Monteagle, got a letter. He took it to the King.

"What's this in your pocket?"

On the night of 4th November, soldiers searched the cellars and found Guy Fawkes with the gunpowder.

"You haven't told us all the names."

"Yes, I have. I've told you everything."

After days of torture in the Tower, Guy Fawkes at last told his story.

"Long live the King! Remember, remember the fifth of November!"

In January 1606, Guy and Tom went to their deaths.

EXERCISE 5

Put the sentences in the right order and tell the story.

But before long the King heard of the plot.
But then they found an empty room.
The first plan was a tunnel under the Parliament.
Guy and Tom went home to England, and the plotters told them what they wanted to do.
Guy Fawkes's end came not long after that.
It all started with Tom Winter's visit to Guy Fawkes.
On the day before the King's visit to the Houses of Parliament, soldiers found Guy Fawkes in the cellar.
They brought some barrels of gunpowder and left them in the room.
They took him to the Tower and got some information from him.

➡ It all started with …

Unit 4 **TEXT 1**

EXERCISE 6

Which is the correct answer?

1. The gunpowder plot was against …
   a) Catholics.
   b) Guy Fawkes and his friends.
   c) the King and Parliament.   d) Spain.
2. The plotters wanted Guy Fawkes in the plot because …
   a) he had a house near the Parliament.
   b) he knew about gunpowder.
   c) he was a friend of King James.
3. The plotters didn't finish the tunnel because they found …
   a) water in it.   b) a letter.
   c) another room in the right place.
4. The gunpowder was in …
   a) bags.   b) barrels.   c) baskets.   d) bottles.
5. Who told Lord Monteagle about the plot?
   a) Guy Fawkes   b) The King
   c) Robert Catesby   d) We don't know.
6. The soldiers searched the cellar late on …
   a) 6th October.   b) 4th November.
   c) 5th November.   d) 16th January.
7. The soldiers found Guy Fawkes with the gunpowder, and for him this meant …
   a) money from the King.
   b) burning on a bonfire.
   c) torture and death.

EXERCISE 7

Find the words in the text.

➨ It's the last part of the day.
   evening

1. It's the opposite of 'good'.
2. It travels on water.
3. It means the same as 'awful'.
4. It's the opposite of 'far'.
5. It means the end of life.
6. It's an underground room.
7. It's the opposite of 'remember'.
8. When you do this, you are looking for something.
9. It means that there is nothing in it.
10. It comes after winter and before summer.

COMMUNICATION   051

Asking what the matter is

Fragen, was los ist

What's the matter/problem?
~ I've just remembered. It's my dad's birthday today.

What's wrong?
~ I can't find my money. I'm sure it was in my pocket.

What is it?
~ I don't know. I feel a bit ill.

EXERCISE 8

Complete the dialogues.

➨ *Mum*   What's the matter?
   Jade   I've hurt my arm.
1. *Jack*   … ?
   Daniel   I've … my mobile. Can I use yours?
2. *Kirsty*   … ?
   Amy   It's half past two. I'm going to be … for basketball.
3. *Teacher*   … ?
   Kate   I want to download this, but I … do it. Can you … me?
4. *Amy*   … ?
   Lehka   Oh, I just … a bit tired, that's all.

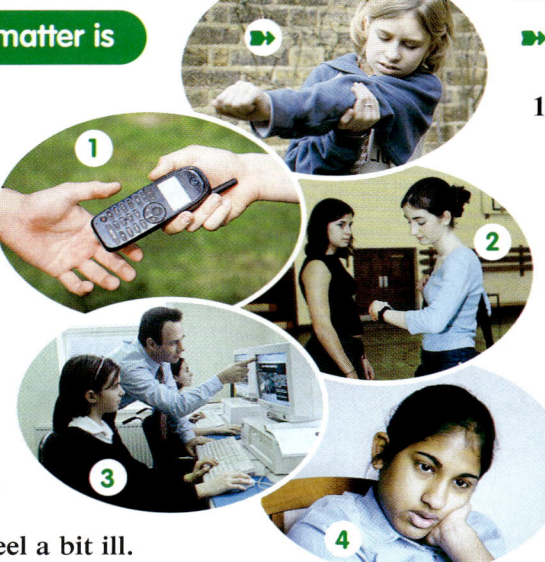

54   fifty-four

ACTIVITIES 1

1 VALENTINE CARDS

Would you like to send a Valentine card?
Here are some messages you can use:

Roses are red
Violets are blue
It's time you know
What I think of you!
Be my Valentine!

U R 2 good
2 B 4got10
ILY!
Do UL me?

Roses are red
Violets are blue
God made me beautiful
But what happened to you?

Remember that night
We kissed in the hall
I missed your lips
And kissed the wall.

To Ricky
Happy Valentine
from ...

Which message do you like best?
Which message would you not like to get?

Make Valentine cards for pupils in your class. Remember: don't write your name on the card!

2 GOING TO RAP

SONG 052

One, two,
we're going to say atshou!
Three, four,
we're going to slam the door!
Five, six,
we're going to look like pigs!
Seven, eight,
we're going to come home late!
Nine, ten,
we're going to sing again!

3 PICTURES TALK

2,3   5,6   3,5,1   2,3   6,2,3   2,4   5   5,7,8

fifty-five 55

Unit 4 — INTRODUCTION 2

SITUATION 3

053

Ben   Is tea ready yet?
Mum   No, not yet. You can do a bit of homework first.
Ben   Oh, I've already done my homework. I've just finished it.
Mum   Already?
Ben   It was easy – maths and English.
Mum   I hope you're doing your best at school, Ben.
Ben   Of course I am.
Mum   Well, I haven't made the tea yet, but maybe you can lay the table.

> I've just phoned my friend.
> He's already bought his ticket.
> Kirsty hasn't asked her parents yet.
> → page 123

EXERCISE 9

Complete the dialogue. Put in these words: *already, has, have, just, yet.*

Oliver   … the game started …?
Kirsty   Started? It's … finished. You're hopeless, Oliver. Where … you been?
Oliver   I've … seen Mr Williams about my maths homework. And I've lost my watch. I don't know what time it is.
Kirsty   Well, everyone here has … seen a great game.
Oliver   … we won?
Kirsty   Yes, we … . And we're top of the league. We've … won six games this term, and we haven't lost a game … .

EXERCISE 10

We can't always do what we want. You must say why. Use sentences with *n't … yet.*

➡ *Emily*   Sorry, Simon, I can't go to a disco now. I **haven't done** my homework **yet**. (do my homework)

1 *Dad*   There's a job to do before you go and see Jessica, Sophie. You … (make your bed)
2 *Kirsty*   No, I can't send an e-mail to Thomas. I … (find out his address)
3 *Mum*   I'm sorry, Ben. You can't play basketball now. … (tidy your room)
4 *Mum*   Amy can't come out at the moment, Kirsty. … (finish her tea)
5 *Jessica*   No, I can't tell you the answers to the quiz. … (look at the questions)

EXERCISE 11

Do you and your friends do enough to help at home? Ask and answer these questions with a partner. One of you is mum or dad and asks the questions. The other answers *Yes, I have* or *No, I haven't.*

1 Have you tidied your room this week?
2 Have you washed the car?
3 Have you done the shopping?
4 Have you helped in the house in the last few days?
5 Have you helped in the garden?
6 Have you taken the dog out?
7 Have you made a cup of tea or coffee for your parents?
8 Have you laid the table this week?
9 Have you made breakfast?
10 Have you washed up?
11 Have you fed a pet?
12 Have you done other jobs?

INTRODUCTION 2

SITUATION 4

Ben and Royston are at a newspaper shop.

Ben   There are some football magazines here.
Royston   Are there any magazines on in-line skating?
Ben   I can't see any. I want to buy this football magazine. And maybe a comic. Can you lend me some money?
Royston   Sorry, I haven't got any money.
Ben   Oh, never mind. I haven't got enough for a magazine, but I've got enough for some chocolate. Would you like some?
Royston   Oh, great. Thanks, Ben.

I've got some food.

I haven't got any food.

→ page 124

Have you got any food?

Yes, would you like some?

EXERCISE 12

Say what they've got or what they haven't got. Use *some* or *any* and these words: *cornflakes, crisps, e-mails, ice-cream, presents, sheep, shoes, skates.*

▶ He's got some presents.
▶ She hasn't got any cornflakes.

EXERCISE 13

Complete the dialogue. Put in *some* or *any*.

Amy   Let's go to the pop concert next week.
Lehka   We're too late. There aren't … tickets.
Amy   Yes, there are. They've got … at the music shop.
Lehka   Well, I'd like to go if we can get tickets. There are going to be … good bands.
Amy   Have you got … money, Kirsty?
Kirsty   No, not enough for a ticket. And I haven't got … time. I must do … work on my project.
Lehka   Can you lend me … money for a ticket, Kirsty?
Kirsty   I've just said I haven't got … .
Lehka   What about you, Amy? Have you got … money?
Amy   Yes, but I don't want to go if Kirsty doesn't go. Would you two like to come to my house and play … music?
Lehka   Have you got … All Saints CDs?
Amy   Yes, of course.
Lehka   OK, but it isn't the same as a concert.

Unit 4 **TEXT 2**

🔴 The one o'clock gun

055

A few weeks ago, in the half-term holiday, the Sharmas visited the Patels, their
⁵ relatives in Scotland. Ravi and Anita's aunt and uncle and their three cousins live in Edinburgh. Sanjay is 18, and the two girls, Usha and Tara, are 14 and 12. Mr Patel
¹⁰ is a hospital doctor, and his wife also works at a hospital. The family live only two miles from the city centre.

The school holiday was at the same time as Diwali, the Hindu festival of light. The Patels lit candles in their house, and in the evening they went with the Sharmas to
¹⁵ the temple and saw the lights and the fireworks. There were a lot of people there, and everyone enjoyed it.

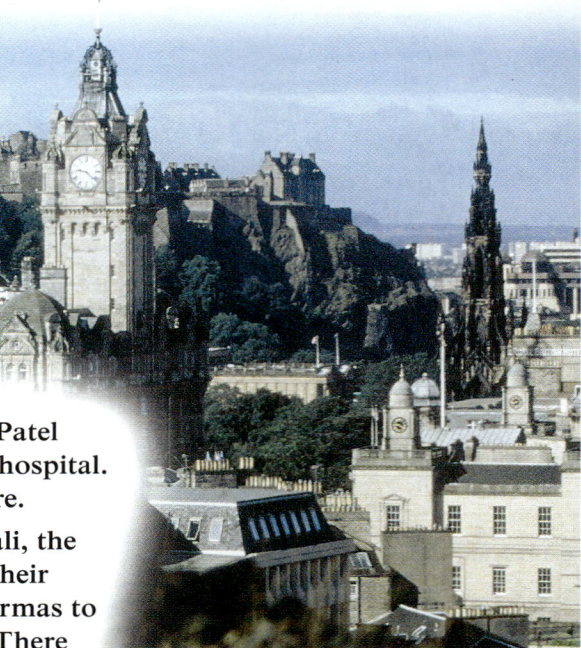

Edinburgh city and castle

On the second day of their visit, the Sharmas went into the city centre with Usha and Tara. The two girls wanted to show them the sights. 'Would you like to see the castle?' asked Usha. They were in Princes Street, where the big shops are. High above them
²⁰ was the castle. 'Yes, I'd like to,' said Mrs Sharma. 'Me too,' said Anita. 'Let's walk up and look at the view.'

They walked up the road to the castle.

'I like Edinburgh, and I'm glad we've come, but it's like winter here,' said Ravi.
²⁵ 'Colder than London.' 'You're soft,' said Tara. 'That's because you live in the warm south. We're tough here in Scotland.'
'I'm hungry, too,' said Ravi. 'It's quarter to one, and we haven't had lunch yet.'
³⁰ 'You can't be hungry, Ravi,' said Anita. 'You've just eaten all those sweets.'

One o'clock gun

ONE O'CLOCK GUN
FIRED EVERY DAY, EXCEPT SUNDAYS, AT ONE O'CLOCK. THE FIRST GUN WAS FIRED IN 1861 TO PROVIDE AN AUDIBLE TIME SIGNAL FOR SHIPS IN THE PORT OF LEITH.
🔊 37 🔊

At the entrance to the castle, Mr and Mrs Sharma bought the tickets. 'The café is this way, Ravi,' said Tara. 'Let's go and look at the menu.' 'Wait a minute,' said Mr Sharma. 'We want to look at the view.'
³⁵ 'It's a great view, but we've already looked at it,' said Ravi. 'I'm going with Tara.' The two of them hurried ahead to the café.

'Now,' said Usha to the others. 'I must warn you. In a minute something is going to happen.'

Tara and Ravi were on their way to the café when … BANG!! … there was a big bang. 'Oh, my God!' shouted Ravi. 'What's happened?'
⁴⁰ Tara laughed. 'It's the one o'clock gun,' she said. 'Don't worry, it's just a time signal. They fire the gun every day at this time. If you don't know about it, it can be a bit of a shock.'
'Yes, it was a shock. You knew and you didn't warn me.' 'It was just a joke, Ravi. Come on, let's go and look at the menu. Or have you lost your appetite now?'

EXERCISE 14

Put in the missing words. Put one word in each space.

The Sharmas have got some ... in Scotland. Anita and Ravi have got three ... : Sanjay, Usha and Tara. The Sharmas went to Edinburgh in the half-... holiday, at the time of Diwali, the ... of light. They all went to the park and saw some ... . The next day Usha and Tara took the Sharmas into the city ... , and they walked up the ... to the castle. Ravi was ... , so he wanted to find a café. Tara and Ravi left the others behind and went ... to the café. Usha ... the others about the one o'clock ... , but Tara ... warn Ravi. When he heard the gun, it was a ... for him. Tara said it was just a ... .

EXERCISE 15

What are they going to do, what are they doing and what have they done?

He's going to post the letter.

He ... the letter.

He ... the letter.

She's ... make a cake.

She ...

She has made a cake.

Now make more sentences.
Use *I, she, we, they* and these phrases:
build a house, *draw a picture*, *eat a hamburger*, *feed the cat*, *win a prize*.

EXERCISE 16

Imagine you are Ravi or Tara. Tell one of your friends the story of the joke. You can start like this.

Ravi At half term we visited our relatives in Edinburgh. On the second day ... OR

Tara At half term our relatives came from London and stayed with us. On the second day ...

EXERCISE 17

Listening

A boy and a girl are talking about what they did in the half-term holiday. Look at the questions and listen to the conversation. Then copy the questions into your exercise book and write the answers.

	Girl	Boy
How was the half-term holiday?	Great.	All right.
Where did they go?	...	...
What did they do?	...	...
What was the best part	...	...
When did they get home?	...	...

EXERCISE 18

Listen and repeat.

[ɑː]   [ʌ]
d**a**rk d**u**ck

Listen to the words and put them in the right group.

dark • above • another • argument • aunt • castle • come • country • last • laugh • part • young • up

Now listen again and check.

TEXT 2

Unit 4 — ACTIVITIES 2

1 WHAT DOES IT LOOK LIKE?
058

Loch Ness

Last weekend the Patels went to Drumnadrochit in the Highlands to have a picnic at Loch Ness. It was the first time the girls visited Loch Ness. But, of course, they knew the stories about Britain's largest lake and its strange animals. Usha and Tara had their sandwiches and ran down to the water to throw some stones. Suddenly the girls were back. They were very excited.

Tara   We have seen Nessie!
Usha   It looked out of the water fifty metres away from us!
Tara   With a long neck and it's all green and blue!
Usha   No, it is dark blue and purple with long and dangerous teeth.
Tara   This friendly monster isn't dangerous! There were birds on her back and …
Usha   Well, I didn't see its back, just the small head and its tail. The tail has yellow spots and … ugghhh …
Tara   Ha, Usha was afraid of it!
Usha   No, I wasn't afraid, YOU were afraid!
Tara   Nonsense, it looked so nice and funny. Come on, let's go to the water! We can show Nessie to you!

Mr and Mrs Patel looked out on the water, but they didn't see anything. Just some shadows of the clouds on the water. There wasn't any noise. Only some tourists watched the lake with their cameras. Their mother smiled.

Mum   Well, I guess you two are famous now. Not many people have seen the Loch Ness monster …

At home in Edinburgh, the girls drew a picture of Loch Ness and its strange monster. They found it hard to sleep that night.

What do YOU think Nessie looks like? What does it eat? Where does it hide? … Draw a big picture and write some information about your monster on it. These are nice posters for your classroom!

2 LUCKY LETTERS!

Find a word that starts with the last letter of your friend's word. Be quick!

➡ *Florian*	pupi**l**
Lisa	**l**esson
Ann-Kathrin	**n**ic**e**
Alexander	**e**a**t**
Steffi	easy
everyone	You're out! Sit down!
Kristina	te**a**
Marco	**a**fternoo**n**
Sabine	**n**onsens**e**

ACTIVITIES 2

3 SCOTTISH SHORTBREAD FINGERS

This is what you need.

*300 g of soft butter,
200 g of sugar,
500 g of flour,
and a little salt.*

To make them:

➤ Mix the butter, the sugar, the flour and the salt until you have a ball.
➤ Roll it out until it's about 1 cm thick.
➤ Bake it for half an hour at 180° C.
➤ Cut the hot shortbread into long fingers.

Enjoy your Scottish shortbread fingers with a nice cup of tea or coffee!

SONG 059 4 YELLOW SUBMARINE
by Lennon / McCartney 1966

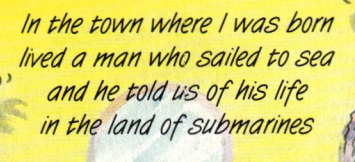

In the town where I was born
lived a man who sailed to sea
and he told us of his life
in the land of submarines

so we sailed into the sun
till we found the sea of green
and we lived beneath the waves
in our yellow submarine

we all live in a yellow submarine
yellow submarine, yellow submarine
we all live in a yellow submarine
yellow submarine, yellow submarine

as we live a life of ease
everyone of us has all we need
sky of blue and sea of green
in our yellow submarine

we all live ...

Unit 4 **PRACTISE YOUR ENGLISH**

1 The Sharmas' plans for Diwali. Say what the Sharmas are going to do.

1 We can see our relatives in Scotland.
2 Five days in Edinburgh – that's fantastic.
3 Where's that guidebook about Edinburgh castle?
4 Don't forget my books and comics.
5 Have you seen my camera?
6 Don't forget to buy some presents, Mum.

▶ stay with   1 be away for   2 visit   ▶ They are going to stay with
3 read   4 take photos   5 buy   their relatives in Scotland.

2 Getting ready for the trip.

The Sharmas have to do lots of things before they can go to Edinburgh. Say what they have done and what they haven't done yet.

▶ Mr and Mrs Sharma have written all the Diwali cards.
▶ Anita hasn't got any presents for the Patels yet.

▶ write all the Diwali cards	Mr and Mrs Sharma	✓
▶ get some presents for the Patels	Anita	
1 buy some candles	Mrs Sharma	
2 wash the car	Ravi	✓
3 load the cases in the car	Mr Sharma	
4 tidy your room	Ravi	✓
5 close all windows	Mr Sharma	
6 post some letters	Anita	
7 check the car	Mr Sharma	✓
8 ring Auntie Sita	Mrs Sharma	✓

3 Find the missing words.

▶ a lot / big   1 east / west   2 school / teacher   3 summer / hot   4 one o'clock / time
a bit / small   north / …   hospital / …   winter / …   blue / …

5 down / bottom   6 eat / eaten   7 funny / smile   8 one / first   9 plane / flew
up / …   tell / …   very funny / …   two / …   bike / …

62   sixty-two

PRACTISE YOUR ENGLISH

4 How can you find information? Put the words in the right places.

> click on • computer • DVD •
> e-mail • find out • internet •
> library • museum shop •
> newspapers • postcards • pictures •
> print • project • radio • screen •
> telephone • type • video • websites

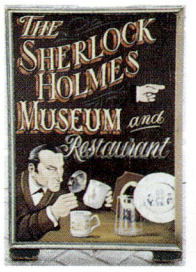

If you want do a *project* about Sherlock Holmes, for example, you can go to a … and look at all the Sherlock Holmes stories to … about this famous detective. If you've got a computer at home, maybe you've also got an encyclopedia on CD-Rom or … . You put it in your … and … what you want. Then you can read the information on the … or … out the pages. If you are on the … , the information comes along the … line to your computer. You … in 'Sherlock Holmes' and the computer searches for … on the detective. On some websites you can even find … from Sherlock Holmes films. Sometimes you can also find interesting information on television or on the … . Or you can send an … to a friend in Britain. If he lives near London he can visit the Sherlock Holmes Museum in 221b Baker Street and get some … or posters for you. In the … you can also buy Sherlock Holmes films on … , Sherlock Holmes T-shirts, old … and magazines and many other things.

5 Can you talk to Erisha about Diwali? Your partner is Erisha.

You	*Erisha*
Du triffst Erisha und sagst, dass du wissen möchtest, was sie normalerweise an Diwali macht.	Du antwortest, dass du in den Tempel gehst und dort mit Freunden spielst.
Du fragst, ob sie auch Geschenke bekommt.	Du sagst, dass viele Leute in euer Haus kommen, wenn du vom Tempel zurückkehrst. Sie geben dir Geld und Süßigkeiten.
Du möchtest wissen, an welchem Tag Diwali ist.	Du antwortest, dass es am 9. November stattfindet. (Schau auf deine Uhr.)
Du möchtest wissen, was los ist.	Du antwortest, dass du deinen Computerkurs vergessen hast und dass du zu spät kommen wirst.

6 Listen to Usha, Tara, Anita and Ravi. Then finish the sentences.

060

1. Anita got up at … .
2. The Sharmas started their trip to Edinburgh at … .
3. They stopped at Tesco's to … .
4. At one o'clock they … .
5. … went on a sightseeing tour.
6. In the park they … .

UNIT 5
HAVE YOU GOT A JOB?

WORDS AND PICTURES

A These people have got jobs.
061

Mr Sharma is a postman. He delivers letters. He likes his job, but it's not so good when it's raining.

Mrs Foster works in a bank. She helps people with their money problems.

Kirsty's mum works at a supermarket in Wimbledon.

Jessica's dad works in a factory. The company makes jam, marmalade and honey. Mr Hurst is the manager.

WORDS AND PICTURES

B Young people can have jobs, too.
062

Lehka sometimes helps her uncle. He sells clothes in the market on Saturday.

Simon delivers newspapers on Sunday morning. He gets up at seven o'clock.

Kirsty's sister Lauren sometimes washes cars. Her pocket money isn't enough. She wants to earn some extra money. This car was very dirty, but Lauren got it clean.

C Tell a partner about someone's job. Make sentences like these.
063
- My uncle is a farmer. He's got a lot of cows. He keeps sheep, too.
- My sister works in a sports shop. She doesn't earn much money, but she enjoys it.
- Our neighbour is a taxi driver. Sometimes he works in the evening.

Do you know someone with an interesting job?

D What job would you like to do when you're older? Would you like to work in an office
064 or a factory? With people or machines? Or with animals? Would you like to be a vet? Or maybe you'd like to be a footballer, a singer or a TV presenter?

Tell the other kids what you want to do. Say why you think it's the best job for you.

sixty-five **65**

Unit 5   **INTRODUCTION 1**

SITUATION 1
065

What about the future? What about life twenty-five years from now? Well, computers and robots will do all our work for us. People will have more spare time. They'll have long holidays. Maybe you'll fly to Venus for a winter holiday. It'll be nice and warm there.

| Robots
Emily
The letter | will | do all our work.
be 16 next month.
get there on Thursday. |

→ page 125

EXERCISE 1

Madame Zara is telling Sophie about her future. Make sentences with *will*.

▶ (have) a very long life.
  You'**ll have** a very long life.
▶ Exciting things (happen) to you.
  Exciting things **will happen** to you.
1 (have) four lovely children.
2 Your husband (be) a famous film star.
3 (meet) a lot of interesting people.
4 (live) in Hollywood.
5 All your friends (come) and visit you there.
6 Ten years from now (travel) round the world.

EXERCISE 2

Can you do these puzzles?

1 Oliver is doing his maths homework. There are five problems. Each problem takes fifteen minutes. Oliver started the homework at ten past seven. What time will he finish?
2 A man and a half can dig a garden and a half in a day and a half. A man is going to dig a garden. How long will it take?
3 Next week at school some interesting things are going to happen. There will be a disco, a football game, a sports day, a visit to the museum and a visit to the zoo. There will be something different every day. There is never any sport on Monday. Football games are always on Thursday or Friday. The zoo will be open every day. The museum opens only on Wednesday, Thursday and Friday. Discos are always at the end of the school week. What will happen on each day from Monday to Friday?

SITUATION 2
066

Ben's mum is getting the tea ready.

Mum I'm late today. I'll be as quick as I can, but tea won't be ready until six. Oh, no! We haven't got any beans.
Ben I'll go to the shop and get some.
Mum Oh, will you, Ben? Thanks, that'll be a help. Get two tins. And some bread, please. Oh, and some butter.
Ben OK. Beans, bread and butter.
Mum There's some money in my purse.
Ben I won't be long.
Mum It's cold. Don't forget your coat.

66 sixty-six

INTRODUCTION 1

EXERCISE 3

These people are all helping. What are they saying? Use these words: *answer it, carry this case, feed the dog, lay the table, look at our e-mail, post your letter, take a photo of you, wash up.*

➡ I'll wash up.

EXERCISE 4

Complete the dialogue. Use *will* or *won't* with the verbs. Then act out the dialogue with a partner.

Amy Kirsty is in the basketball team. **Will you come** (you/come) with me and watch the game?
Lehka No, … (I/not/come). I don't like basketball much.
Amy Come on. It's Kirsty's big day. We must support her. And … (it/be) good fun.
Lehka Well, what time … (it/finish)?
Amy … (it/not/be) very long.
Lehka I don't want to be late home, or my parents … (worry).
Amy Just half an hour. … (it/not/be) any fun on my own.

Lehka OK, but I don't know the rules.
Amy It's all right. … (I/explain) the rules to you. Then … (you/enjoy) it, I'm sure.

You can play this game. Ask a question and find out who has got the right answer. Put the question and answer together.

Will you be at the disco on Saturday?

I will be if I can get a ticket.

sixty-seven **67**

Unit 5 — TEXT 1

🔴 Bad news

067

Kirsty's mum and dad have arrived home from work. They're getting the tea ready.

Lauren Can I help?
Mum You can lay the table, Lauren. These plates are clean.
Lauren Are you all right, mum? What's the matter?
Dad We've got some bad news.
Lauren What? What's happened?
Mum Well, it isn't the end of the world, but in two weeks I'll be without a job.
Lauren Oh, no! Why?
Mum The company say they don't need so many people. They want to save money. In two weeks my job won't exist.
Lauren Oh, mum, that's awful.
Mum It's all right. Worse things have happened.
Dad You lay the table, Lauren. I'll put the potatoes on.

Kirsty What time will tea be? I'm hungry.
Dad It'll be ready soon.
Kirsty What's the matter? Is something wrong?
Lauren Mum's lost her job.
Kirsty Oh. What did you do, mum? Steal some sausages?
Dad It isn't funny, Kirsty.
Kirsty Sorry.
Mum They say they don't need so many people, Kirsty.
Dad Things will be a bit more difficult now, you know.
Kirsty What do you mean?
Dad Well, I mean your trip to California will be very difficult.
Kirsty Oh, no. That's not fair.
Dad It's not fair that your mum's lost her job.
Mum We'll see. Maybe you can go to America. I'll get some extra money from the company when I finish. I don't know how much.
Lauren And you'll soon find another job, mum.
Mum Yes, maybe.
Kirsty I can earn some money. I can deliver newspapers or wash cars like Lauren does. I'll soon earn the price of a ticket.
Lauren It'll be holidays soon. You won't earn hundreds of pounds before then. And that's what a flight to San Francisco costs.
Dad It's a nice idea, Kirsty, but Lauren is right. And you're too young. You can't work at your age.
Kirsty Lehka has got a job. She works in the market.
Dad You've got your school work.
Mum The potatoes! Quick!
Dad Oh, damn!
Mum Be careful. It's hot.
Dad Yes, I know it's hot. … OK, tea will be in about twenty minutes.

68 sixty-eight

TEXT 1

EXERCISE 5

Are the sentences right or wrong?
Look at the text and find the information.

▶ Mum and dad are in the kitchen at home. That's right. It says they 'have arrived home' and are 'getting the tea ready'.
1. Lauren can see that there is something wrong.
2. Soon Mrs Jewell will have no job.
3. A new person will do her job.
4. Lauren thinks it's bad news.
5. The family won't have as much money as before.
6. Mrs Jewell is sure Kirsty can't go to California.
7. She knows she will get an extra £500 from the company when she leaves.
8. Lauren thinks Kirsty can't earn enough money for her trip.
9. Dad thinks Kirsty hasn't got time and she isn't old enough.

EXERCISE 6

Look at each sentence and say if it is about the past, the present or the future.

1. Tea will be ready at six.
2. The Jewell family are sitting around the table.
3. Mum started her job at the supermarket five years ago.
4. She's going to look for another job.
5. When did they tell you the news?
6. The family are all talking about it.
7. It won't be easy.

EXERCISE 7

Find the best word for each verb. Then put the words in a short dialogue.

lay	earn	a bag	a letter
draw	close	a coat	some money
post	carry	the door	a picture
ride	wear	a game	relatives
win	visit	a horse	the table

▶ **lay the table** Can I lay the table for you?
  ~ Oh, yes, please.
▶ **draw a picture** Did you draw that picture?
  ~ Yes, I did.
  ~ It's very good.

Reacting to news

Auf eine Nachricht reagieren

Good news

I've found my bag.	I've won a hundred pounds.
~ Oh, good.	~ Fantastic!
We aren't going to do a maths test.	Someone is going to sponsor our team.
~ That's great.	~ That's wonderful news.

Bad news

| My brother can't find a job. | Anita has lost her purse with all her money in it. |
| ~ Oh, dear. That's a pity. | ~ Oh, no! Poor Anita. How awful. |

COMMUNICATION

068

EXERCISE 8

What can you say when you hear the news? Think of an answer and then practise the dialogues with a partner.

1. Someone has stolen Amy's coat.
2. It's a holiday tomorrow.
3. They've got some really cheap CDs at the music shop.
4. There's a hole in your sweater, look.
5. Don't use that phone. There's something wrong with it.
6. Germany are winning 2-1 against England.

Unit 5

ACTIVITIES 1

1 WHAT'S MY JOB?

Look at these jobs and start working.
Can your friends find out who you are?

> Are you a secretary, window-cleaner, weatherwoman, tourist guide, taxi driver, police officer, singer, robot, postman, teacher, elephant keeper, fire fighter, tennis player, TV presenter, doctor, actor, prince or princess, model, juggler, hockey player, guitar player, farmer, football player, criminal, paramedic, pet shop assistant, Formula One driver, … ?

Here are some questions the others can ask.

Do you sell something? Do you work on a farm? Are you on TV? Do you work with animals? Is your job dangerous?
Do you get much money?
Would you really like
to do this job? …

2 MY STORY

Your teacher gives you the beginning of a sentence. Write it on top of a piece of paper and add a short sentence. BUT: Always start your sentences with one of the blue words below! Fold the paper so that the other pupils can't see what you've written. Give it to your neighbour. He or she writes down something, folds it, …
Repeat this as often as you like. In the end read out some of these crazy stories.

Start every sentence with one of these words: *and, but, or, because, that's why, when, before, so*

➡ *Yesterday I went to the swimming-pool* … *because I wanted to bake a cake* … *or watch Star Trek* … *but I liked it very much there* … *that's why* …

3 LIMERICKS

There was a young
   man in Peru,
who found he had
   nothing to do.
So he sat on a chair
And counted his hair
And found he
   had seventy-two.

There was a young
   woman called Duck,
Whose life was full
   of bad luck.
But she went out one day,
Feeling happy and gay,
And got hit by a
   twenty-ton truck.

INTRODUCTION 2

SITUATION 3

Oliver has bought a TV guide. He bought it yesterday on his way home from school.

Oliver   It's Star Trek 6 on TV tonight. Have you seen that?
Royston   Yes, I have.
Oliver   I haven't seen it. Did you see it on video?
Royston   No, I saw it in the cinema last year. I went with Adam. You didn't come because you were ill.
Oliver   Oh, I remember. Was it good?
Royston   No, I didn't like it much.

EXERCISE 9

Look at the pictures and complete the sentences. Say what has happened and when it happened. Use the correct form of these verbs: *buy, do, earn, hurt, make, print, take*.

→ page 126

I've just finished my homework, look.

I finished mine half an hour ago.

▶ Lauren **has earned** some money. She **earned** it last week.
1. Oliver … some skates. He … them at the weekend.
2. Mr Williams … some tea. He … it five minutes ago.
3. Usha and Tara … some photos. They … them yesterday.
4. Ben … the information. He … it ten minutes ago.
5. Amy … her hand. She … it on Saturday at judo.
6. The boys … their homework. They … it yesterday evening.

Unit 5 INTRODUCTION 2

EXERCISE 10

Look at the information about our friends in Wimbledon. Write sentences with *n't*.

➡ Royston has seen Star Trek 5 (not Star Trek 6). He **hasn't** seen Star Trek 6.
➡ Ben saw the film in the cinema (not on video). He **didn't** see the film on video.
1. Thomas went to Madame Tussaud's (not the Tower of London) last year.
2. Ravi has been to Edinburgh (not Glasgow).
3. Cindy sent an e-mail to Ben (not Royston).
4. Ben has saved a bit of money (not a lot of money).
5. The Hurst family stayed in the New Forest (not the Black Forest).
6. Kirsty's mum (not her dad) has lost her job.
7. Royston has done in-line skating (not judo) before.
8. Kirsty did a project on baseball (not basketball).

SITUATION 4

070

Kirsty Have you ever done trampolining?
Amy Yes, once or twice.
Kirsty I've never done it. But it looks good fun.
Amy It's great. There's a club here. We can do it on Saturday mornings.
Kirsty Well, why not?

EXERCISE 11

Look at these dialogues. Work with a partner. Ask questions and answer them. Use *never, once, twice, three times, about ten times, hundreds of times* and so on.

➡ *Eva* Uwe, have you ever been to England?
Uwe No, **never**. But I'd like to go.
➡ *Uwe* Have you ever played tennis?
Eva Yes, **three or four times**.

1. Have you ever ridden a horse?
2. Have you ever talked to a famous person?
3. … (do) in-line skating?
4. … (make) a chocolate cake?
5. … (have) a caravan holiday?
6. … (see) a badger?
7. … (be) in a go-kart race?

Have you ever eaten a sausage sandwich?

No, never.

→ page 126

INTRODUCTION 2

EXERCISE 12

Practise this dialogue with a partner. Find a path through the dialogue.

- **Q** Have you ever played mini-golf?
  - **A** Yes, I played it on holiday last summer. — **Q** Did you enjoy it?
    - **A** Yes, I did.
    - **A** No, I didn't.
  - **A** No, I haven't. — **Q** Would you like to?
    - **A** Yes, why not?
    - **A** I'm not sure.

Now make more dialogues with these words.

played mini-golf: seen 'Spiceworld', done trampolining, stayed a night at your friend's house, been to New York
played it: saw it, etc.
on holiday last summer: at Christmas, last year, last week, two years ago
No, I haven't: No, never, No, not yet
Yes, I did: Yes, it was good, It was OK
No, I didn't: No, it wasn't very exciting
Yes, why not?: Yes, I would
I'm not sure: I don't know, Maybe not

You can play this game. Where have you been?

Heiko Have you ever been to Manchester?
Sabine No, I've never been to Manchester, but I've been to Munich.

Gabi Have you ever been to Australia?
Sandra No, I've never been to Australia, but I've been to America.

If you like, your answer can be silly.

Jens Have you ever been to Spain?
Anne No, I've never been to Spain, but I've been to a shopping centre.

EXERCISE 13

Look at the words in black. Which go with the simple past (*I did*) and which go with the present perfect (*I have done*)?

Write the words in two groups like this.

Simple past: last summer, …
Present perfect: ever, …

I was ill on Saturday, but I felt better yesterday.

Come on. I've already eaten my sandwiches, and you haven't started yours yet.

Did you see the Simpsons yesterday evening? I've never laughed so much in my life.

I started my homework at four o'clock, and I've just finished it now.

We went to North Wales last year. Have you ever been there?

These shoes hurt because I haven't worn them before. I bought them three weeks ago.

TEXT 2

The garage sale

On Friday evening Kirsty looked in the cupboard in her room. She found some old toys, games, books and comics. She put them all in a box and carried them down to the garage. She took a piece of paper and painted two words on it in big letters: GARAGE SALE.

In the morning Kirsty put all her things on two old tables outside the garage. She also got some lemonade and some biscuits. Then she fixed the piece of paper to the gate.

Soon Ben arrived. He had a bag full of things.

Ben Hi. I like the sign on the gate. Oh, you've found a lot of things. I haven't brought so much. But my mum gave me these old plates.
Kirsty Oh, they're good. Someone will buy them.
Ben And some clothes. This coat is too small for Jade now.

About an hour later Oliver and Royston were on their way to the park. In Wood Road they saw the sign on Kirsty's gate.

Oliver Let's go and look at this sale. Hi, you two!
Ben Hello. Come in.
Royston What's the idea?
Kirsty We need some money for our tickets to America. So we're selling these things.
Royston You didn't tell me about it. I haven't got enough money for a ticket.
Kirsty Sorry, but we only thought of it last night.
Oliver Have you ever in your life seen so much rubbish, Royston?
Royston No, I don't think I have. These cassettes are very old.
Oliver That racket is broken. And it's dirty. Who's going to buy that?
Kirsty It's really cheap. Only fifty p.
Ben We've already sold some books. A girl bought three.

Kirsty Would you like a glass of lemonade and a biscuit?
Oliver Oh, yes, please. We'd like a drink.
Ben That's thirty p each, please.
Royston Oh, we haven't got any money.
Ben Oh, well, that's OK. You're friends.

Oliver You aren't going to make enough money for a flight to America.
Kirsty That's what my sister said. But we've got eight pounds already. It's better than nothing.
Oliver My mum says maybe a company can sponsor you.
Ben You mean someone will pay for our tickets?
Royston Well, why not? Let's talk to Mr Coleman about it next week.
Kirsty OK, but we'll still need to make some money. So who wants to buy this Oasis CD? It's only a pound. Or this Baywatch poster? Or this diary for last year? I've never written in it, and it's really cheap …

TEXT 2

EXERCISE 14

Make sentences from the table.

Kirsty found some old things	some plates and clothes.
She put them all on two tables	on the gate.
She painted the words 'Garage Sale'	can sponsor the team.
She put the sign	for their plane tickets.
Ben brought	some lemonade and a biscuit.
They sold some books	because they didn't bring any money.
They need some money	in the garage.
Oliver thought most of their things were	to a girl.
Oliver and Royston had	Mr Coleman about it.
They didn't pay	in her cupboard.
Oliver's idea is that someone	rubbish.
They're going to ask	on a piece of paper.

➡ Kirsty found some old things in her cupboard.

EXERCISE 15

072

Listen and repeat.

[ʃ]   [tʃ]
wa**sh**   wa**tch**

Now listen to the words and find the missing letters.

*irt • *ips • *ips • *eep •
*eap • tor*ure • sear* •
informa*on • *oe •
Mar* • *ess • *elf • *ed

Listen and check your answers, then put the words in two groups in your exercise book.

[ʃ]   [tʃ]
shirt   **ch**ips

Now listen and check.

EXERCISE 16

Look at the pictures. What can you see in Kirsty and Ben's garage sale?

➡ a coat
➡ some toys

EXERCISE 17

73

Listening

Amy is telling Kirsty about her new dress. Which of these labels is on Amy's dress?

SALE Colour: RED Price: £12·99 AGE 11-12
SALE Colour: BLUE Price: £18·99 AGE 11-12
SALE Colour: RED Price: £18·99 AGE 13-14
SALE Colour: BLUE Price: £12·99 AGE 13-14

Unit 5 **ACTIVITIES 2**

1 RICKY AND THE GARAGE SALE

Now, Ricky, what do you want to give away?

I don't want to give them away, mum, but this will get me about £20 for a new bike.

Ricky wants a new bike. So she must sell some toys at the garage sale.

I'll give you £2.50 for this elephant

OK, here you are.

I must think of my new bike, I must think of my new bike ...

It's really hard for her to give away her toys ...

What are you selling?

Well, books, CD-ROMs, teddy bears, in-line skates, ...

In-line skates? Yes! They are my size!

Great! In-line skates for £20 – and I got £15 for my old toys!

... but she has already done a good job.

Let me guess. £10 for your new bike?

O happy day!

Mum, look, what I've got!

Oooops, the new bike! Well, at least I've got some wheels.

What a nice surprise for mum!

76 seventy-six

ACTIVITIES 2

2 FIVE QUESTIONS

Your partner is selling one of these things at his/her garage sale. Try to find out what. You can ask FIVE questions and your partner answers only with 'YES' or 'NO'! Take turns!

Here are some questions you can ask. Think of new ones yourself.

- Have you got this thing in your room?
- Can I use it at school?
- Did you play with it when you were small?
- Have you read it?
- Is it blue and red?
- Did you buy it at a ... shop?
- Is it a book? — No.
- Is it a ...? — ....

3 THE WEATHER

The south wind brings wet weather,
the north wind wet and cold together,
the west wind always brings us rain,
the east wind blows it back again.

SONG 4 WEATHER RAP
074

Monday morning – it's snowing,
I can't go to school today!
Tuesday morning – it's raining,
I can't go to school today!
Wednesday morning – it's so cold,
I can't go to school today!
Thursday morning – it's so hot,
I can't go to school today!
Friday morning – it's windy,
I can't go to school today!
Saturday morning – it's sunny,
let's go out and play, hooray!

UNIT 6
WHAT'S ON TELEVISION?

WORDS AND PICTURES

A 075 These are some TV programmes for young people in Britain.

TV programmes for young people

Grange Hill
Sunday 4pm BBC 2
The school soap opera with all your favourite characters.

Home Farm Twins
Sunday 7.30pm BBC 1
A drama series about twin girls Helen and Hannah. They move from the city to the country, where they buy animals for their farm.

Giggly Bitz
Sunday 8.30pm ITV
A comedy show with four young presenters. If you know a good joke, you can come on the show and tell it to everyone.

Wild Track
'Serengeti' Monday 5.15pm BBC 1
A series about two real-life teenagers on safari in Africa.

How II
'Inside your computer' Tuesday 6pm ITV
Learn something interesting from this popular science programme.

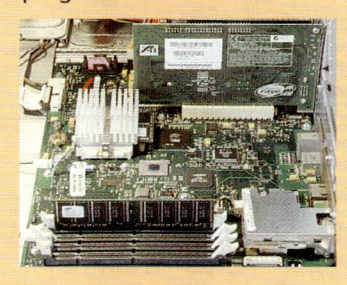

Spider
Wednesday 6.30pm ITV
Cartoon fun.

The Crash Zone
Friday 5pm Ch 4
In this drama five children test new computer games. They also look for answers to their own problems.

Newsround Extra
Saturday 2pm BBC 1
News reports for young people. Everything from India's flying doctors to football schools for the stars of tomorrow.

Polterguests
Saturday 5.30 pm Ch 5
In this comedy drama three ghosts live in a hotel. What happens when the guests meet the ghosts?

Which of the programmes would you like to watch and why?

▶ I'd like to watch 'Wild Track' because I'm interested in wild animals. I like programmes about animals.

WORDS AND PICTURES

B

Soap operas are the most popular TV programmes in Britain. A lot of young people watch soaps like 'Neighbours', 'Home and Away' and 'East Enders'. Newspapers and magazines often have news about the characters and the actors in soap operas. Drama and comedy shows are also popular. The BBC makes great documentaries. Some years ago there was a famous one called 'Walking with Dinosaurs'. The dinosaurs were all models but they looked very real.

C

'Who Wants To Be A Millionaire?' is a quiz show. It first started in Great Britain in 1998 and is very popular in the USA, too. If you want to become rich you can ring a telephone number and answer an easy question. If you get it right (and you are lucky) the TV company invites you to the show. There you've got to answer questions. The questions become more difficult with each round. You've got to decide: do you want to go on or take the money for that round? The highest prize is one million pounds (or dollars in the USA).

D

What German TV programmes do you like? Think of three or four. Can you say something about the programmes to a young visitor from Britain?

➡ You must watch 'Marienhof'. It's a soap opera. It's really good.

Unit 6 **INTRODUCTION 1**

● SITUATION 1
079

Oliver and Ben are at school. They're talking about yesterday afternoon.

Oliver   I rang you yesterday at about quarter past five, but you weren't in.
Ben   No, I was at Royston's house.
Oliver   What were you doing there?
Ben   We were watching 'Home and Away.'
Oliver   Oh, I don't watch that.
Ben   It was good. Vinnie was really sad because Justine has left him.
Oliver   I was doing my maths homework – well, trying to do it.
Ben   So why did you ring?
Oliver   Because I wasn't doing it right. I don't understand maths. I wanted to ask you about it.
Ben   Oh, I haven't looked at it yet. I expect I'll do it tonight.
Oliver   I'll ring you later, and you can explain it to me.

I he was watching she it	you we were watching they
	→ page 127

EXERCISE 1

Look at the table and make sentence pairs.

Ravi was at home yesterday evening. Adam and Ben were in the park after school. Jade and her mum were at the toy shop yesterday. Sophie was at the music club on Thursday. Royston was at the skate park on Saturday. Kirsty and Amy were at the disco last night. Mr Coleman was in the computer room at lunch time. Mr and Mrs Williams were at the seaside last Sunday. Oliver was in the library yesterday afternoon.	He She They	was were	dancing with their friends. buying a new football for Ben's birthday. watching TV. sending some e-mails. doing his project. sitting on the beach. playing football. skating with his friends. learning the guitar.

➭ Ravi was at home yesterday evening. He was watching TV.

INTRODUCTION 1

EXERCISE 2

Ben had a very strange dream last night. Look at the scenes from his dream and say what was happening.

▶ The postman was delivering bananas.
1 A juggler ... for a bus.
2 Two elephants ... a cup of tea.
3 A house ... through the air.
4 A policeman ... on a caravan.
5 A queen ... on a sheep.
6 A woman ... a newspaper.
7 Two dogs ... musical instruments.

Have you had a strange dream? Tell the other kids about your dream.

EXERCISE 3

Here are some words for clothes.

a jacket   a coat   a sweater
a shirt   a dress   a skirt

Now say what these people were wearing when you saw them.

▶ yesterday morning / Oliver / red shirt
1 at the weekend / Mr Batty / green jacket
2 on Saturday / Mrs Parry / blue coat
3 yesterday evening / Daniel / black jacket
4 not long ago / Simon / yellow sweater
5 yesterday / Tessa / red and white dress
6 on Sunday / the twins / blue skirts

▶ I saw Oliver yesterday morning. He was wearing a red shirt.

eighty-one 81

Unit 6 TEXT 1

🔴 Holiday Monday

080

Last Monday was a holiday. After lunch Jessica's mum and dad drove Jessica and her friend Sophie to Hampton Court. It's only a short journey from Wimbledon.

'We have to be home for 'Neighbours',' said Jessica as they were driving along the busy main road. 'It's at half past five.' 'Oh, we'll be home before then, don't worry,' said her mum.

'I watch 'Neighbours' too,' said Sophie. 'But 'East Enders' is better.'
'They're all rubbish, those soap operas,' said Mr Hurst. 'I can't understand why you watch them.'

'But 'Neighbours' isn't rubbish,' said Jessica. 'It's really exciting this week. Mike is going to have an argument with Libby.'

At Hampton Court there's an old royal palace, some gardens and a big park. There's also a famous maze. Jessica and Sophie wanted to go in the maze.
'Will you two be all right on your own?' asked dad.
'Of course we'll be all right,' said Jessica.
'I know the way. We'll just go to the middle and then come out. Sophie says she can push me if I get tired.'
'You're lucky to have a friend like Sophie,' said mum. 'OK, then. We'll look round the gardens, and we'll meet you here in about half an hour. Have fun!'
'Thanks. We will.'

Inside the maze the two girls followed the path between the hedges. They came to a turning where three people were standing and talking.
'Which way is it?' – 'Right, I think.'
The three people turned right. Sophie and Jessica turned left. Soon they came to a dead end. They turned back. At the next turning they stopped.
'Is this where we turned left?' asked Sophie.
'I'm not sure. I can't remember.'
'So you don't know the way?'
'Yes, I do, but I've forgotten.'
'Oh, that's great.'
'Well, let's get to the middle, where the trees are.'
'OK, I can see the trees. They're over there. Let's go straight on here.'

Jessica's mum and dad walked around the gardens. Soon they were back at the entrance to the maze. Twenty minutes later they were still waiting.
'Where are they?' said Mr Hurst.
'Oh, I expect they've lost their way. They'll probably be here soon.'

When the girls at last came out of the maze, they looked hot and tired.
'Sorry,' said Jessica. 'We got lost. But that woman showed us the way out.'
'Which woman?' mum asked.
'Over there – the woman with dark hair in the blue dress.'
'That was nice of her,' said dad.
'Are you all right?' her mum wanted to know.
'Yes, we're OK. What time is it?'
'Almost five o'clock. Would you like a drink now?'
'Oh, can we go, or I'll miss 'Neighbours'?'
'Don't worry,' said Mr Hurst. 'We'll be home in twenty minutes.'

TEXT 1

EXERCISE 4

Answer the questions.

1. Who went to Hampton Court?
2. Why did Jessica want to be home before half past five?
3. What does Mr Hurst think about soap operas?
4. What did they all do at Hampton Court?
5. Does Jessica know the way around the maze?
6. Where were Jessica's parents waiting?
7. What time did the girls come out of the maze?
8. How did they find their way out?
9. Were Jessica's parents angry?
10. How long is the car journey home to Wimbledon?

EXERCISE 5

Put in these words: *along, at, between, from, in, on, round, to, with*.

➡ They travelled **along** the main road.
1. They went in the maze … their own.
2. East Enders is really good … the moment.
3. Mum and dad are going to look … the gardens.
4. Let's go … the middle of the maze.
5. The path was … two hedges.
6. I don't want an argument … you.
7. Hampton Court is only about eight miles … Wimbledon.
8. We'll be home … half an hour.

EXERCISE 6

What's the opposite?
Put in the missing words.

➡ Did you remember the ticket, or did you **forget** it?
1. We don't go left here. We go … .
2. The concert isn't next week. It was … week.
3. This isn't the way in. It's the way … .
4. Are we going to leave before lunch or … lunch?
5. Did you say quarter past eleven or quarter … eleven?
6. It isn't a long way. It's a really … journey in the car.
7. I lost my watch, but I … it again the next day.
8. The entrance isn't here. I think it's over … .
9. No, I don't feel better. I feel … .
10. This cup isn't clean. It's … .

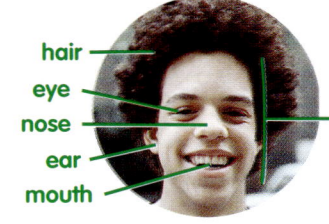

Describing people

Menschen beschreiben

My friend is fifteen **years old**.

She's about one metre sixty **tall**.

He's got dark /brown /fair **hair** and brown / blue **eyes**.

She usually **wears** blue jeans and a sweater.

hair
eye
nose
ear
mouth
face

EXERCISE 7

You are looking for these people in the maze. Can you describe them?

➡ Have you seen a short man, about 40 years old? He's got dark hair, and he's wearing a brown jacket.

COMMUNICATION

081

eighty-three 83

Unit 6

ACTIVITIES 1

1 FAMOUS PEOPLE

082 Let's call him Bill. He was born in England in 1982 as a member of a very rich family. He has got blue eyes and fair hair and he is very tall. A lot of girls fancy him just like the star of a soap opera on TV. He loves his brother, the Spice Girls and having parties with his friends. His father has got big ears. His mother sadly died in 1997.

Who is he? Would you like to be in his place for a day? Do you know any other members of this family? Find his name from the list below.

Let's call him Chuck. He moved from London to the USA at 21. His real name was Mr Spencer and he was a clown like his father. Everyone knows his black and white films – they are very funny. In these films, the actors don't talk – they sometimes hold up signs with the words they want to say. Chuck usually played poor, unlucky but warm-hearted people. In one film, he was so poor and hungry that he ate his shoe. He died in 1977 when he was more than eighty years old.

Who was this actor? Can you walk like he did?

Do you want to find out more about your favourite star? Try the internet and look for www.biography.com.

Let's call her Gaga (but we aren't sure if it's a girl).
British and German TV programmes show her every evening. This 'person' is yellow, has got big eyes and ears, a TV on her belly and can't say very much, but she makes sounds like 'oh, oh'. She's got three friends and they often play with a vacuum cleaner. You can sing songs with her name. Little boys and girls love her, but they must be very, very little!

Do you know who she is? Do you know her friends' names?

Will Smith	Buddy Holly	Posh Spice
Chris Evans	Buster Keaton	Pocahontas
David Beckham	Winston Churchill	Charlotte Church
Ronan Keating	Charlie Chaplin	Tubby Laa-Laa
Leonardo DiCaprio	Frank Sinatra	The Queen
Prince William	Alfred Hitchcock	Caroline of Monaco
Prince Naseem	Walt Disney	Snow White

Who do you think Bill is?

Maybe it's … … Chris Evans?

Rubbish!

84 eighty-four

ACTIVITIES 1

2 GUESS WHAT I AM DOING

WALK, sadly, talk, angrily, sing, quietly, shout, eat, read, slowly, run, QUICKLY, play, HAPPILY, jump, nervously

Are you a good actor? Your teacher will give you two pieces of paper. One has a verb and one has an adverb. Act out what's on the pieces of paper. Your friends must guess what you are doing:

➡ Are you singing happily? Are you walking quietly?

3 FAMOUS LAST WORDS

What did Little Red Riding Hood say to the wolf?

➡ All the better to hug you with, my dear.

1. All the better to see you with, my dear.
2. All the better to hear you with, my dear.
3. All the better to eat you with, my dear! Rooooaaaar!

➡ What big arms you've got, grandmother!

4 READY, STEADY, GO

Write down these umbrella words.

letter	at school	food	5 letter words	numbers	animals	stars	hobbies	points
C	canteen	chips	clean	—	cow	—	cycling	25

Your teacher or one of the pupils says a letter – and now your answers for each umbrella word must start with this letter. So hurry to find and write down all the words. When you have written down all the answers, say *stop*. Everybody must stop writing then.

Now let's count your points. You get five points for every correct answer.
Would you like to go on with another letter?
Who is the first pupil with 100 points?

Unit 6 **INTRODUCTION 2**

SITUATION 2

083

Sophie You read quickly, Jessica. You've almost finished that book, and you only started it yesterday.

Jessica I can read a book easily in a weekend. This is great. It's a story about the Internet and time travel. You can read it after me.

Sophie OK, thanks. And you can have mine. It's about two girls. They're twins. One is nice and the other is horrible.

Adjectives

Please be quick.
That was an easy question.

Adverbs

Come quickly.
I answered it easily.

→ page 128

EXERCISE 8

Read this paragraph from a story. Then say which of the words in blue are adjectives and which are adverbs.

It was hot in the bedroom. Laura lay quietly and sadly on her bed. It was tea time, but she wasn't hungry. She thought about the terrible news. It all happened so suddenly. One moment she was talking happily with her friends, and the next moment everything was different. She lay on the bed and looked at her new poster on the wall, but she didn't see it. Then she heard someone at the door, and she quickly got up from the bed.

Adjectives: hot, …   **Adverbs:** quietly, …

EXERCISE 9

Find the best adverb and make sentences.

Oliver's arm hurt	happily.
The man shouted	carefully.
All the children played	hungrily.
The dogs ate	cheaply.
The red team won the game	**badly.**
You can buy shoes in the market very	correctly.
The boys carried the plates	slowly.
The pupils answered all the questions	angrily.
Emily was tired, so she walked	easily.

▶ Oliver's arm hurt badly.

Are you a good actor? Can you say these sentences in different ways?

Just look at these photos.

We've already bought our tickets for the journey.

I've got news for you.

Can you say them happily, sadly, quickly, slowly, angrily and nervously?

86 eighty-six

INTRODUCTION 2

SITUATION 3

Oliver	That's good, Ben!
Royston	He can do that really well.
Oliver	He can go fast, too. I can't go as fast as Ben.
Royston	I expect you can if you try hard.
Ben	Look, I can do it on one leg!
Royston	That's great!
Ben	Oh no! … Ow!
Oliver	Oh, dear. Are you OK, Ben?

Adjectives	Adverbs
Take the fast train.	We're going fast.
This is hard work.	You work too hard.
That was good.	You did well!
	→ page 129

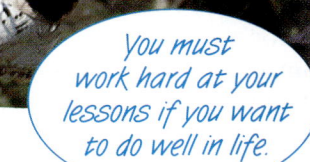

You must work hard at your lessons if you want to do well in life.

EXERCISE 10

Which adverb is right? Make the sentences.

→ She's going **fast** / **slowly**
➡ She's going **fast**.

1. He's driving **carefully** / **dangerously**.
2. It's going **quickly** / **slowly**.
3. They're talking **nervously** / **happily**.
4. He's playing **badly** / **nicely**.
5. She's smiling **happily** / **sadly**.
6. She's doing **hopelessly** / **well**.
7. They're talking **angrily** / **quietly**.
8. He's doing **badly** / **well**.

Unit 6 TEXT 2

Can you do me a favour?

085

Mr and Mrs Hurst, Jessica and Sophie left Hampton Court at five o'clock. 'We can get home easily in half an hour,' said Mr Hurst. But soon they were in a long queue of traffic.

Jessica	Why are we going so slowly?
Mum	It's a holiday. It's busy. Everyone is going home at the same time.
Dad	I think this is going to take a long time.
Jessica	Oh no! We must be home at half past five.
Mum	Well, it's your fault if we're late. You were so long in the maze.
Jessica	But I can't miss 'Neighbours'.
Mum	Don't be silly, Jessica. Look at all this traffic. What can we do?

At twenty-five past five they were still going very slowly.

Sophie	We need a mobile phone.
Dad	I didn't bring mine. Do you want to ring someone, Sophie?
Sophie	I thought maybe someone can record the programme for Jessica.
Jessica	Oh, good idea. There must be a phone box around here. Dad, turn left here. We can look for a phone box.
Dad	Oh, all right. Maybe we should get out of this traffic. I expect we can find a quicker way home.
Mum	You can't ring Daniel. He's out.
Jessica	Is Adam or Emily at home, Sophie?
Sophie	I don't know, but if we can find a phone box, I'll ring and find out.

They turned left off the main road. It wasn't so busy now. They came to some houses. On the right there were some shops and a phone box. They stopped, and Sophie quickly jumped out, ran to the phone box and dialled the number.

Adam	Hello?
Sophie	Adam, it's me, Sophie. Look, can you do me a favour? It's for Jessica. Can you record 'Neighbours' for her?
Adam	A favour? How much is it worth? 50p?
Sophie	Come on, Adam. Don't be mean.
Adam	Go and ask her how much.
Sophie	Adam!
Adam	All right, but say please.
Sophie	Can you record 'Neighbours', please?
Adam	Maybe. Yes, all right.

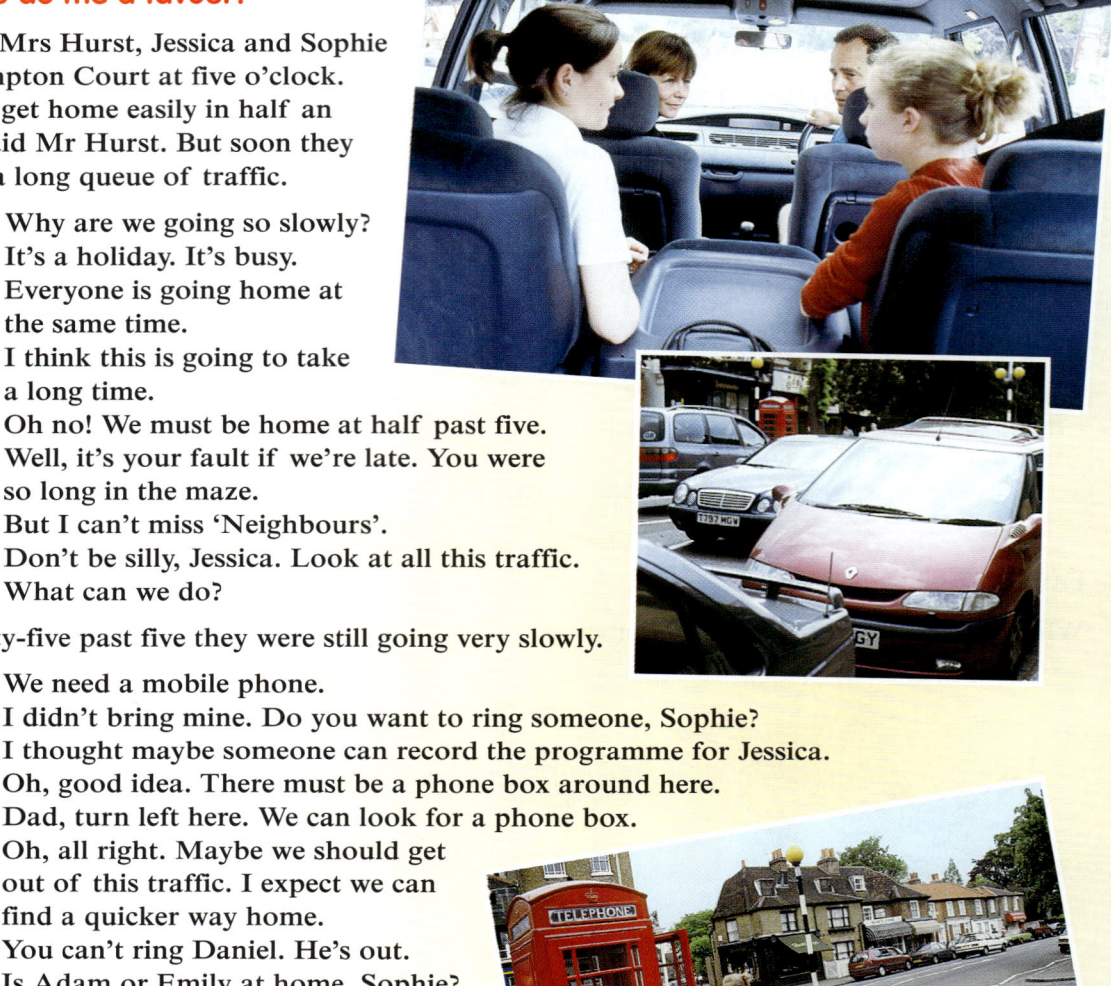

Sophie	It's starting now. It's on BBC 1.
Adam	OK.
Sophie	And the roads are very busy. Tell mum and dad I'll be late for tea.
Adam	OK, I'll tell them.
Sophie	Now hurry up and record that programme.
Adam	What channel is it? BBC 2, did you say?
Sophie	BBC 1! Stop it, Adam! Hurry up! Bye!

Sophie got back in the car.

Sophie	No problem. Adam is recording it now.
Jessica	Great. Thanks, Sophie.
Sophie	I'll bring the tape round after tea. Well, at half past eight, after 'East Enders'. Terry's got a lot of problems at the moment. I want to see what he does next.

EXERCISE 11

Make sentences from the table.

They started the journey home	his mobile phone.
The traffic was moving	BBC 1.
Jessica didn't want to miss	at five o'clock.
Mr Hurst didn't bring	rang home.
Jessica wanted to find	'Neighbours'.
Sophie ran to the phone box and	'East Enders'.
Someone answered the phone.	
It was	very slowly.
The programme was on	Adam.
Sophie wanted to watch	a phone box.

▸ They started the journey home at five o'clock.

EXERCISE 12

Next day Sophie told another friend about her afternoon out. Tell the story for her.

Yesterday I went with Jessica and … to Hampton Court. When we got there, Jessica's parents looked round the … , and we went into … . But we didn't know the … , and we got … . We were in there a long … . We got hot and … . When we … out, … waiting for us. The time was … , and Jessica wanted to … at half past. On the way back the traffic … very slowly. We turned off … and found a … . I quickly rang … , and he … for Jessica. After tea I … 'East Enders', and then I … house, and we … together.

TEXT 2

EXERCISE 13

Find the word pairs.

TV	towns	science
toys	sweater	newspapers
summer	life	bricks
rivers	CDs	bread
friends	husband	letters

games	winter	magazines
butter	radio	postcards
relatives	skirt	death
cassettes	stones	streams
wife	villages	technology

▸ TV and radio

EXERCISE 14

Listen and repeat.

[uː]   [ʊ]
Luke   look

Which words don't have [uː] or [ʊ]?

afternoon • book • cool • door • floor • food • foot • good • look • room • school • soon • wood • zoo

Listen and check your answers.

Put the rest of the words in two groups.

[uː]   [ʊ]
aftern**oo**n   b**oo**k

Listen and check your answers.

EXERCISE 15

Listening

Daniel is ringing Jessica about a TV programme. She's going to record it for him. Listen to the conversation and then complete the sentences.

1 The name of the programme is … .
2 It starts at … .
3 It finishes at … .
4 The channel is … .

Unit 6 ACTIVITIES 2

1 OFF TO A NEW WORLD

088

Five hundred years ago, most kings and queens in Europe had a dream. They wanted gold, silver, silk and other fine things from India.

Send my men to India! I want to be the richest queen in the world!

Queen Isabella of Spain wasn't any better.

But the problem was how to get there. It was dangerous and expensive to travel to India over land and the sea route to the east meant a long and rough journey around South Africa.

Let me look for a western route to India! That must be much shorter!

Nonsense! You'll fall into nowhere at the end of the seas!

Good joke!

Just look at him!

Then, Cristoforo Colombo, a young man from Italy, had a great idea.

But Christopher Columbus, as the British and American people call him now, told them about his new idea. Some people thought that the earth was not flat, but ...

All the people thought he was silly.

They say the earth is round like this ball. So I can travel to the west and it's an easy and short journey to India.

Well, the question was how far India lay to the west of Spain. Columbus thought that the earth was much smaller than it really is. He thought he could get to India in just a few weeks. But he had a problem. No one wanted to give him ships, food or money for a crew to discover the new western sea route across the Atlantic. It was a journey into nowhere. But at last, Queen Isabella and King Fernando of Spain helped the tall, quiet man with the red hair.

And most of these people thought he was silly, too.

More than five hundred years ago, on August 3rd, 1492, he left Europe with three small ships. The Santa Maria, his biggest ship, was just 23 metres long. The journey was rough ...

ACTIVITIES 2

We're tired!
Captain, there's no land out there!
Let's go home!

… after 30 long days …

50 days for nothing!
We're ill!
We'll fall off the earth …
Just another few days – we'll find India soon!
I hope…

… after 50 long days …

We have arrived!
India is ours!
No more fish!
Oh happy day!

To his death Columbus never knew that he didn't find India – but that he was discovering lands that no one imagined to be there – the Bahamas, another wonderful place.

After 70 days in nowhere they came to an island on the morning of October 12th, 1492.

(AMERICA)
PORTUGAL
Lisbon
(BAHAMAS)
(CUBA) (HAITI)

My dear Indian friends, tell me: Where can I find gold?

He didn't find any gold on the island. And it wasn't fair and friendly of him to kidnap seven new friends as a present to King Fernando and Queen Isabella.

After all, he was not the first person to discover America. People lived there more than 20 000 years before him. And the Vikings arrived around the year 1 000. But it was Columbus's journey which turned a page in world history.

The people on this island were friendly and ready to help.

ninety-one **91**

Unit 6   **PRACTISE YOUR ENGLISH**

1 Find the missing letters and put the words in the right group.

b**n • br**d • b*tt*r • c**t • c*ff** • c*k* •
r • *y* • f*c* • j*ck*t • j*m • jns •
l*m*n*d* • m*rm*l*d* • m**th • n*s* •
*r*ng* j**c* • sk*rt • sw**t*r • w*t*r

clothes	drinks	food	head
coat, ...			

2 Look at this word spider for 'Holidays'. Can you add more words?

wonderful • mountains • Spain • hotel • seaside • car • HOLIDAYS • games • train • caravan • swimming • the Black Forest

Now make a word spider for 'Television'.

3 At four o'clock yesterday these people were in Conway Street. What were they doing?

➡ A boy was eating an ice-cream.

92   ninety-two

PRACTISE YOUR ENGLISH

4 What have they already done? What are they going to do?

➤ **Mum** Please tidy your room now, Adam. (OK – an hour ago)
 Adam I've already tidied my room. I tidied it an hour ago.
➤ **Kirsty** Can you finish that book, Amy? I want to read it, too. (not yet – this afternoon)
 Amy I haven't finished the book yet, but I'm going to finish it this afternoon.
1 **Dad** Sophie! Can you phone Grandad today? (OK – after lunch)
2 **Mum** Royston, don't forget to invite Adam to your party. (not yet – after tea)
3 **Adam** Take the book on Guy Fawkes back to the library, Oliver. (OK – two days ago)
4 **Ben** Don't forget to feed Softy, Jade. (OK – ten minutes ago)
5 **Emily** Have you bought a present for mum's birthday, Sophie? (not yet – tomorrow)
6 **Simon** Can you buy the cinema tickets for tonight, Emily? (OK – yesterday)
7 **Ravi** Can you put my walkman in your case, Anita? (OK – this morning)
8 **Amy** Have you done your homework, Lehka? (not yet – later)

5 Do you need an adjective or an adverb?

➤ Mr Foster is a careful driver. He drives carefully. (careful)
1 This is an … exercise. You can do it … . (easy)
2 Amy sings … . She has got a … voice. (wonderful)
3 All the children were … . They played … in the park. (happy)
4 Rocky is always … . He ate … . (hungry)
5 Lehka's neighbour is an … old man. He often shouts … . (angry)
6 Arsenal won yesterday. They are a … team. They played … . (good)
7 Jade is … . Softy has run away again. 'I haven't found Softy yet,' she said … . (sad)
8 We're on a … train today. It's going really … . (fast)

6 Someone has stolen your walkman. Work with a partner. Your partner is the policeman.

You

Auf der Polizeiwache erzählst du einem Polizisten, dass du den Mann gesehen hast, der dir deinen Walkman auf dem Markt gestohlen hat.

Du sagst, dass er 20 oder 25 Jahre alt und 1,70 groß war und dass er blonde Haare hatte, Jeans und einen roten Pullover trug.
Du antwortest, dass du es nicht weißt.

Policeman

Du reagierst erfreut und fragst, ob er/sie den Mann beschreiben kann.

Du fragst, wohin er rannte.
Du reagierst enttäuscht, bedankst dich aber für seine/ihre Hilfe.

7 089 What do we know about the first guest in the quiz show? Write the answers in your exercise book.

Name …
She's from … .
She wants to go to … .
Age … .
She's got … children.
The famous person is … .

UNIT 7
THE GOLDEN STATE

WORDS AND PICTURES

A *090* What is the Golden State? It's California, the most exciting state in the US.

The coast of California is 1,264 miles long. There are some wonderful beaches. Surfing is a popular activity.

Everyone has heard of Hollywood in Los Angeles. Hollywood means movies.

In the north of the state you can see huge redwood trees, the tallest in the world. Some are 110 metres high. You can drive a car through some of them.

California has a coast, lakes, forests, deserts and mountains. There are three national parks in the Sierra Nevada mountains. The most famous is Yosemite with its many waterfalls. In winter, the mountain ridges in Yosemite like Badger Pass are popular skiing resorts.

WORDS AND PICTURES

The Golden Gate Bridge in San Francisco is one of the great sights of America. The famous cable cars go up and down the steep hills.

California is famous for its oranges and for its wine. There's also Silicon Valley, around San Jose, the home of computer companies.

The first Europeans in California were from Spain. They built missions along the coast. The four largest cities in the state – Los Angeles, San Diego, San Jose and San Francisco – all have Spanish names.

B Is California in the east or the west? Is it on the Atlantic Ocean or the Pacific? Find it on a map. Where would you like to go in California, and what would you like to do?

SONG This land is your land

1. This land is your land, this land is my land,
From California to the New York Island,
From the redwood forest to the gulf stream waters,
This land was made for you and me.

2. As I was walking along the highway,
I saw above me that endless skyway,
I saw below me that golden valley,
This land was made for you and me.

3. This land is your land, …

Unit 7 **INTRODUCTION 1**

SITUATION 1
093

Rocky What's this program?
Girl It's a movie. It's about a family on vacation in Disneyland.

Ricky What's this programme?
Boy It's a film. It's about a family on holiday in Disneyland.

Who's British and who's American? How do you know?

Ricky We both speak English.
Rocky Yes, but sometimes we use different words.

Some words have different spellings.

BRITISH	AMERICAN
TV programme	TV program
centre	center
colour	color → page 110

EXERCISE 1

Look at the pictures and find the British and American words.

🇬🇧	🇺🇸
a holiday	a movie
a main road	mail a letter
chips	a vacation
petrol	a highway
post a letter	french fries
a film	gas
lorry	truck

➡ A holiday is a vacation.

SITUATION 2
094

Royston and Ben are at school.

Royston What are you doing?
Ben It's our English project.
Royston You've done a lot of work on it. How many pages have you written?
Ben Oh, not many. Well, about twenty. But there are lots of pictures.
Royston Well, stop now because I've got some news. A company is going to sponsor our trip to California.
Ben Oh, that's great! How much money are they going to give us?

Royston I don't know. Mr Coleman wants to see all the team at one o'clock. So come on, we haven't got much time.
Ben OK, I'm coming.

INTRODUCTION 1

lots of plates / a lot of plates

not many worms

not much water

→ page 129

How much are these apples?

25p each. How many would you like?

EXERCISE 2

Say what they've got. Use *a lot of, lots of, many* or *much*.

➡ She's got **a lot of** telephones.
➡ He hasn't got **many** CDs.
➡ There isn't **much** toast.

1 He hasn't ... . 3 She's ... . 5 She ... . 7 She ... .
2 There aren't ... . 4 There ... . 6 There ... . 8 He's ... .

EXERCISE 3

Complete the conversation. Put in *a lot of, lots of, many* or *much*.

Sophie I don't like this place. It isn't **much** fun. This isn't a very good holiday.
Dad But Sophie, it's lovely here. There are ... nice views.
Sophie There aren't ... young people here. Most of the tourists are old people.
Dad It's nice and quiet here. That's what I like. There isn't ... noise. It's because there aren't ... cars on the road. It's so different from London, where there's ... traffic.
Sophie There aren't ... shops here.
Dad Oh, I'm sure there are enough for you.
Sophie Really? And how ... discos are there?
Dad You go to discos at home. You can do something different here. There are ... nice places where you can walk.
Sophie Yes, dad.

ninety-seven 97

Unit 7 TEXT 1

Welcome to California

095

The baseball team from Brookfield School has just arrived in Sonoma, California. The Americans are welcoming them with a barbecue at Mrs Avery's house. She runs a baseball club for girls in Sonoma.

Cindy Ben! Hi!
Ben Oh, hi, Cindy. Hello Mrs Scott.
Mrs Scott Hello, Ben. It's lovely to see you here.
Ben It's nice to see you, too. It's great to be here.
Mrs Scott How are you? Did you have a good flight?
Ben It was OK. I watched a film.
Mrs Scott How's your mother, Ben?
Ben Oh, she's fine, thanks.
Mrs Scott And Jade?
Ben Yes, she's OK.
Cindy Ben, are your mom and Jade on vacation at the moment?
Ben Yes, they're camping with some friends in Wales.
Mrs Scott Oh, that sounds like a lot of fun.
Ben Jade wanted to come to California, but she can't, of course.
Cindy Ben, what would you like to do tomorrow? Would you like to go bowling?
Ben Yes, that'll be great.

Meanwhile Mrs Avery is talking to Royston.

Mrs Avery Hey, I like your baseball cap.
Royston Oh, thanks.
Mrs Avery What's 'World Sports'?
Royston It's a company in London. They make sports equipment. They gave us these caps and some shirts for the team. They sponsored our trip here. It was great news for me because my mum hasn't got much money – well, she didn't have enough for my ticket.
Mrs Avery Well, I'm glad you're here. And I hope you have fun.
Royston Thank you.
Mrs Avery Are you OK?
Royston Sorry. I'm a bit tired. I think it's jet lag. I've been tired all evening. It must be the middle of the night in England now.
Mrs Avery Oh, you'll probably be OK in a day or two. Would you like some potato salad?
Royston Not for me, thank you.

Kirsty is making a new friend.

Justin Hi, I'm Justin.
Kirsty Oh, hi. I'm Kirsty.
Justin So you're a baseball player from England?
Kirsty Well, I play at school with the others here. One of our teachers started the club – Mr Coleman, that's him over there. He's from Chicago.
Justin The tall man in the blue shirt?
Kirsty That's right. He runs the club. But we haven't played many games. I expect you're all much better than us.
Justin Well, I don't know about that. But we'll see on Sunday. That's when our first game is.
Kirsty Are you in your school team?
Justin I was on the team last year. I'm a catcher.
Kirsty Oh, really? Catcher is my favourite position.
Cindy Would you two like another burger? And some cola?

98 ninety-eight

TEXT 1

EXERCISE 4

That's wrong! What are the correct sentences?

➡ The Scotts are saying goodbye to some visitors from Australia. The Scotts are welcoming some visitors from England.
1 Of the Preston family, only Ben and his mum are in California.
2 Jade is staying at a hotel in London.
3 West End Sports sponsored the barbecue and gave the team some shoes.
4 When it's evening in America, it's the end of the afternoon in Europe.
5 Mrs Avery thinks Royston must see a doctor.
6 Kirsty is telling Cindy who Mrs Coleman is.
7 The first baseball game is on Monday.
8 There are pizzas and coffee at the barbecue.

EXERCISE 5

Can you say it in English? The sentences are all in the text.

➡ Schön, dich hier zu sehen.
   It's lovely to see you here.
1 Hast du einen guten Flug gehabt?
2 Wie gehts deiner Mama?
3 Was würdest du morgen gerne machen?
4 Meine Mama hat nicht viel Geld.
5 Ich bin den ganzen Abend müde gewesen.
6 Der große Mann im blauen Hemd?
7 Ihr seid alle sicher viel besser als wir.
8 Möchtet ihr noch einen Hamburger?

EXERCISE 6

Can you say it a different way? Put in the missing words.

➡ They were a group of baseball players. = They were a baseball **team**.
1 Where is your sister at the moment? = Where is your sister ... ?
2 These caps were free. = We didn't ... for these caps.
3 They sponsored our trip. = They gave us some ... for our tickets.
4 I hope you have fun. = I hope you have a ... time.
5 You'll probably be OK. = I ... you'll be OK.
6 I don't know about that. = I'm not ... about that.
7 Baseball is my favourite sport. = I ... baseball the most.

EXERCISE 7

Listening

A boy called Mark and a girl called Kim are talking at a barbecue. Which picture shows what they were doing last weekend? Then say if these sentences are right or wrong.

1 Mark arrived late at the party.
2 Kim's brother helped her with her homework.
3 Mark is feeling fine.
4 Only ten people are at the barbecue.
5 Kim likes her job.
6 Mark had a wonderful time at the weekend.

Unit 7 ACTIVITIES 1

1 THIS IS NO TEDDY BEAR!

In some national parks in California there are still bears. Be careful! Grizzly bears are never afraid. They win every fight. And they are fast: they can move their 600 kilos across 100 metres in 7 seconds. (Can you go faster?) Mister Rocky Mountains can even open your car if he wants to. These bears are probably the most dangerous animals in the world. When you meet one of them, you have a problem. Here are some rules to help you.

- Sing loudly when you walk in the mountains. The bears will not want to meet you then.
- Never go nearer than forty metres! If you do, they will get nervous.
- Don't play with little baby bears. Mummy doesn't like it and she'll be there in seconds.
- Never try to feed a bear! Grizzly will enjoy the sweets – and you as his lunch!
- Put your food into bags and hang them between two trees three metres above the ground.
- Be careful when you make your meals. The bears can smell very well and will be interested.
- Burn the rest of your food.
- Leave your dog at home. First it finds a bear and then the bear finds you.

But when you meet a grizzly: talk quietly to the bear, no matter what you say. Move back slowly and wait until it is bored and leaves. Good luck!

DON'T BE BEAR CARELESS

2 GRIZZLY BEAR
by Mary Austin

If you ever, ever, ever meet a grizzly bear,
You must never, never, never ask him where
he is going.
Or what he is doing.
For if you ever, ever dare
To stop a grizzly bear,
You will never meet another grizzly bear.

3 CARTOON

Excuse me, have you seen Mr and Mrs Tanaka?

ACTIVITIES 1

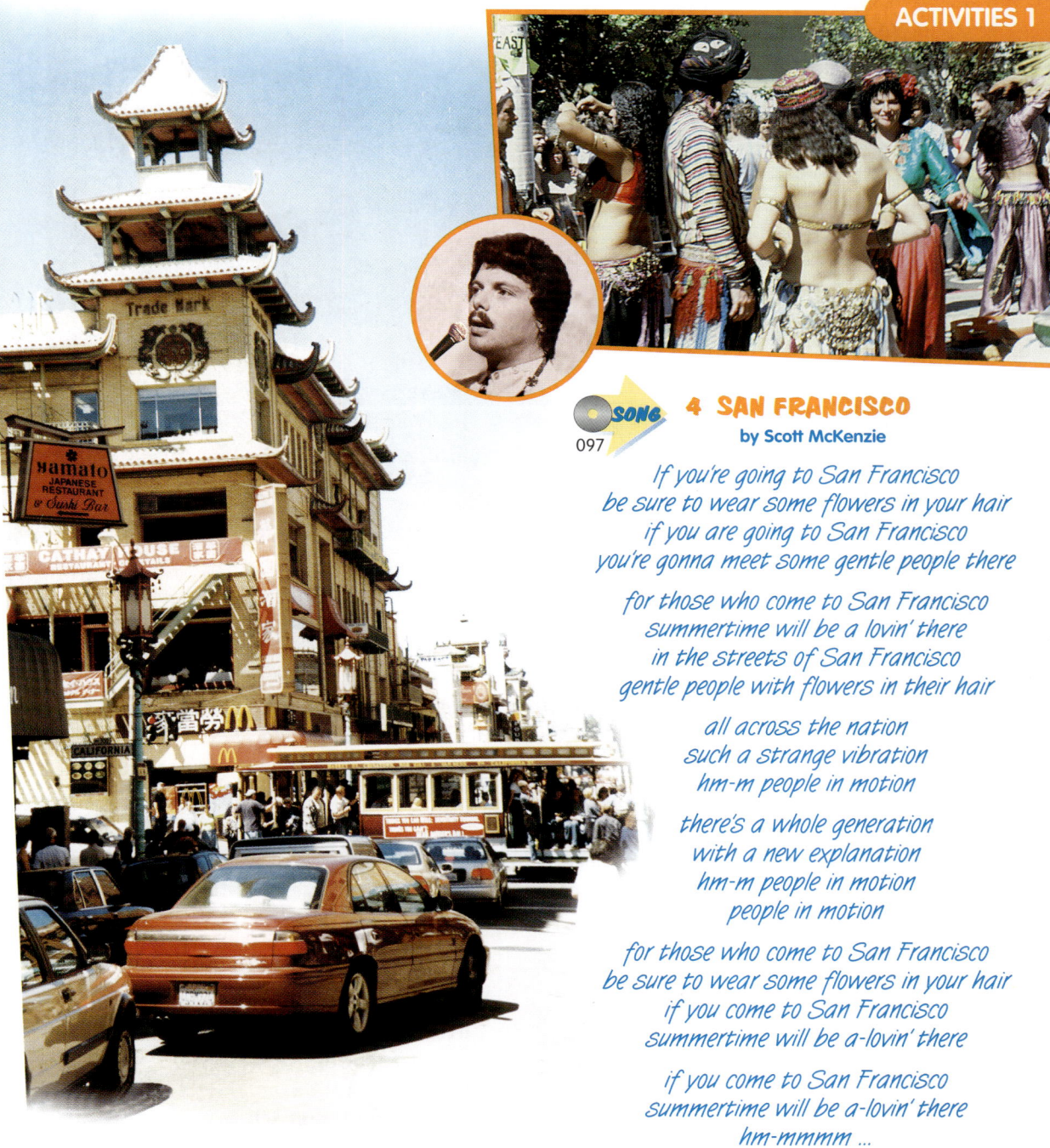

🎵 SONG
097

4 SAN FRANCISCO
by Scott McKenzie

If you're going to San Francisco
be sure to wear some flowers in your hair
if you are going to San Francisco
you're gonna meet some gentle people there

for those who come to San Francisco
summertime will be a lovin' there
in the streets of San Francisco
gentle people with flowers in their hair

all across the nation
such a strange vibration
hm-m people in motion

there's a whole generation
with a new explanation
hm-m people in motion
people in motion

for those who come to San Francisco
be sure to wear some flowers in your hair
if you come to San Francisco
summertime will be a-lovin' there

if you come to San Francisco
summertime will be a-lovin' there
hm-mmmm ...

5 SHORT MESSAGES

Do you sometimes send e-mails with your computer? Here is a trick to make some words shorter. Now you can write longer messages and you're really up-to-date.

Use these codes for your messages:

ASAP   4E   BBL   BFN   CUL   HAND

Guess what they mean. Here are the answers:

1   Bye for now.
2   See you later.
3   Forever yours.
4   Have a nice day!
5   I'm going to be back later.
6   I'm going to do this as soon as possible.

one hundred and one   **101**

Unit 7　**INTRODUCTION 2**

🔵 **SITUATION 3**

098

These are baseball players. The player who throws the ball is called the pitcher. The player who hits the ball is the batter. And the person who stands behind the batter and catches the ball is the catcher.

| The pitcher is the player | who | throws the ball. |
| The batter is the person | | hits the ball. |

→ page 130

EXERCISE 8

Look at the table and write the sentences.

| A | farmer
postman
guide
pupil
manager
doctor
neighbour
tourist | is | a person
someone | who | delivers letters.
runs a company.
works on the land.
shows you the way.
lives in the next house or flat.
goes to school.
travels on holiday.
makes you better when you are ill. |

➡ A farmer is someone who works on the land.

EXERCISE 9

Can you explain what these words mean?

➡ a visitor – A visitor is a person who visits your house.
1　an ambulance driver
2　a singer
3　a footballer
4　a European

The person who dropped that is an idiot.

102　one hundred and two

INTRODUCTION 2

SITUATION 4

Ben Where can I put this rubbish?
Cindy Rubbish?
Ben I've got some things that I want to throw away.
Cindy Oh, sorry. We say 'garbage'.
Ben OK, garbage. And what about these magazines? Is this something that you recycle?
Cindy Yes, of course. I'll take them.

| Rubbish is something | that | you throw away. |
| A newspaper is a thing | | you read every day. |

→ page 130

EXERCISE 10

Put in these words: *actions, a bell, clothes, an e-mail, food, a pen, sights.*

➡ **Food** is something that you eat.
1 ... is a message that you send to a computer.
2 ... are things that you wear.
3 ... are interesting things that people visit.
4 ... is a thing that you can ring.
5 ... are things that you do.
6 ... is something that you use when you're writing.

EXERCISE 11

Put the words in the right order and write sentences in your exercise book.

➡ is / a / CD / that / listen / you / something / to.
  A CD is something that you listen to.
1 Mr / Chicago / the / IT teacher / comes / who / from / Coleman / is.
2 who / baseball / girls / Avery / is / the / woman / runs / a / club / for / Mrs.
3 an / is / letter / you / e-mail / on / the / a / computer / that / write.
4 is / famous / someone / who / a / star / is / very.
5 you / can / something / that / a / prize / is / win.

EXERCISE 12

Complete the sentences and explain what the words mean.

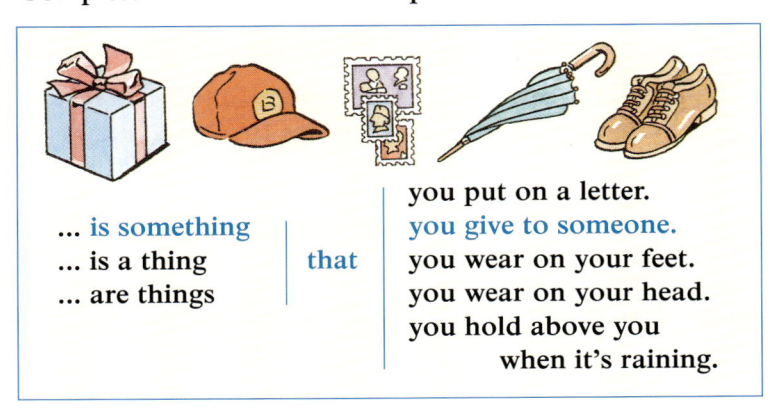

| ... is something
... is a thing
... are things | that | you put on a letter.
you give to someone.
you wear on your feet.
you wear on your head.
you hold above you when it's raining. |

➡ A present is something that you give to someone.

Now you can play this game. One pupil thinks of something and then says three things about it.

Heike I've thought of something that you can light. You can see it in the dark. And it's something that you see at New Year.
Anton Is it a candle?
Heike No, it isn't.
Regina Is it a firework?
Heike Yes, it is.
Regina Now it's my turn. It's a thing you can listen to …

Unit 7 TEXT 2

🔊 Kirsty's diary

Saturday 10th August
We're here at last! Yesterday we flew from Heathrow to San Francisco. The journey was boring, but we watched films. We are five boys and five girls – a baseball team and one extra for luck! Mr and Mrs Coleman are with us. At the airport Mr and Mrs Avery were waiting for us. They drove us to Sonoma, the town where we're staying. It's in the 'Wine Country'. My family are called Anderson, and they're really nice and friendly. Their daughter Nicole is in the baseball club here. After we arrived there was a barbecue for everyone at the Averys' house. I talked to a boy called Justin.

Today Nicole took me into Sonoma. We went to the Plaza, a big square in the middle of the town. There were some old buildings and the mission. I bought a lot of postcards. Later we met the others, and we all went bowling. Justin was there. It was great.

Monday 12th August
We played our first game yesterday – and lost. It was England (girls and boys) against America (girls and boys). Justin was their best player. He can catch and hit. We didn't play so well. Royston says it's jet lag.

We drove to a beach today. Some of the Americans came with us. We swam in the sea. The water was cold! Justin splashed me, so I splashed him back. Cindy fancies Ben. She talks to him all the time, but Ben and Royston stay together. I expect Ben is too young for girlfriends.

Tuesday 13th August
In the morning Mr and Mrs Anderson drove Nicole and me out into the country, and we visited a farm. In the afternoon our team played softball with some of the Americans. It's a game that American girls play. It's like baseball but not exactly the same. It sounds like a game for little kids, but the ball isn't really soft. If it hits you, it hurts! But it was good fun. With all this activity we're all very very tired. I'm sure I'll sleep well tonight.

Justin wasn't at the softball game. Will he be on the trip to San Francisco tomorrow?

Main Street, Sonoma

Sonoma Plaza

Thursday 15th August

Yesterday was a big day because we went to San Francisco. It's only 45 minutes away. We drove along Highway 101 over the Golden Gate Bridge. In the city we took a cable car up a hill. It's called Nob Hill, and it's really really steep.

In the afternoon we went to a part of the city called Fisherman's Wharf and looked at all the boats. Then we looked round an old chocolate factory and ate some wonderful chocolate. I bought a box for my mum and dad.

In the evening we drove to 3 Com Park, where the San Francisco Giants play. We saw their National League game against the San Diego Padres. The Giants won 5-4. Justin sat next to me, and we talked about the game. Later, when we got back to Sonoma, he gave me a kiss.

Today we played another game against the Americans, and this time was better. We didn't win, but we played OK. Maybe we've learned something. This was our last day. We've had a fantastic time here. Justin is going to come to the airport with us tomorrow. He says he's going to write to me. I haven't written my postcards yet!

Fisherman's Wharf

View from Powell Street

TEXT 2

EXERCISE 13

Say which day these things happened.

➡ They went to a beach.
  They went to a beach on Monday.
1 They visited San Francisco and watched a big baseball game.
2 They had a game of softball.
3 The American kids played baseball against the English for the first time.
4 The English kids played better in the second game.
5 The group arrived in California.
6 They flew back to London.
7 Kirsty had her first conversation with Justin.

EXERCISE 14

When Ben got home from California, his mum asked him about the trip. Put in the missing verbs.

Mum Well, did you have a good time?
Ben We had a great time. It was fantastic. All the Americans ... so nice and friendly.
Mum How did the baseball go?
Ben Well, we ... two games against them, but we ... both times. They ... much better than us. We ... softball, too, and that ... fun.
Mum And did you see something of California?
Ben Yes, the Americans ... us to some interesting places, and we ... a lot of exciting things. And we ... over the Golden Gate Bridge.
Mum How was San Francisco?
Ben Great. We ... the Giants against San Diego. Everyone ... it. Oh, and one day we ... bowling. And we ... in the sea.
Mum I expect you're tired now.
Ben Yes, a bit, but I ... most of the time on the plane.

one hundred and five 105

Unit 7 **TEXT 2**

EXERCISE 15

Kirsty forgot her postcards, but Royston didn't. On Tuesday evening he wrote a card to his mum. Can you complete the card?

Dear Mum,
I think it's ... here. ... all enjoying it. We ... here OK on Friday. I was ... because I had ... lag, but I'm ... now. Our first ... against the American team was on ... , and we ... . Yesterday we ... and ... . This afternoon we ... with ... . Tomorrow it's our trip ... . We're going to watch a ... . It's against ... . I'm looking ... to it. I'll see you on ... .
Love, Royston

EXERCISE 16

Put four of these words in each group.

ambulance, beans, bus, car, castle, coat, crisps, factory, hit, hospital, jacket, jump, lake, ocean, palace, potato, push, river, run, sausage, sea, skirt, sweater, taxi

Buildings: castle, ...
Water: ...
Food: ...
Traffic: ...
Clothes: ...
Actions: ...

EXERCISE 17

101 Listen and repeat.

[tʃ]   [dʒ]
ri**ch**   ri**dge**

Listen and find the missing letters.

a∗e • bea∗ • ca∗e • ∗ips • fu∗ure •
hu∗e • ∗udo • lar∗e • ma∗or • pic∗ure •
ques∗on • tea∗ • tor∗ure • wa∗

Listen and check. Then put the words [tʃ] [dʒ] in two groups in your exercise book.   bea**ch** a**ge**

102 Now listen again and check.

COMMUNICATION

Explaining words

Wörter erklären

Short explanations

A movie is a film.
An ocean is a big sea.
A millennium is a thousand years.
A wardrobe is a cupboard for clothes.
A cottage is a small house in the country.

Where

A playground is a place where children play.
A cinema is a building where people watch films.

Who and that

A fan is someone who supports a team.
A letter is a message that you write to someone.

EXERCISE 18

Find the right explanation for each word and write the sentence.

➡ a parent	an underground ... .
1 a child	a room ... you eat.
2 a dining-room	a mother or ... .
3 the afternoon	a meal ... you eat in the morning.
4 an actor	a ... person.
5 a teenager	the middle part of the ... .
6 breakfast	someone between 13 and 19 ... old.
7 a cellar	someone ... works in films or television.

➡ A parent is a mother or father.

EXERCISE 19

Can you explain these words?

1 weekend
2 a library
3 an American
4 a city
5 a bus-stop
6 a nest
7 a zoo
8 homework
9 your grandma

ACTIVITIES 2

1 BAKED POTATOES

At a barbecue you often eat baked potatoes. But they are also nice when you do them at home in the oven. This is what you need to feed two hungry pupils:

➤ Wash the potatoes.
➤ Cut them once.
➤ Put some oil under and on the potatoes. Use salt and herbs as you like.
➤ Bake the potatoes for 45 minutes at 200° C. When they are soft, they are done.
➤ Have a salad together with your potatoes.

Hmmm ... enjoy one of my favourite meals!

2 DO YOU REMEMBER?

Who said:

1 Well, it isn't the end of the world, but in two weeks I'll be without a job.
2 Remember, remember, the fifth of November!
3 I've got my mobile. I can ring 999.
4 You're hopeless. You're the most hopeless sister in the world.
5 Well, I know all about gunpowder.
6 Hey, I like your baseball cap.
7 Maybe we can find a quicker way home.
8 You're soft. That's because you live in the warm south. We're tough here in Scotland.

3 CAN YOU READ THIS?

Does your American boyfriend or girlfriend love you when he or she writes:
I C U R 2 much 4 me...
And what's the best answer to this message:
What about a B-B-Q 4 U 2 N 8?

one hundred and seven 107

Unit 7 POEMS

OCTOPUS
103 by John Paton

I'd like to be an octopus,
With arms on every corner,
I'd scare my granny close to death;
I wouldn't even warn her.

MULES
104 Anon.

On mules we find two legs behind
And two we find before.
We stand behind – before we find
What those behind are for.
We find before the two before
Just what they, too, are for.
So stand before the two behind
And behind the two before.

A SEA SERPENT
105 Anon.

A sea serpent saw a big tanker,
Bit a hole in her side and then sank her,
It swallowed the crew,
In a minute or two,
And then picked its teeth with the anchor.

POEMS

A GORILLA
by Sarah Mills

A gorilla once visited Spain,
And said crossly, 'I'll not come again,
A land full of farmers
Who can't grow bananas
And it's true what they say about rain.'

DOCTOR BELL
Anon.

Doctor Bell fell down the well
And broke his collar-bone.
Doctors should attend the sick
And leave the well alone.

LIMERICK

There was an old lady from Riga,
Who rode with a smile on a tiger.
They came back from the ride,
With the lady inside,
And a smile on the face of the tiger.

TWELVE MONTHS

January comes with frost and snow,
February brings on winds that blow,
March has winds and happy hours,
April brings us sun and showers,
Pretty is the month of May,
June has flowers sweet and gay,
July begins our holiday,
August bears us all away,
September takes us back to school,
October days begin to cool,
November brings the leaves to earth,
December, Christmas with its mirth.

American English Amerikanisches Englisch

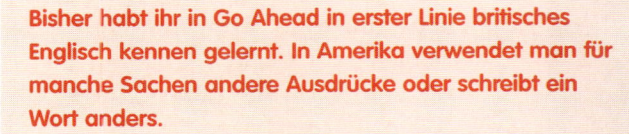

trailer

gas station

fall

Bisher habt ihr in Go Ahead in erster Linie britisches Englisch kennen gelernt. In Amerika verwendet man für manche Sachen andere Ausdrücke oder schreibt ein Wort anders.

Here are some American words. Do you remember the British words? They are all in the vocabulary list.

truck

yard

subway

garbage

Grammatical terms Grammatikalische Fachausdrücke

adjective [ˈædʒɪktɪv]	Eigenschaftswort, Adjektiv	*big, good, bad, dangerous, expensive, …*
adverb [ˈædvɜːb]	Adverb	***very** big, **usually**, …*
adverb of frequency [ˈædvɜːb əv ˈfriːkwənsi]	Adverb der Häufigkeit	*always, often, never, …*
adverb of manner [ˈædvɜːb əv ˈmænə]	Adverb der Art und Weise	*carefully, slowly, well, …*
article [ˈɑːtɪkl]	Geschlechtswort, Artikel	*a, an, the*
auxiliary verb [ɔːgˈzɪliəri vɜːb]	Hilfsverb	***don't** know, **is** swimming, **has** seen*
comparative [kəmˈpærətɪv]	Komparativ, erste Steigerungsform	*bigger, better, more interesting, …*
comparison of adjectives [kəmˈpærɪsn əv ˈædʒɪktɪvz]	Steigerung der Adjektive	*big – bigger – biggest; as big as, bigger than*
conjunction [kənˈdʒʌŋkʃn]	Bindewort, Konjunktion	*and, or, but, after, when, …*
consonant [ˈkɒnsənənt]	Mitlaut, Konsonant	*b, c, d, f, g, k, …*
future with *going to* [ˈfjuːtʃə]	Futur mit *going to*	*I'm **going to leave** now.*
future with *will* [ˈfjuːtʃə]	Futur mit *will*	*I **will come** tomorrow.*
imperative [ɪmˈperətɪv]	Befehlsform, Imperativ	*Now **listen**. **Don't talk** to your neighbour.*
infinitive [ɪnˈfɪnətɪv]	Grundform, Infinitiv	*to go, to see, to eat, to run, to work, …*
***ing*-form** [ˈɪŋfɔːm]	*-ing*-Form	*singing, dancing, sitting, …*
irregular verb [ɪˌregjʊlə ˈvɜːb]	unregelmäßiges Verb	*do – **did** – **done**, buy – **bought** – **bought**, …*
long form [ˈlɒŋ fɔːm]	Langform	*He **is** reading. She **does not** work.*
main verb [meɪn ˈvɜːb]	Vollverb	*work, dance, read, write, play, …*
modal auxiliary [məʊdl ɔːgˈzɪliəri]	Modalverb	*can, must, …*
negative statement [ˈnegətɪv steɪtmənt]	verneinter Aussagesatz	*Emily does**n't** like tennis.*
noun [naʊn]	Namenwort, Nomen, Substantiv	*house, book, tea, plan, idea, …*
object [ˈɒbdʒɪkt]	Satzergänzung, Objekt	*She likes **pop music**.*
***of*-phrase** [ˈɒvfreɪz]	Fügung mit *of*	*the name **of** the game*
past progressive [pɑːst prəˈgresɪv]	Verlaufsform der Vergangenheit	*She **was** reading. We **were** watching TV.*
personal pronoun [pɜːsənl ˈprəʊnaʊn]	persönliches Fürwort, Personalpronomen	*I, you, she, … , me, us, them, …*
plural [ˈplʊərəl]	Mehrzahl, Plural	*books, letters, dogs, wom**en**, child**ren**, feet*
positive [ˈpɒzətɪv]	Positiv, Grundform des Adjektivs	*good – better – best, **interesting** – more interesting – most interesting*
positive statement [ˈpɒzətɪv steɪtmənt]	bejahter Aussagesatz, Erzählsatz	*I speak English and French.*
possessive adjective [pəˈzesɪv ædʒɪktɪv]	adjektivisch gebrauchtes besitzanzeigendes Fürwort, Possessivpronomen	*my, your, his, her, its, our, your, their*
possessive form [pəˈzesɪv fɔːm]	besitzanzeigende Form, *s*-Genitiv	***Adam's** computer, **his friends'** books*
possessive pronoun [pəˈzesɪv prəʊnaʊn]	nominal gebrauchtes Possessivpronomen	*mine, yours, his, hers, its, ours, yours, theirs*

Grammatikalische Fachausdrücke

preposition [prepə'zɪʃn]	Verhältniswort, Präposition	*in, at, on, with, because of, …*
present perfect [preznt 'pɜːfɪkt]	*present perfect* (Perfekt)	*We **have finished** the lesson.*
present progressive [preznt prə'ɡresɪv]	Verlaufsform des Präsens	*I **am watching** TV.*
pronoun ['prəʊnaʊn]	Fürwort, Pronomen	*I, me, my, this, …*
question ['kwestʃn]	Frage, Fragesatz	***Is Adam at school?** – No, he isn't.* *– **Where is Adam?***
question word ['kwestʃn wɜːd]	Fragewort	*what, when, where, who, whose, why, which, how*
regular verb [reɡjʊlə 'vɜːb]	regelmäßiges Verb	*call – called – called, …*
relative clause ['relətɪv klɑːz]	Relativsatz	*The girl **who phoned** was Mary.*
relative pronoun [relətɪv 'prəʊnaʊn]	Relativpronomen	*who, that, …*
sentence ['sentəns]	Satz, Satzgefüge	*I love Star Trek. Do you speak French?*
short answer ['ʃɔːt ɑːnsə]	Kurzantwort	*Do you understand? – **Yes, I do.***
short form ['ʃɔːt fɔːm]	Kurzform	***I've** got a rabbit. **She's** over there.* *– **I can't** see her.*
simple past [sɪmpl 'pɑːst]	einfache Form der Vergangenheit	*I **called** Katie. She **bought** a new skirt.*
simple present [sɪmpl 'preznt]	einfache Form des Präsens	*She **reads** love stories every day.*
singular ['sɪŋɡjʊlə]	Einzahl, Singular	*book, letter, dog, woman, child, foot*
statement ['steɪtmənt]	Aussage, Aussagesatz	*She likes cats. I don't like dinosaurs.*
subject ['sʌbdʒɪkt]	Satzgegenstand, Subjekt	***Jessica** likes maths. **The girl over there** is Sophie.*
superlative [suː'pɜːlətɪv]	Superlativ, höchste Steigerungsform	***biggest**, **best**, **most** interesting, …*
verb [vɜːb]	a) Zeitwort, Verb b) Satzaussage, Prädikat	*be, love, play, get up, … ; can, will, do, …* *She **likes** yoghurt. We **can play** cards.*
vowel ['vaʊəl]	Vokal, Selbstlaut	*a, e, i, o, u*
word order ['wɜːd ɔːdə]	Wortstellung	*subject – verb – object (S – V – O)*
***yes/no* question** [jes'nəʊ kwestʃən]	Entscheidungsfrage	***Is Adam at home?** – Yes, he is. / No, he isn't.*

Classroom phrases

The teacher can say …

Sit down, please.	Bitte nehmt Platz.
Be quiet.	Seid ruhig.
Please speak up.	Sprich bitte lauter.
Open your books at page … .	Öffnet eure Bücher auf Seite … .
Read the text on page … .	Lies den Text auf Seite … .
Do exercise … for homework.	Macht die Übung … als Hausaufgabe.
Write the answers in your exercise book.	Schreibt die Antworten in eure Übungshefte.
That's not very good.	Das ist nicht sehr gut.
Very good. Well done.	Sehr gut. Gut gemacht.

You can say …

Good morning, Mr/Mrs/Miss … .	Guten Morgen, Herr/Frau … .
I'm sorry I'm late.	Es tut mir Leid, dass ich zu spät komme.
My train/bus was late.	Mein Zug/Bus hatte Verspätung.
Can I go to the toilet, please?	Kann ich bitte auf die Toilette gehen?
Can I open/shut the window?	Darf ich das Fenster öffnen/schließen?
I'm not feeling well.	Ich fühle mich nicht wohl.
What page are we on?	Auf welcher Seite sind wir?
What's this in English/German?	Wie heißt das auf Englisch/Deutsch?
What does … mean?	Was bedeutet … ?
I don't understand this word/sentence.	Ich verstehe dieses Wort/diesen Satz nicht.
Can you write this word/sentence on the board, please?	Können Sie dieses Wort/diesen Satz bitte an die Tafel schreiben?
Can you explain it, please?	Können Sie das bitte erklären?
Pardon?	Wie bitte?
Can I ask a question?	Darf ich eine Frage stellen?
I don't know the answer.	Ich weiß die Antwort nicht.
Can you repeat the answer?	Kannst du die Antwort wiederholen?
I'm sorry. I haven't got my homework.	Es tut mir Leid. Ich habe meine Hausaufgabe nicht.
I've got something different.	Ich habe etwas anderes.
What's for homework, please?	Was haben wir auf?
Goodbye/Bye.	Auf Wiedersehen!

GRAMMATIKANHANG

UNIT 1

1 the comparison of adjectives — Steigerung und Vergleich von Adjektiven

a

fast	**faster**	**fastest**
schnell	*schneller*	*am schnellsten*
		der Schnellste

Wenn wir zwei oder mehrere Personen oder Dinge vergleichen, verwenden wir die Steigerung.

b comparison of short and long adjectives — Steigerung kurzer und langer Adjektive

The Spitfire is **old** and **expensive**.

The Morgan car is **old**er and **more** expensive.

The Rolls Royce is **the old**est and **most** expensive.

Im Englischen gibt es zwei Arten der Steigerung: die mit *-er/-est* und die mit *more* und *most*.

Wie ein Adjektiv gesteigert wird, hängt von seiner Länge ab.

c comparison with '-er/-est' — Steigerung mit „-er/-est"

POSITIVE	COMPARATIVE	SUPERLATIVE
cheap	cheap**er**	cheap**est**
short	short**er**	short**est**
nic**e**	nic**er**	nic**est**
big	big**g**er	big**g**est
hot	hot**t**er	hot**t**est

Alle kurzen, **einsilbigen** Adjektive steigern wir, indem wir die Endung *-er/-est* anhängen.

Beachte die Schreibweise:
- stummes *-e* entfällt.
- Verdopplung des Endkonsonanten, wenn der vorangehende Vokal als ein Buchstabe geschrieben wird und betont ist.

Das kommt mir irgendwie bekannt vor.

Ja, das stimmt. Beim present progressive war das auch schon so:
I make → I'm making
I sit → I'm sitting

Grammatikanhang UNIT 1

Beachte die Aussprache bei Adjektiven auf *-ng*!

long [lɒŋ]	long**er** ['lɒŋɡə]	long**est** ['lɒŋɡɪst]
happ**y**	happ**ier**	happ**iest**
eas**y**	eas**ier**	eas**iest**
bus**y**	bus**ier**	bus**iest**

Bei **zweisilbigen** Adjektiven, die auf *-y* enden (*happy*), hängen wir ebenfalls die Endung *-er/-est* an. *-y* wird dabei zu *-i-*.

Steigerung mit „more/most"

comparison with 'more/most'   d

famous	**more** famous	**most** famous
careful	**more** careful	**most** careful
boring	**more** boring	**most** boring
expensive	**more** expensive	**most** expensive
difficult	**more** difficult	**most** difficult

Die meisten anderen **zweisilbigen** Adjektive steigern wir mit *more/most*.

Drei- und mehrsilbige Adjektive werden immer mit *more/most* gesteigert.

Unregelmäßige Steigerungsformen

irregular comparison   e

good	**better**	**best**
bad	**worse**	**worst**
far	**further**	**furthest**
weit	*weiter*	*am weitesten*
much/many	**more**	**most**
viel/viele	*mehr*	*am meisten*

Einige Adjektive haben unregelmäßige Steigerungsformen.

Vergleich

comparison   f

Mme Tussaud's is **more interesting than** Hyde Park.

My brother is **older than** me.

Bei Vergleichen mit einem Komparativ benutzen wir *than* (als). Folgt auf das *than* nur noch ein Pronomen, so steht dieses in der Objektform (*me/you/him/her/us/them*).

The cassettes are **as expensive as** the CDs.

The film is**n't as good as** the book.

Vergleichssätze mit einem Adjektiv in der Grundstufe (Positiv) bilden wir mit *as … as* (so … wie), um auszudrücken, dass etwas gleich ist.

not as … as (nicht so … wie) verwenden wir, wenn etwas nicht gleich ist.

Who is **the oldest** pupil in the class?

Normalerweise steht *the* vor dem Superlativ. Beachte aber: **most** *people* = **die meisten** Leute

one hundred and fifteen   **115**

UNIT 2   **Grammatikanhang**

1 the simple past | Das simple past

Janet and Tom **were** at home yesterday afternoon.

It **rained** all afternoon.

In the evening Janet **worked** on her project but Tom **went** to the cinema with some friends.

Wir verwenden das *simple past*, um über die Vergangenheit zu sprechen. Das *simple past* kommt oft in Berichten, Geschichten und Erzählungen vor.

Meist wird es mit Zeitbestimmungen wie *yesterday*, *last Friday*, *last summer*, *in 1984* usw. gebraucht.

Mit dem *simple past* sagen wir, **wann etwas geschehen ist** oder **wann jemand etwas getan hat**.

2 the simple past of 'be' | Das simple past von „be"

a positive statements with 'was/were' | Bejahte Aussagesätze mit „was/were"

I	was
You	were
He/She/It	was
We	were
You	were
They	were

here last night.

Das *simple past* für *be* lautet *was/were*.

Wie kann man sich merken, wann *was* und wann *were* verwendet wird?

Das ist ganz einfach:

Steht im *simple present* …	**am/is**	**are**
benutzt du im *simple past* …	**was**	**were**

b negative statements with 'was/were' | Verneinte Aussagesätze mit „was/were"

SHORT FORMS	LONG FORMS
I **was**n't	I **was not**
You **were**n't	You **were not**
He/She/It **was**n't there.	He/She/It **was not** there.
We **were**n't	We **were not**
You **were**n't	You **were not**
They **were**n't	They **were not**

Um die Verneinung zu bilden, hängen wir *not* an *was/were* an.

Es gibt bei der Verneinung Kurz- und Langformen.

116   one hundred and sixteen

Grammatikanhang UNIT 2

Entscheidungsfragen mit „was/were"

Bei Entscheidungsfragen mit *was/were* vertauschst du einfach Subjekt (*subject*) und Verb (*verb*).

War das nicht bei *is/are/am* schon so?

Klar, aus *He **is** in London.* wurde ***Is** he in London?*

yes/no questions with 'was/were' c

SUBJECT	VERB	
He	was	in London.

VERB	SUBJECT		
Was	he	in London?	– Yes, he **was**.
			– No, he **wasn't**.

Fragen mit Fragewörtern

Auch hier musst du Subjekt und Verb vertauschen, um eine Frage zu bilden.

Die Fragewörter (*where/what/how/…*) stehen davor, also ganz am Anfang des Fragesatzes.

questions with question words d

	VERB	SUBJECT	
Where	was	he?	– In Spain.
What	was	her name?	– Sophie.
How	was	your visit?	– It was great.

Das simple past: regelmäßige Verben

the simple past: regular verbs 3

Bejahte Aussagesätze

Das *simple past* bildest du aus der Grundform des Verbs und der Endung *-ed*.

Es gibt nur eine Form für alle Personen.

Für die Aussprache der *-ed*-Endung gelten folgende Regeln:

- nach harten (stimmlosen) Lauten → [t]
- nach weichen (stimmhaften) Lauten → [d]
- nach den Lauten [t] und [d] → [ɪd]

Beachte die Schreibung:

- stummes *-e* entfällt.
- *-y* nach Konsonant wird zu *-i-*.
- Endkonsonant wird verdoppelt, wenn der vorangehende Vokal als ein Buchstabe geschrieben wird und betont ist.

positive statements a

I/You
He/She/It **started** at 9 o'clock.
We/You/They

as**ked** [ɑːskt]
ope**ned** ['əʊpənd]
shou**ted** ['ʃaʊtɪd]   nee**ded** ['niːdɪd]

arrive → arriv**ed**   phone → phon**ed**
carry → carr**ied**   tidy → tid**ied**
stop → sto**pped**

UNIT 2   Grammatikanhang

b   **negative statements**

The pony **didn't like** the noise.
Jessica **didn't get** up.
I **didn't see** the film in the cinema.

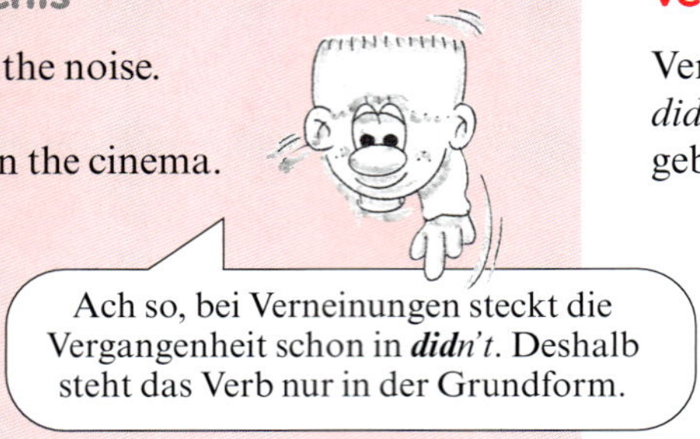

Verneinte Aussagesätze

Verneinungen werden für alle Personen mit *did not/didn't* und der Grundform des Verbs gebildet.

Ach so, bei Verneinungen steckt die Vergangenheit schon in **did**n't. Deshalb steht das Verb nur in der Grundform.

Du hast es erfasst.

c   **questions**

Did you visit the Tower of London?
  – Yes I **did**. / – No, I **didn't**.

Did Sophie do her maths homework?
  – Yes, she **did**. / – No, she **didn't**.

Did they watch a Dracula film?
  – Yes, they **did**. / – No, they **didn't**.

Where did the accident happen?
When did the ambulance arrive?
Why did the accident happen?

Adam wanted to buy it.
↓
Who   wanted to buy the computer game?
Wer wollte …?

An accident happened.
↓
What   happened?
Was geschah?

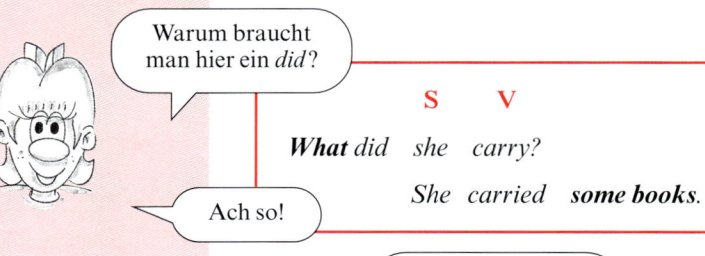

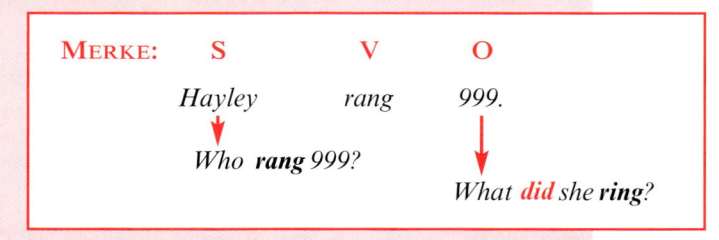

Fragen

Yes/No Fragen im *simple past* werden mit *did* und der Grundform des Verbs gebildet. *did* wird vorangestellt, dann folgen das Subjekt und die Grundform des Verbs.

Bei Fragen mit Fragewörtern (*where/when/why/…*) stehen diese am Satzanfang.

Wenn *who* oder *what* nach dem Subjekt fragt, so steht **kein** *did*.

Warum braucht man hier ein *did*?

        S   V
What did she carry?
       She carried **some books**.

Ach so!

What fragt hier nach dem Objekt (*some books*).

MERKE: S   V   O
     Hayley   rang   999.
       ↓   ↓
     Who **rang** 999?
                    What **did** she **ring**?

Das simple past: unregelmäßige Verben

Einige Verben haben unregelmäßige Formen für das *simple past*.

come → **came**   fall → **fell**   have → **had**

Du musst diese besonderen Formen auswendig lernen. Auf den Seiten 152–153 findest du eine Liste aller unregelmäßigen Verben von **Go Ahead 5** und **6**.

Fragen und Verneinungen bildest du bei den unregelmäßigen Verben genauso wie bei den regelmäßigen Verben.

the simple past: irregular verbs — 4

The children **came** out of the forest.
Jessica **fell** off the pony.
I **had** a funny dream last night.

INFINITIVE	SIMPLE PAST
drive	drove
fall	fell
go	went
have	had

Ravi **flew** to India last summer.
Did he **fly** with his parents? – Yes, he **did**.
                                     – No, he **didn't**.
He **didn't** fly alone.

UNIT 3

Das future mit „going to"

Wir verwenden das *future* mit *going to*, um auszudrücken, …

◆ dass jemand etwas vorhat oder plant:
Liz **is going to** make a sandwich.
Liz hat vor, ein Sandwich zu machen.

◆ dass etwas bald geschehen wird, weil es schon Anzeichen dafür gibt:
Look at the sky. It**'s going to** rain.
Schau den Himmel an. Es wird gleich regnen.

the future with 'going to' — 1 a

Bejahte Aussagesätze

In bejahten Aussagesätzen verwenden wir *am/are/is going to* + Grundform.

positive statements — b

I**'m**
You**'re**
He/She/It**'s**   going to **leave** in a minute.
We**'re**
You**'re**
They**'re**

Man kann diese Form leicht mit dem *present progressive* verwechseln:

I'm going to school.   *Ich gehe (gerade) zur Schule.*
I'm going to go back.   *Ich habe vor zurückzugehen.*

Ja, da muss man unheimlich aufpassen.

one hundred and nineteen

UNIT 3   Grammatikanhang

c negative statements

I'm not
You aren't
He/She/It isn't   going to stop.
We/You/They aren't

Verneinte Aussagesätze

In verneinten Aussagesätzen verwenden wir *am not/aren't/isn't going to* + Grundform.

d questions and short answers

Am I
Are you
Is he/she/it   going to stop?
Are we/you/they

– **Yes**, they are. / **No**, they aren't.

When are you going to **watch** TV tonight?
Who is going to **play** with me?

Fragen und Kurzantworten

Bei Fragen stehen *am/are/is* am Satzanfang vor dem Subjekt.

Fragewörter stehen am Satzanfang.

Wenn *who* und *what* nach dem Subjekt fragen, ist die Satzstellung wie im Aussagesatz.

2 possessive pronouns

Is this **your CD**, Kim? – No, Liz, it's **yours**.
deine CD   *deine*

POSSESSIVE ADJECTIVES		POSSESSIVE PRONOUNS	
my	mein	mine	meine(r,s)
your	dein; Ihr	yours	deine(r,s); Ihre(r, s)
his	sein	his	seine(r,s)
her	ihr	hers	ihre(r,s)
its	sein, ihr	—	
our	unser	ours	unsere(r,s)
your	euer; Ihr	yours	eure(r,s); Ihre(r,s)
their	ihr	theirs	ihre(r,s)

Possessivpronomen

Die Possessivbegleiter (*my/your/his/her/…*) kennst du bereits. Sie stehen immer **vor einem Nomen**.

Die Possessivpronomen (*mine/yours/his/hers/…*) stehen allein, d.h. **ohne Nomen**. Wir verwenden sie, wenn wir ein Nomen, das bereits erwähnt wurde, nicht wiederholen wollen.

Anstelle von:
*This is **your disk** and that's **my disk**.*
kann ich sagen:
*This is **your disk** and that's **mine**.*

Klar.

Grammatikanhang UNIT 4

Das present perfect / the present perfect   1

Wir verwenden das *present perfect*, wenn wir sagen wollen, **dass jemand etwas getan hat** oder **dass etwas geschehen ist**.
Der **genaue Zeitpunkt** des Geschehens ist **unwichtig** und wird **nicht genannt**.

Oft wirkt sich die Handlung auf die Gegenwart oder Zukunft aus.

Tim hat seine Hausaufgaben vollständig gemacht. Wir wissen, **dass** er sie gemacht hat, aber **nicht wann**.

TIM **I've finished** my homework. Now we can play football.

Also, jetzt kann er Fußball spielen.

Das present perfect: regelmäßige Verben / the present perfect: regular verbs   2

Bejahte Aussagesätze / positive statements   a

Das *present perfect* bildest du mit *have/has* und dem Partizip Perfekt (*past participle*).

Bei regelmäßigen Verben hängt man für das Partizip Perfekt *-ed* an die Grundform:
work → work**ed**   talk → talk**ed**

I	**have walked**	home.
You	**'ve walked**	
He/She/It	**has walked**	home.
	's walked	
We	**have walked**	home.
You	**'ve walked**	
They		

one hundred and twenty-one **121**

UNIT 4   Grammatikanhang

b spelling and pronunciation

arriv**e**   have/has arriv**ed**
carr**y**   have/has carr**ied**
sto**p**   have/has sto**pped**

> *I have* used it. heißt „Ich **habe** ihn benutzt." Was heißt aber „Ich **bin** angekommen."?

> *I have* arrived. Egal, ob es im Deutschen „haben" oder „sein" heißt – beim *present perfect* steht immer *have* oder *has*.

Schreibweise und Aussprache

Für die Schreibweise und Aussprache der -*ed*-Endung gelten dieselben Regeln wie für das *past tense* (vgl. S. 117).

Beachte die unterschiedliche Satzstellung im Deutschen:
*They **have used** the computer.*
Sie **haben** den Computer **benutzt**.

c negative statements

I/You	**have not** found **haven't** found	the answer.
He/She/It	**has not** found **hasn't** found	the answer.
We/You/They	**have not** walked **haven't** walked	home.

Verneinte Aussagesätze

Verneinungen werden mit *have not* (*haven't*) oder *has not* (*hasn't*) und dem Partizip Perfekt gebildet.

d questions

Have	I/you		
Has	he/she/it	**start**ed? **been** there?	
Have	we/you/they		

Where	**have**	you	**been**?	
Why	**has**	she	**left**?	

He   **has seen** her.
↓
Who   **has seen** her?

Fragen

Bei Fragen stehen *have* oder *has* vor dem Subjekt.

Kurzantworten werden mit Subjekt + *have* oder *has* gebildet:

*Yes, I/you/we/you/they **have**.*
     *he/she/it **has**.*
*No, I/you/we/you/they **haven't**.*
     *he/she/it **hasn't**.*

Bei Fragen mit Fragewörtern (*where/when/why/…*) stehen diese am Satzanfang.

Wenn *who* oder *what* nach dem Subjekt fragen, ist die Satzstellung wie im Aussagesatz.

Grammatikanhang — UNIT 4

Das present perfect: unregelmäßige Verben | the present perfect: irregular verbs — 3

Unregelmäßige Verben haben für das Partizip Perfekt eine besondere Form, die du wie die *simple past* Form zusammen mit der Grundform lernen musst:

> write – **wrote** – written
> buy – **bought** – bought
> see – **saw** – seen
> be – **was** – been
> have – **had** – had
> do – **did** – done
> send – **sent** – sent

Ab jetzt stehen auch im Vokabelanhang alle drei Formen, wenn ein unregelmäßiges Verb zum ersten Mal vorkommt.

Am besten lernst du alle drei Formen auswendig.

Auf den Seiten 152–153 findest du eine Liste aller unregelmäßigen Verben von **Go Ahead 5** und **6**.

a The children **have brought** their pets to school.
He**'s seen** the show on TV.
I**'ve done** my homework.

Fragen und verneinte Aussagesätze | questions and negatives — b

Fragen und Verneinungen bildest du bei den unregelmäßigen Verben genauso wie bei den regelmäßigen Verben.

Ben **has written** an e-mail to Jürgen.
Has he **written** in English? – **Yes**, he **has**.
 – **No**, he **hasn't**.
Jürgen **hasn't written** an answer.

LIZ Ben, **have** you **sent** an e-mail to Cindy?
BEN No, **I haven't**. My mother **hasn't found** her e-mail address.

Das present perfect mit „already/just/yet" | the present perfect with 'already/just/yet' — 4

Sätze im *present perfect* drücken aus, dass etwas **irgendwann** in der Vergangenheit passiert ist. Wann genau wird nicht gesagt.

Deshalb steht das *present perfect* oft zusammen mit **Adverbien der unbestimmten Zeit** wie *just*, *already* und *yet*.

already und *just* stehen vor dem Partizip Perfekt; *yet* dagegen steht am Satzende.

I**'ve already seen** the new James Bond film.
  schon, bereits

Adam **has just talked** to Ben about it on the phone.
  gerade, soeben

Have you **seen** Royston **yet**? He's got green hair now.
  schon?

No, **I haven't seen** him **yet**.
  noch nicht

one hundred and twenty-three — 123

UNIT 4 Grammatikanhang

5 'some' and 'any' / „Some" und „any"

a

There are **some sandwiches** on the table, but there
(einige/ein paar) Sandwiches
… is**n't any** tea.
kein Tee

Wir verwenden *some* und *any* zusammen mit Substantiven, um über eine **unbestimmte Menge oder Zahl** zu sprechen.

Zählbare Nomen (*sandwiches, cups*) stehen dabei im Plural,
nicht zählbare Nomen (*tea*) im Singular.

b positive statements / Bejahte Aussagesätze

Lehka wanted **some tickets** for the pop concert.

Royston had **some water**.

There's no **cola** in the cellar. Let's go and buy **some**.

In bejahten Aussagesätzen verwenden wir *some*.

Vor Nomen im Plural hat *some* meistens die Bedeutung „einige/ein paar".

Bei nicht zählbaren Nomen hat *some* oft keine Entsprechung im Deutschen. Es bedeutet „ein bisschen, etwas".

some kann auch alleine, anstelle eines vorher erwähnten Nomens (*cola*) stehen.

c negative statements and questions / Verneinte Aussagesätze und Fragen

There aren't **any tickets**.
Es gibt keine Eintrittskarten.
I haven't got **any money**.
Ich habe kein Geld.

Are there **any tickets** left?
Sind noch Eintrittskarten da?
Have you got **any money**?
Hast du Geld?

Are there **any magazines** on history?
Sorry. We have**n't** got **any**. *Wir haben keine.*

Can you lend me **some money**?
Would you like to listen to **some CDs**?

any steht vor allem
◆ in verneinten Aussagesätzen

◆ und in Fragen.

Es hat meist keine Entsprechung im Deutschen.

Auch *any* kann alleine stehen, wenn ein Nomen (*magazines*) vorher erwähnt wurde.

some wird jedoch **in Fragen** gebraucht, wenn man um etwas **bittet** oder etwas **anbietet**.

Grammatikanhang UNIT 5

Das future mit „will"
the future with 'will' — 1a

Das *future* mit *will* verwenden wir,

◆ wenn wir sagen, **was in Zukunft geschehen wird**. Oft geht es um Dinge, die wir nicht beeinflussen können.

◆ wenn wir **gerade**, während des Sprechens, eine **Entscheidung treffen**.

Laura **will be** 15 in November.
It **will rain** in the South tomorrow.

I think I**'ll go** to the youth club tonight.

Bejahte Aussagesätze
positive statements — b

Wir bilden das *will-future* mit *will* und der Grundform des Verbs. Alle Personen haben dieselbe Form.

I/You
He/She/It   **will**   **be** here tomorrow.
We/You/They   **'ll**

Vorsicht, *will* nicht mit „wollen" verwechseln!

Verneinte Aussagesätze
negative statements — c

Verneinte Aussagesätze werden mit *will not*/*won't* und der Grundform des Verbs gebildet.

I/You
He/She/It   **will not**   **come** today.
We/You/They   **won't**

Fragen
questions — d

Bei Fragen steht *will* vor dem Subjekt.

Will I/you he/she/it we/you/they **arrive** tomorrow?

Kurzantworten werden wie folgt gebildet:

Yes, I/you/he/she/it/we/you/they **will**.
No, I/you/he/she/it/we/you/they **won't**.

Bei Fragen mit Fragewörtern stehen diese am Satzanfang.

When **will** he **arrive**?
What **will** they **do**?

one hundred and twenty-five

UNIT 5   Grammatikanhang

2 present perfect or simple past | Present perfect oder simple past

I've seen Jurassic Park.
I saw it at the cinema years ago.

Beide Zeitformen werden verwendet, um über die Vergangenheit zu sprechen. Sie sind jedoch nicht (wie oft im Deutschen) austauschbar.

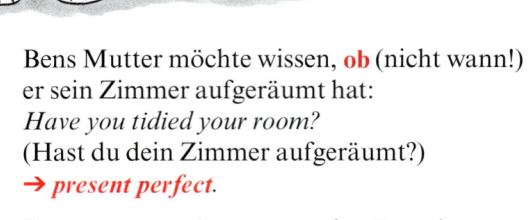

Bens Mutter möchte wissen, **ob** (nicht wann!) er sein Zimmer aufgeräumt hat:
Have you tidied your room?
(Hast du dein Zimmer aufgeräumt?)
→ *present perfect*.

Ben antwortet, **dass** er es aufgeräumt hat:
Yes, I have.
→ *present perfect*.

Er fügt hinzu, **wann** er es getan hat:
I tidied it two hours ago.
(Ich habe es vor zwei Stunden aufgeräumt.)
→ *simple past*.

MUM **Have** you **tidied** your room?
BEN Yes, I **have**. I **tidied** it two hours ago.

Wir drücken mit dem **present perfect** aus, **dass** oder **ob** etwas geschehen ist.	Häufige Zeitangaben sind: *already, ever, just, never, yet.*
Wir drücken mit dem **simple past** aus, **wann** etwas geschehen ist.	Häufige Zeitangaben sind: *yesterday, last week, three days ago, in 1998, … when?*

3 the present perfect with 'ever' and 'never' | Das present perfect mit „ever" und „never"

Wir können *ever* und *never* zusammen mit dem *present perfect* verwenden. Dabei steht *ever* oft in Fragen.

Ever bedeutet „jemals in deinem ganzen Leben bis jetzt" und *never* bedeutet „nie". Wann genau wird jedoch nicht gesagt. Deshalb stehen diese **Adverbien der unbestimmten Zeit** zusammen mit dem *present perfect*.

Have you **ever ridden** a pony?
   jemals

No, **never**. But I've **never been** on a farm.
   niemals

Grammatikanhang UNIT 6

Das past progressive / the past progressive

1 a

Wir verwenden das *past progressive*, um auszudrücken, was **zu einem bestimmten Zeitpunkt in der Vergangenheit** gerade geschah.

War das nicht schon beim present progressive so ähnlich?

*Ja, aber beim present progressive tut jemand etwas jetzt gerade – beim past progressive **tat** er es damals gerade.*

Ach so.

At nine o'clock Liz and Kim **were danc**i**ng** at the disco.

Bejahte Aussagesätze / positive statements

b

Wir bilden das *past progressive* mit *was/were* und der *-ing*-Form des Verbs.

I	**was sitt**i**ng**
You	**were sitt**i**ng**
He/She/It	**was sitt**i**ng** in the garden after tea.
We / You / They	**were sitt**i**ng**

Verneinte Aussagesätze und Fragen / negative statements and questions

c

Verneinte Aussagesätze im *past progressive* bilden wir mit *wasn't/weren't* und der *-ing*-Form des Verbs.

Bei Fragen stellen wir *was/were* vor das Subjekt des Satzes.

BEN I phoned at 7 o'clock last night. What **were** you **do**i**ng**? Were you in the garden with Rusty?
ADAM No, I **wasn't play**i**ng** with Rusty.
BEN Oh, **was** it **rain**i**ng**?
ADAM Yes, but we were in the shed. Dad and I **were repair**i**ng** my bike.
I hope you **weren't wait**i**ng** for me.

UNIT 6   Grammatikanhang

2 adverbs of manner — Adverbien der Art und Weise

a

Steve was eating **quickly**.

ADJECTIVE
Mr Foster is a **careful** driver. … *ein vorsichtiger Fahrer.*

He is always **careful**. *Er ist immer vorsichtig.*

ADVERB
Mr Foster always drives **carefully**.
Mr Foster fährt immer vorsichtig.

Adverbien der Art und Weise drücken aus, wie etwas geschieht.

Wie aß Steve? – Schnell.

Adjektive geben an,
◆ wie eine Person oder Sache **ist**. Sie beziehen sich auf ein Substantiv oder Pronomen.

Adverbien der Art und Weise (*adverbs of manner*) geben an,
◆ wie jemand etwas **tut**. Sie beziehen sich daher oft auf ein Verb.

b the formation of adverbs from adjectives — Die Bildung von Adverbien aus Adjektiven

ADJECTIVE	ADVERB
nervous	nervous**ly**
careful	careful**ly**
polite	polite**ly**
safe	safe**ly**
horrib**le**	horrib**ly**
simp**le**	simp**ly**
eas**y**	eas**ily**
angr**y**	angr**ily**
fantast**ic**	fantast**ically**

Ausnahme: publi**c** (*öffentlich*) → public**ly**

Die meisten Adverbien sind von Adjektiven abgeleitet. Wir bilden sie, indem wir *-ly* an das Adjektiv anhängen.

Beachte: Stummes *-e* entfällt bei der Bildung von Adverbien **nicht**. (*polite* → *politely*)

Besonderheiten bei der Schreibung der Adverbien:

◆ *-le* fällt vor *-ly* weg.

◆ *-y* wird vor *-ly* zu *-i-*.

◆ Bei Adjektiven auf *-ic* hängen wir *-ally* an.

c special forms — Sonderformen

Royston ran a **good** race. Royston ran **well**.
ein gutes Rennen   lief gut

He's **well** again. *Er ist wieder gesund.*

◆ *good* bildet die Adverbform *well*.

Beachte: *well* kann auch ein Adjektiv sein.

Adverbien, die die gleiche Form wie Adjektive haben

Einige Adverbien haben die gleiche Form wie Adjektive. Dies sind:

far	weit
fast	schnell
free	frei, kostenlos
hard	hart, schwer
high	hoch
late	spät
left	links
long	lang
near	nahe
right	richtig, rechts
straight ahead	geradeaus
wrong	falsch

adverbs with the same form as adjectives

ADJECTIVE	ADVERB
It was a **fast** race.	They all drove **fast**.
I did some **hard** work.	I worked **hard**.
Emily is **late** again.	She always arrives **late**.

MUM Why are you writing so **slowly**?
TOM I'm writing a letter to *grandma*. She can't read very **fast**.

Much, many, a lot of/lots of

A lot of/lots of, *much* und *many* drücken aus, dass etwas in großer Menge oder Anzahl vorhanden ist.

Bejahte Aussagesätze

Wir verwenden *a lot of/lots of* eher in **Aussagesätzen** sowohl zusammen mit einem
◆ Nomen im Plural (*comics*)
◆ als auch mit einem nicht zählbaren Nomen (*noise*).

Verneinte Aussagesätze und Fragen

In **verneinten Aussagesätzen** und in **Fragen** steht normalerweise
◆ *many* zusammen mit Nomen im Plural.
◆ *much* bei nicht zählbaren Nomen.

Nach *too* und *so* werden *much* bzw. *many* auch in Aussagesätzen gebraucht.

much, many, a lot of/lots of

There are **lots of** tourists in California.
You don't see **many** tourists in South Wales.
Is there **much** traffic in Sonoma?

positive statements

There are **a lot of visitors** in Disneyland.
He's bought **lots of magazines** and **comics**.

And there's **a lot of noise** in the disco.
We had **lots of homework** last Friday.

negative statements and questions

There aren't **many cars** on the road.
Do you see **many tourists** there?

We haven't got **much time** for our visit.
How **much homework** did you have?

You've bought **too many CDs**.
There's **so much traffic** on the road.

UNIT 7   Grammatikanhang

2 relative clauses / Relativsätze

a

A person **who travels on holiday** is a tourist.

A message **that you send to a computer** is called an e-mail.

Es ist manchmal erforderlich, ein Nomen (*person, message*) näher zu erläutern, damit man weiß, von wem oder was gesprochen wird. Deshalb verwenden wir oft Relativsätze, wenn wir eine Definition geben.

Die Relativpronomen (*who, that*) stehen nach dem Nomen und am Anfang des Relativsatzes.

b who / Who

```
                 S      V       O
I know the girl  who   wrote   this diary.
                (She   wrote   this diary.)
```

Ich kenne das Mädchen, das dieses Tagebuch geschrieben hat.

Relativsätze haben die normale Wortstellung:

S – V – O

Das Relativpronomen *who* steht nur für Personen (*the girl*).

c that / That

```
                    O     S    V
That's the video   that   I   bought   last week.
(I bought the video.)
```

Das ist das Video, das ich letzte Woche gekauft habe.

That's the watch **that** I bought very cheaply.

The person **who** made it made a small mistake.

Steht das Relativpronomen für das Objekt, so ist die Wortstellung:

O – S – V

Das Relativpronomen *that* steht für Sachen und Tiere (*the video*).

Ich merke mir das so:

wh**o** → Pers**o**n   th**a**t → S**a**che

d where / Where

This is the place **where** the riding accident happened.
A zoo is a park **where** people can see wild animals.

Wir können auch *where* benutzen, um einen Ort näher zu bestimmen.

Using the vocabulary list Erklärung des Wörterverzeichnisses

In den Englischstunden kommen immer wieder neue Wörter vor, die dir dein Lehrer oder deine Lehrerin erklärt. Zu Hause musst du diese Vokabeln dann lernen. Dabei hilft dir dein Englischbuch mit verschiedenen Verzeichnissen:

➡ Das **WÖRTERVERZEICHNIS** (S. 133–151) enthält die neuen Wörter in der Reihenfolge, in der sie in den einzelnen Units auftreten. So ist das Wörterverzeichnis aufgebaut:

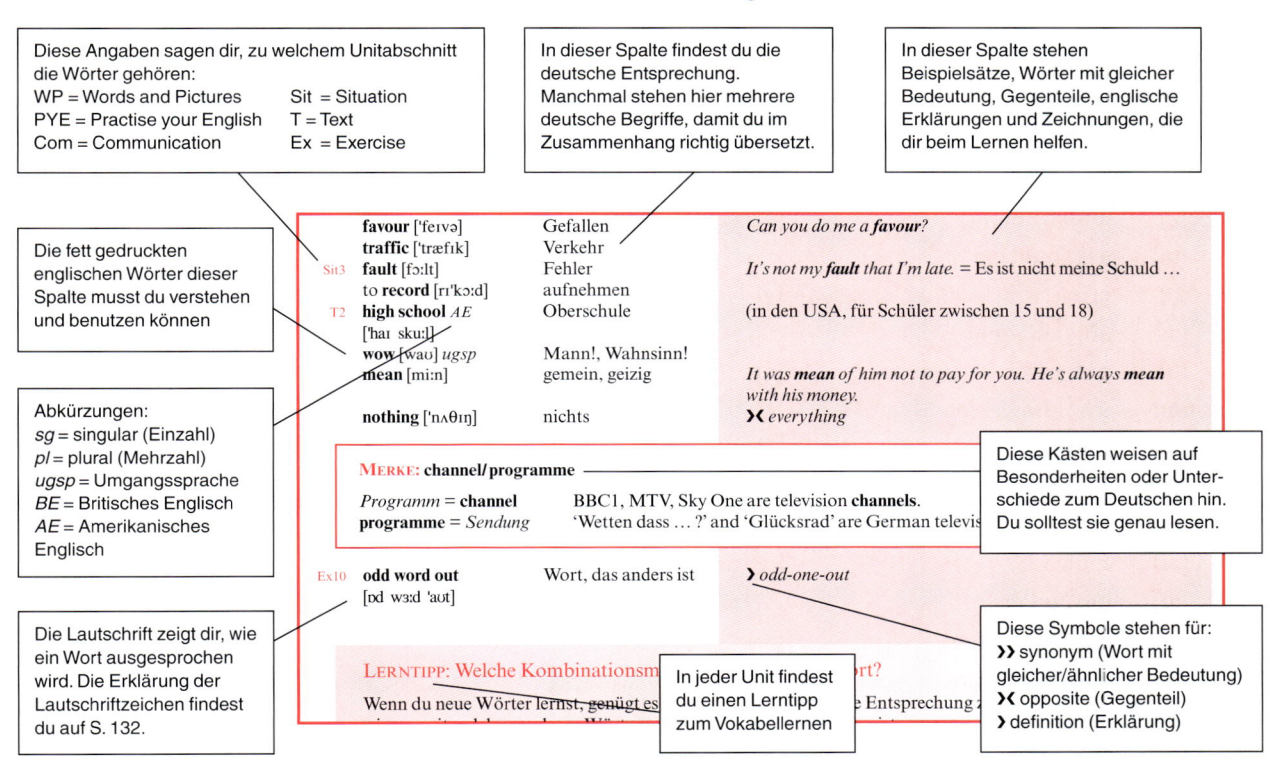

Diese Angaben sagen dir, zu welchem Unitabschnitt die Wörter gehören:
WP = Words and Pictures   Sit = Situation
PYE = Practise your English   T = Text
Com = Communication   Ex = Exercise

In dieser Spalte findest du die deutsche Entsprechung. Manchmal stehen hier mehrere deutsche Begriffe, damit du im Zusammenhang richtig übersetzt.

In dieser Spalte stehen Beispielsätze, Wörter mit gleicher Bedeutung, Gegenteile, englische Erklärungen und Zeichnungen, die dir beim Lernen helfen.

Die fett gedruckten englischen Wörter dieser Spalte musst du verstehen und benutzen können

Abkürzungen:
sg = singular (Einzahl)
pl = plural (Mehrzahl)
ugsp = Umgangssprache
BE = Britisches Englisch
AE = Amerikanisches Englisch

Die Lautschrift zeigt dir, wie ein Wort ausgesprochen wird. Die Erklärung der Lautschriftzeichen findest du auf S. 132.

	favour [ˈfeɪvə]	Gefallen	*Can you do me a **favour**?*
	traffic [ˈtræfɪk]	Verkehr	
Sit3	**fault** [fɔːlt]	Fehler	*It's not my **fault** that I'm late.* = Es ist nicht meine Schuld …
	to record [rɪˈkɔːd]	aufnehmen	
T2	**high school** *AE* [ˈhaɪ skuːl]	Oberschule	(in den USA, für Schüler zwischen 15 und 18)
	wow [waʊ] *ugsp*	Mann!, Wahnsinn!	
	mean [miːn]	gemein, geizig	*It was **mean** of him not to pay for you. He's always **mean** with his money.*
	nothing [ˈnʌθɪŋ]	nichts	✕ *everything*

MERKE: channel/programme
Programm = **channel**   BBC1, MTV, Sky One are television **channels**.
programme = *Sendung*   'Wetten dass …?' and 'Glücksrad' are German televi…

Ex10	**odd word out** [ˌɒd wɜːd ˈaʊt]	Wort, das anders ist	⟩ *odd-one-out*

Diese Kästen weisen auf Besonderheiten oder Unterschiede zum Deutschen hin. Du solltest sie genau lesen.

In jeder Unit findest du einen Lerntipp zum Vokabellernen

LERNTIPP: Welche Kombinationsm… …rt?
Wenn du neue Wörter lernst, genügt es …

Diese Symbole stehen für:
⟫ synonym (Wort mit gleicher/ähnlicher Bedeutung)
✕ opposite (Gegenteil)
⟩ definition (Erklärung)

➡ Im **INDEX** (S. 158–166) findest du alle Wörter von **Go Ahead 5** und **6** in alphabetischer Reihenfolge. Hier kannst du schnell nachschlagen, wenn dir die Bedeutung eines Wortes nicht mehr einfällt.

auntie Tante **5-U1**, Song
autumn Herbst **6-U4**, WPB
away weg, fort **5-U1**, Sit6
awful schrecklich **5-U1**, Sit2

englisches Stichwort	deutsche Übersetzung	Band	Unit	Abschnitt
away	weg, fort	5	1	Situation 6

➡ Du findest die Aussprache der **VOR- UND NACHNAMEN** auf S. 154. Andere **EIGENNAMEN** und **ORTSNAMEN** stehen mit einer kurzen Erklärung auf den Seite 155–7.

➡ Alle **GRAMMATIKALISCHEN FACHBEGRIFFE** werden auf S. 111–112 erläutert.

➡ Eine Zusammenstellung von Ausdrücken, die oft im Englischunterricht verwendet werden (**CLASSROOM PHRASES**), steht auf S. 113.

➡ Eine Liste aller **UNREGELMÄSSIGEN VERBEN** von **Go Ahead 5** und **6** findest du auf den Seiten 152–3.

English sounds Erklärung der Lautschriftzeichen

Vowels
Selbstlaute, Vokale

[iː]	eat, week, he
[i]	party, very, ready
[ɪ]	in, give, film
[e]	end, get, many
[æ]	add, man, black
[ʌ]	under, come
[ɑː]	ask, half, car
[ɒ]	often, what, coffee
[ɔː]	all, four, door
[ʊ]	put, good, woman
[uː]	who, June, blue
[ɜː]	learn, girl, work
[ə]	again, policeman, sister
[eɪ]	eight, table, play
[aɪ]	I, nice, by
[ɔɪ]	boy, toilet
[əʊ]	old, road, know
[aʊ]	out, house, now
[ɪə]	we're, here, near
[eə]	wear, chair, there
[ʊə]	your, pure, sure

Consonants
Mitlaute, Konsonanten

[p]	pen, speak, map
[b]	book, rabbit, job
[t]	table, letter, sit
[d]	desk, radio, old
[k]	car, basketball, back
[g]	get, bigger, bag
[f]	father, left, cliff
[v]	very, every, have
[θ]	thank, birthday, bath
[ð]	this, father, with
[s]	see, classes, dance
[z]	zoo, thousand, please
[ʃ]	shop, sugar, English
[ʒ]	television, usually
[tʃ]	child, kitchen, watch
[h]	help, who, home
[m]	mouse, number, film
[n]	name, window, pen
[ŋ]	sing, morning, long
[l]	like, blue, all
[r]	read, borrow, very
[j]	yes, you, year
[w]	walk, where, quiz

The English alphabet
Das englische Alphabet

a	[eɪ]
b	[biː]
c	[siː]
d	[diː]
e	[iː]
f	[ef]
g	[dʒiː]
h	[eɪtʃ]
i	[aɪ]
j	[dʒeɪ]
k	[keɪ]
l	[el]
m	[em]
n	[en]
o	[əʊ]
p	[piː]
q	[kjuː]
r	[ɑː]
s	[es]
t	[tiː]
u	[juː]
v	[viː]
w	[ˈdʌbl juː]
x	[eks]
y	[waɪ]
z	[zed]

Erklärung der Symbole im Wörterverzeichnis

Act	=	Activities	List	=	Listening	⟩ =	definition
Com	=	Communication	PYE	=	Practise your English	⟩⟩ =	synonym
Ex	=	Exercise	Sit	=	Situation	⟩⟨ =	opposite
Intro	=	Introduction	W&P	=	Words and Pictures	≠ =	false friend

Wörterverzeichnis

Unit 1

WPA
city ['sɪti]	Stadt, Großstadt	⚠ one *city* – two *cities*
lively ['laɪvli]	lebendig, rege, lebhaft	❯ full of life
exciting [ɪk'saɪtɪŋ]	spannend, aufregend	A day in London can be very **exciting**.
famous ['feɪməs]	berühmt	❯❯ well-known
		London is **famous** for its red buses.
sights [saɪts]	Sehenswürdigkeiten	the **sights** of London
centre ['sentə]	Zentrum	Piccadilly Circus is in the **centre** of London.
tour [tʊə]	Rundfahrt, Führung	a **tour** of the city, a **tour** of the Tower of London
interesting ['ɪntrəstɪŋ]	interessant	
fire-eater ['faɪəri:tə]	Feuerschlucker/in	
juggler ['dʒʌɡlə]	Jongleur/in	
parliament ['pɑ:ləmənt]	Parlament	⚠ Achte auf die Schreibung: *parliament*
by [baɪ]	an, bei, neben	❯❯ near
		Let's have a party **by** the swimming-pool.
		The Rhine is a **river** in Germany.
river ['rɪvə]	Fluss, Strom	
bell [bel]	Glocke, Klingel	
tower ['taʊə]	Turm	
palace ['pæləs]	Palast	
prison ['prɪzn]	Gefängnis	
bridge [brɪdʒ]	Brücke	
queen [kwi:n]	Königin	
millennium [mɪ'leniəm]	Jahrtausend, Millennium	
dome [dəʊm]	Kuppel	
south [saʊθ]	Süden	
east [i:st]	Osten	*south-east* = Südosten

WPB
underground *BE* ['ʌndəɡraʊnd]	U-Bahn, Untergrund	❯❯ tube
tube [tju:b] *BE*	U-Bahn	The **underground/tube** station is at Piccadilly Circus.
central ['sentrəl]	zentral	❯ in the centre of
line [laɪn]	Linie, Zeile	
which [wɪtʃ]	welche(r, s)	
circle ['sɜ:kl]	Kreis	
street [stri:t]	Straße	*in the street* = auf der Straße

Song
fair [feə]	*hier:* schön, liebreizend	
lady ['leɪdi]	Dame	
to build [bɪld]	bauen	to **build** a house, a road, a plane
built, built [bɪlt, bɪlt]		
wood [wʊd]	Holz	
clay [kleɪ]	Lehm	
to wash away [ˌwɒʃ ə'weɪ]	wegspülen	
brick [brɪk]	Ziegelstein	
stone [stəʊn]	Stein	

UNIT 1 Wörterverzeichnis

Sit1	**husband** ['hʌzbənd]	Ehemann	
	daughter ['dɔːtə]	Tochter	
	son [sʌn]	Sohn	
	west [west]	Westen	
	aunt [ɑːnt]	Tante	
	cousin ['kʌzn]	Cousin, Cousine	
	wife [waɪf]	Ehefrau	
	pl. **wives** [waɪvz]		

husband   wife   uncle   aunt

son   daughter   cousin

Ex2	**footballer** ['fʊtbɔːlə]	Fußballspieler/in	
Sit2	**a lot (of)** [ə 'lɒt əv]	eine Menge, viel	I've got **a lot of** videos. Have you got videos? – Yes, **a lot**.
	tourist ['tʊərɪst]	Tourist/in	
	popular (with) ['pɒpjələ wɪð]	beliebt (bei)	The Tower of London is **popular with** tourists.
	museum [mjuˈzɪəm]	Museum	
	waxwork ['wækswɜːk]	Wachsfigur	
	cheap [tʃiːp]	billig	✗ expensive
	queue [kjuː]	Warteschlange	a long **queue** at a bus-stop
	if [ɪf]	wenn, falls	
Ex3	**short** [ʃɔːt]	kurz	✗ long
Ex4	**form** [fɔːm]	Form	
	way [weɪ]	Art und Weise	
T1	**ticket** ['tɪkɪt]	Fahrkarte; Eintrittskarte	
	to **worry** ['wʌri]	sich sorgen	Don't **worry**. = Mach dir keine Sorgen.
	to **look after** [ˌlʊk 'ɑːftə]	sich kümmern um	My sister is only three. I often **look after** her.
	no [nəʊ]	kein(e)	I've got **no** time for you now.
	argument ['ɑːgjumənt]	Streit	
	chamber of horrors [ˌtʃeɪmbər əv 'hɒrəz]	Gruselkabinett	
	part [pɑːt]	Teil	
	busy ['bɪzi]	beschäftigt, belebt	This road is very **busy**. (belebt) Can you help me, Rachel? – Sorry, I'm **busy**. (beschäftigt)
	pocket ['pɒkɪt]	Tasche	Tasche = *bag* *pocket*
	hopeless ['həʊpləs]	hoffnungslos	
	world [wɜːld]	Welt	
Ex5	to **look forward to** [ˌlʊk 'fɔːwəd tə]	sich freuen auf	I'm **looking forward to** the holidays.
Ex8	**missing** ['mɪsɪŋ]	fehlend, nicht vorhanden	
Com	**more** [mɔː]	mehr	
	polite [pəˈlaɪt]	höflich	It's **polite** to say 'please' and 'thank you'.
Sit3	**than** [ðən]	als	Cars are faster **than** bikes. ⚠ **than** = als
	to **cross** [krɒs]	überqueren	
Ex10	**rule** [ruːl]	Regel	I can't play chess. I don't know the **rules**.
Sit4	**outside** [aʊtˈsaɪd]	draußen	
	better ['betə]	besser	good – **better** – best
	joke [dʒəʊk]	Witz, Scherz	
	worst [wɜːst]	am schlechtesten	✗ best

Wörterverzeichnis UNIT 1

	worse [wɜːs]	schlechter	✘ *better* bad – **worse** – worst
Ex13	**rain** [reɪn]	Regen	
Ex14	**advertisement** [əd'vɜːtɪsmənt]	Reklame	
	slogan ['sləʊgən]	Slogan, Parole, Wahlspruch	
Sit5	**as … as** [əz əz]	so … wie	*Royston's bike is **as** old **as** Ben's bike.*
	boring ['bɔːrɪŋ]	langweilig	✘ *interesting*
T2	to **look** [lʊk]	aussehen	*Wie sieht er aus? What does he **look** like?*
	presenter [prɪ'zentə]	Moderator/in	*Thomas Gottschalk is the **presenter** of 'Wetten, dass…'.*
	to **smile** [smaɪl]	lächeln	
	singer ['sɪŋə]	Sänger/in	
	king [kɪŋ]	König	✘ *queen*
	president ['prezɪdənt]	Präsident/in	
	royal ['rɔɪəl]	königlich	*the **royal** family, a **royal** palace*
	he's fed up [hiz ˌfed 'ʌp]	er hat die Nase voll	*What's wrong? You look really **fed up**.*
	princess [ˌprɪn'ses]	Prinzessin	
	over there [ˌəʊvə 'ðeə]	dort drüben	
	on your own [ɒn jɔːr 'əʊn]	(ganz) allein	*He lives **on his own**. = Er lebt allein.*
	never mind [ˌnevə 'maɪnd]	macht nichts, vergiss es	❯ *Don't worry about it.*
	criminal ['krɪmɪnl]	Verbrecher/in	
	scene [siːn]	Szene	
	torture ['tɔːtʃə]	Folter, Qual	
	horrible ['hɒrəbl]	fürchterlich, schrecklich	❯❯ *terrible, awful*
Ex19	**pig** [pɪg]	Schwein	
	letter ['letə]	Buchstabe	*The alphabet has got 26 **letters**.*
Ex20	**model** ['mɒdl]	Modell, Fotomodell	
Ex21	to **show** [ʃəʊ]	zeigen	*Can you **show** me your homework?*
	showed, shown [ʃəʊd, ʃəʊn]		

LERNTIPP: Was muss ich beim Vokabellernen beachten?

Auch in diesem Schuljahr musst du wieder eine ganze Menge neuer Vokabeln lernen. Vielleicht erinnerst du dich noch an die wichtigsten Tipps aus dem vergangenen Schuljahr:

- Falls du CDs zu deinem Englischbuch besitzt, so höre dir vor dem Wörterlernen mehrmals die entsprechenden Texte an.
- Lerne Wörter in Gruppen von nicht mehr als 10–12 Vokabeln.
- Schreibe die Wörter in Kleingruppen von 5–6 Vokabeln auf und lass dazwischen immer eine Zeile frei. Zeichne oder klebe möglichst ein Bild dazu. Markiere besonders schwierige Wörter mit Textmarkern oder Farbstiften.
- Wenn du mit einer Vokabelkartei arbeitest, so lerne nicht zu lange, aber regelmäßig. 5–10 Minuten jeden Tag sind genug.
- Wiederhole auch regelmäßig die „alten" Wörter.
- Falls du einen Computer zu Hause hast, so frage deine(n) Englischlehrer/in nach geeigneten Programmen.

show, showed, shown

Wörterverzeichnis

Unit 2

WPA	country ['kʌntri]	Land	*The Jewells are on holiday **in the country**.* (auf dem Land)
	farm [fɑːm]	Bauernhof	
	cottage ['kɒtɪdʒ]	Hütte, kleines Landhaus	
	grandparents ['grændpeərənts]	Großeltern	❯ *the mother and father of your mother or father*
	cow [kaʊ]	Kuh	
	sheep [ʃiːp]	Schaf	
	pl. sheep [ʃiːp]		
	pony ['pəʊni]	Pony	
	animal ['ænɪml]	Tier	
	horse [hɔːs]	Pferd	
	hen [hen]	Henne, Huhn	
Song	everywhere ['evriweə]	überall	
WPB	lovely ['lʌvli]	schön, hübsch	*a **lovely** day/ view/ film/ party/ holiday*
	young [jʌŋ]	jung	❯❮ *old*
	to lie [laɪ]	liegen	*The dog **is lying** on the floor.*
	lay, lain [leɪ, leɪn]		
	ground [graʊnd]	Grund, Boden	
	deer [dɪə]	Reh, Hirsch	
	pl. deer [dɪə]		
	stream [striːm]	Bach	
	bird [bɜːd]	Vogel	
	air [eə]	Luft	
	swallow ['swɒləʊ]	Schwalbe	
	flower ['flaʊə]	Blume	
Sit1	you were [ju wɜː]	du warst, ihr wart, Sie waren	*You **weren't** at home. Where **were** you?*
	yesterday ['jestədeɪ]	gestern	
Ex1	ill [ɪl]	krank	*Adam is **ill** today. He can't go to school.*
Sit2	diary ['daɪəri]	Tagebuch	*Every evening Lehka writes in her **diary**.*
	last [lɑːst]	letzte(r, s)	❯❮ *first*
	project ['prɒdʒekt]	Projekt	
	to stop [stɒp]	anhalten, aufhören	❯❮ *to start*
	to wash [wɒʃ]	(sich) waschen	
	hair [heə]	Haar	*Your **hair** is short. Deine Haare sind kurz.*
	day-dream ['deɪdriːm]	Tagtraum	
	everyone ['evriwʌn]	jede(r), alle	❯❯ *everybody*
	someone ['sʌmwʌn]	jemand	
	tomorrow [tə'mɒrəʊ]	morgen	*yesterday → today → tomorrow*
Ex3	to happen ['hæpən]	passieren, geschehen	*The accident **happened** at 5.30.*

Wörterverzeichnis UNIT 2

Irregular simple past forms (1) — Unregelmäßige Verben: Simple Past

to come, **came**	kam		to read, **read**	las
to drive, **drove**	fuhr		to ride, **rode**	ritt
to fly, **flew**	flog		to say, **said**	sagte
to go, **went**	ging		to see, **saw**	sah
to lie, **lay**	lag		to take, **took**	nahm
to make, **made**	machte		to think, **thought**	dachte

Alle unregelmäßigen Verben findest du auf S. 152–153.

Sit3
- **village** ['vɪlɪdʒ] — Dorf
- **forest** ['fɒrɪst] — Wald, Forst
- **sea** [si:] — Meer, die See
- **sun** [sʌn] — Sonne

- **did** [dɪd] — tat
- **past** [pɑːst] — Vergangenheit

T1
- to **love** [lʌv] — lieben
- **story** ['stɔːri] — Geschichte
- **ago** [ə'gəʊ] — vor

*A week **ago** I was in England.* Vor einer Woche …

MERKE: vor
I was in France a year **ago**. (vor einem Jahr) — zeitlich
I always get up **before** 7 o'clock. (vor sieben Uhr) — zeitlich
It's five **to** seven. (fünf vor sieben) — zeitlich

Our car is **in front of** the house. (vor dem Haus) — örtlich

- **coast** [kəʊst] — Küste — *on the **coast** = an der Küste*
- **wild** [waɪld] — wild, ungezügelt
- **through** [θruː] — durch — ⚠ ***through** = durch; **thought** = dachte*
- **badger** ['bædʒə] — Dachs
- **dark** [dɑːk] — dunkel
- **light** [laɪt] — Licht
- **noise** [nɔɪz] — Lärm — *Don't make so much **noise**.*
- **guide** [gaɪd] — Führer/in — *The **guide** showed us the Tower of London.*
- **cool** [kuːl] — kühl — *a **cool** place/evening/day; **cool** water/air*
- **at the front** [frʌnt] — vorne, an vorderster Stelle — *There is a large garden **at the front** of the house.* (vorne) *He rode **at the front** of the group.* (an vorderster Stelle)
- **along** [ə'lɒŋ] — entlang — *They walked **along** the river.*
- **side** [saɪd] — Seite — *Let's go to the other **side** of the street.* ⚠ *Buchseite = **page***

- **into** ['ɪntə] — hinein, in
- to **feel** [fiːl] — (sich) fühlen
- **felt, felt** [felt, felt]
- **moment** ['məʊmənt] — Moment

Ex6 to **end** [end] — beenden
Ex7 to **guess** [ges] — raten, schätzen
- **head** [hed] — Kopf, Oberhaupt

into the room — *in the room*

UNIT 2   Wörterverzeichnis

Sit4   to **sleep** [sliːp]   schlafen
slept, slept [slept, slept]

Irregular simple past forms (2)   Unregelmäßige Verben: Simple Past

to buy, **bought**	kaufte	to fall, **fell**	fiel
to catch, **caught**	fing	to find, **found**	fand
to drink, **drank**	trank	to get, **got**	bekam
to eat, **ate**	aß	to wear, **wore**	trug

Alle unregelmäßigen Verben findest du auf S. 152–153.

---

to **be afraid of**   Angst haben   *She's afraid of dogs.*
[bɪ əˈfreɪd əv]

Ex9   to **catch a bus**   einen Bus erreichen
[ˌkætʃ ə ˈbʌs]
caught, caught [kɔːt, kɔːt]
to **interview** [ˈɪntəvjuː]   interviewen

Ex10   **against** [əˈgenst]   gegen   ✗ *for   I'm against your plan.*
Sit5   **both** [bəʊθ]   beide   *Both (of) my sisters like chess.*

MERKE: both

Both (of) my sisters like chess.	**Both of** them can come.	We can **both** swim.	They **both** like comics.
I can't buy **both** books.	She phoned **both of** us.	We are **both** tired.	You **both** look tired.
both (of) + **noun**	both of + **pronoun**	**auxiliary** + both	both + **verb**

Ex13   **conversation**   Gespräch
[ˌkɒnvəˈseɪʃn]

T2   to **ring** [rɪŋ] *bes BE*   anrufen   *Kirsty rang when you were at school.* (rief an)
rang, rung [ræŋ, rʌŋ]   *The telephone is ringing.* (klingelt)
suddenly [ˈsʌdnli]   plötzlich   ***Suddenly** everyone was quiet.*
to **lift** [lɪft]   hochheben
off [ɒf]   von … herunter, weg
to **fall off** [ˌfɔːl ˈɒf]   herunterfallen   *He **fell off** the wall and hurt his foot.*
fell [fel], **fallen** [ˈfɔːlən]
to **land** [lænd]   landen
back [bæk]   Rücken
shock [ʃɒk]   Schock
strange [streɪndʒ]   merkwürdig
voice [vɔɪs]   Stimme   *She sings in a pop group. She's got a good **voice**.*
to **keep back** [ˌkiːp ˈbæk]   zurückbleiben,
kept, kept [kept, kept]   zurückhalten
still [stɪl]   ruhig

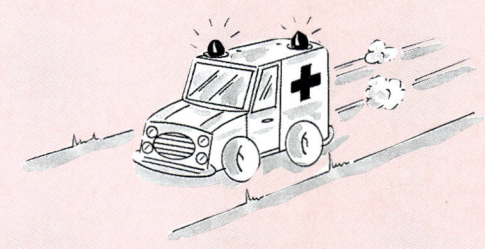

ambulance [ˈæmbjələns]   Krankenwagen
mobile (phone)   tragbares Telefon,
[ˌməʊbaɪl ˈfəʊn]   Handy
to **explain** [ɪkˈspleɪn]   erklären   *Can you **explain** the problem **to** me, please?*

Wörterverzeichnis **UNIT 2**

paramedic [ˌpærəˈmedɪk] Rettungsassistent/in
to **carry** [ˈkæri] tragen

> **MERKE: tragen**
>
> Kleidung   The paramedics **are wearing** a uniform.
> Gegenstand   They**'re carrying** a stretcher.

stretcher [ˈstretʃə] Tragbahre
nothing [ˈnʌθɪŋ] nichts   ✗ *everything*
bored [bɔːd] gelangweilt
sad [sæd] traurig   ✗ *happy*

> **Irregular simple past forms (3)**   Unregelmäßige Verben: Simple Past
>
> to hear, **heard**   hörte   to speak, **spoke**   sprach
> to hurt, **hurt**   verletzte   to tell, **told**   erzählte
> to ring, **rang**   rief an, klingelte   to win, **won**   gewann
>
> Alle unregelmäßigen Verben findest du auf S. 152–153.

Ex16 **odd word out**   Wort, das anders ist   ›› *odd one out*
[ɒd wɜːd ˈaʊt]

LERNTIPP: Wörter abfragen – aber wie?

Wie du mit einer Vokabelkartei arbeitest, weißt du noch vom letzten Schuljahr. Hier noch einmal das Wichtigste:

1 Jeden Tag 5 Minuten wiederholen ist besser als einmal pro Woche 1 Stunde.
2 Du hast das Wort gewusst: Karte wandert ein Fach weiter.
3 Du hast das Wort vergessen: Karte kommt zurück ins erste Fach.
4 Fächer 2 bis 5 voll: nur je ¼ von vorn nach hinten bearbeiten.

Die Karten lassen sich auch nach Sachgruppen ordnen, z.B. suchst du alle Wörter, die etwas mit 'Computer' zu tun haben. Sachgruppen sind sinnvoll, wenn du zu einem Thema einen Text verstehen oder verfassen sollst.

Wenn du lieber mit einem Freund oder einer Freundin Wörter wiederholst, könnt ihr Folgendes ausprobieren:

1 Ihr prägt euch beide einen Abschnitt im Vokabelanhang ein. Seht euch dabei besonders die Aussprache und die dritte Spalte gut an.
2 Nun schließt dein Partner das Buch und du liest ihm die Sätze in der 3. Spalte vor. Das fett gedruckte neue Wort ersetzt du dabei aber durch das erfundene Wort 'gubble'.
3 Dein Partner muss nun den Satz nachsprechen und das gesuchte Wort einsetzen.
4 Du überprüfst, ob alles richtig ist, und gehst zum nächsten Satz.
5 Steht in der 3. Spalte kein Satz, sondern ein *synonym* (››), ein *opposite* (✗), eine Umschreibung oder eine Erklärung (›), so liest du diese vor und dein Partner sagt das dazugehörige Wort.

Am Ende lässt du dich in gleicher Weise abfragen.

> Adam is **gubble** today.
> He can't go to school.

> Adam is **ill** today.
> He can't go to school.

one hundred and thirty-nine

Wörterverzeichnis

Unit 3

	to **find out** [ˌfaɪnd 'aʊt] **found, found** [faʊnd, faʊnd]	herausfinden	How can we **find out** where the elephants are?
WPA	**elephant** ['elɪfənt]	Elefant	
WPB	**DVD** [ˌdiː viː 'diː]	DVD (digitale Videodisk)	
	disc [dɪsk]	Disk	
	to **click on** ['klɪk ɒn]	anklicken	
	screen [skriːn]	Bildschirm, Leinwand	
	to **print (out)** [prɪnt]	(aus)drucken	Can you **print (out)** the letter for me?
WPC	the **internet** ['ɪntənet]	Internet	
	to **type** [taɪp] **(in)**	(ein)tippen	
	phrase [freɪz]	Ausdruck, Phrase, Satzglied	A group of words together is a **phrase**.
	to **search (for)** ['sɜːtʃ fə]	suchen (nach)	You can **search for** everything on the internet.
	website ['websaɪt]	Website	
	million ['mɪljən]	Million	❯ 1,000,000
	everything ['evriθɪŋ]	alles	❳ nothing
	result [rɪ'zʌlt]	Ergebnis	
	news [njuːz]	Neuigkeit(en), Nachricht(en)	It's eight o'clock. Here **is** the **news**. ⚠ **news** ist immer im Singular.
	to **send** [send] **sent, sent** [sent, sent]	schicken	
	message ['mesɪdʒ]	Mitteilung, Nachricht, Botschaft	Adam isn't at home. Can I give him a **message**?
	e-mail ['iːmeɪl]	E-mail	An **e-mail** is an electronic message.
WPD	**up-to-date** [ˌʌptə'deɪt]	aktuell, modern	
	newspaper ['njuːspeɪpə]	Tageszeitung	
WPE	**history** ['hɪstri]	Geschichte	Our next lesson is **history**. We want to read about Caesar.
Sit1	**forecast** ['fɔːkɑːst]	Vorhersage	Here's the **forecast** for tomorrow: Rain in the South ...
	to **be going to** [bi 'gəʊɪŋ tə]	werden	Look at the clouds. It**'s going to** rain.
	warm [wɔːm]	warm	❳ cold
	to **look round** [ˌlʊk 'raʊnd]	sich umschauen	
	grandma ['grænmɑː]	Oma	❯ grandmother
Ex2	**resolution** [ˌrezə'luːʃn]	Vorsatz, Beschluss	
Ex3	**tiger** ['taɪgə]	Tiger	
Ex4	**card** [kɑːd]	Karte	
T1	to **teach** [tiːtʃ] **taught, taught** [tɔːt, tɔːt]	unterrichten	Mr Batty **teaches** music at Brookfield School.
	technology [tek'nɒlədʒi]	Technik	
	member ['membə]	Mitglied	❯ someone in a group
	league [liːg]	Bündnis, Liga	
	and so on [ənd 'səʊ ɒn]	und so weiter	
	major ['meɪdʒə]	größer, bedeutend	❯❯ bigger, very great ⚠ Steht nur vor einem Nomen.
	report [rɪ'pɔːt]	Bericht	Did you read the newspaper **report** of the game?
	to **download** [ˌdaʊn'ləʊd]	herunterladen	
	address [ə'dres]	Adresse	⚠ English: **address** – German: Adresse

140 one hundred and forty

Wörterverzeichnis **UNIT 3**

Ex7	**onto** ['ɒntə]	auf … (hinauf)	
Sit2	**yours** [jɔːz]	deine(r, s)	
	mine [maɪn]	meine(r, s)	
	hers [hɜːz]	ihr(e, s)	
	forgot [fə'gɒt]	vergaß	
	left [left]	(ver)ließ	
Sit3	**ours** ['aʊəz]	unsere(r, s)	
	theirs [ðeəz]	ihre(r, s)	
T2	**wrote** [rəʊt]	schrieb	
	to **be interested in** [bɪ 'ɪntrəstɪd ɪn]	interessiert sein (an)	✗ *to be bored with*

My book	**mine**	our book	**ours**
Your book	**yours**	your book	**yours**
His book	**his**	their book	**theirs**
Her book	**hers**		

MERKE:
| to **be interested in** | interessiert sein an | to **be bored with** | gelangweilt sein von |
| **an interesting website** | eine interessante Website | **a boring website** | eine langweilige Website |

	to **switch on** [ˌswɪtʃ 'ɒn]	anschalten, einschalten	**Switch on** the light, please.
	high school *AE* ['haɪ skuːl]	Oberschule	(in den USA, für Schüler zwischen 15 und 18)
	serious ['sɪəriəs]	ernst	✗ *funny*
	softball ['sɒftbɔːl]	Softball	
	to **fancy** ['fænsi] *ugsp*	mögen	I think he **fancies** you.
	to **get** [get]	bekommen, werden	Can you close the window? I'm **getting** cold.
	got, got [gɒt, gɒt]		
	wow [waʊ] *ugsp*	Mann!, Wahnsinn!	
Ex14	**glass** [glɑːs]	Glas	

LERNTIPP: Was sind falsche und echte Freunde?

Eine ganze Reihe von englischen Wörtern sind deutschen Wörtern sehr ähnlich. Sie werden fast genauso geschrieben und du hast keine Schwierigkeiten, zu verstehen, was sie bedeuten. Dies sind die **true friends** (wahre Freunde):

project   wild   side   to end   parliament   interview   to land   president
slogan   museum   tourist   postcard   hotel   taxi

Du solltest aber immer nachprüfen, wie diese Wörter ausgesprochen werden, bevor du sie selbst benutzt. Manchmal gibt es auch kleine Unterschiede in der Schreibung.

Es gibt aber auch eine ganze Reihe von **false friends** (falschen Freunden), d.h. Wörter, die einem deutschen Wort sehr ähnlich sind, aber eine völlig andere Bedeutung haben:

So heißt **floor** nicht „Flur", sondern „Fußboden". Eine **map** ist keine „Mappe", sondern eine „Landkarte". **False friends** werden in Zukunft immer so im Vokabelanhang dargestellt werden:

cakes = Kuchen ≠ Kekse = **biscuits**   **stream** = Bach ≠ Strom, Fluss = **river**

Du solltest dir in deinem Vokabelheft eine besondere Abteilung für die **false friends** anlegen.

Wörterverzeichnis

Unit 4

WPA	special ['speʃl]	spezial, besonder(e,er)	
	bonfire ['bɒnfaɪə]	Freudenfeuer, Guy-Fawkes-Feuer	
	to light [laɪt]	anzünden	*to light a firework*
	lit, lit [lɪt, lɪt]		
	fireworks ['faɪəwɜːks]	Feuerwerk	
	guy [gaɪ]	Typ, Bursche	›› *man*
	to burn [bɜːn]	(ver)brennen	› *to be on fire*
	burnt, burnt [bɜːnt, bɜːnt]		
	fire ['faɪə]	Feuer	*Let's make a **fire** behind the house.*
	to blow up [ˌbləʊ 'ʌp]	in die Luft jagen, explodieren	
	blew, blown [bluː, bləʊn]		
WPB	autumn ['ɔːtəm]	Herbst	› *the time after summer and before winter*
	festival ['festɪvl]	Fest, Festival	
	Hindu ['hɪnduː]	Hindu	
	candle ['kændl]	Kerze	
	temple ['templ]	Tempel, Kultstätte	
	a bit [ə 'bɪt]	etwas, ein wenig	›× *very*
WPC	another [ə'nʌðə]	ein(e) andere(r, s), noch ein(e, es)	*This pen doesn't write. Can I have **another**?* (einen anderen) *Would you like **another** cup of coffee?* (noch eine)
WPD	fool [fuːl]	Narr, Dummkopf	› *a stupid person*
	fun [fʌn]	Spaß	
	it's fun [ɪts 'fʌn]	es macht Spaß	*Swimming in the sea is **fun**.*

> **MERKE: fun/funny**
> Kirsty and Lehka always have **fun**. (… haben immer Spaß)
> April Fool's Day is **fun**. (… macht Spaß)
> The comic is **funny**. (… ist witzig)

Sit1	spider ['spaɪdə]	Spinne	*I'm looking for my watch. **I lost** it last week.*
	to lose [luːz]	verlieren	
	lost, lost [lɒst, lɒst]		
	cup [kʌp]	Tasse; Pokal	
Ex1	pair [peə]	Paar	*a **pair** of shoes*
Ex2	tonight [tə'naɪt]	heute abend	›› *this evening*
Ex3	prize [praɪz]	Preis, Gewinn	*You can win a **prize** on this TV show.*
Sit2	a few [ə 'fjuː]	ein paar	

Irregular past participle forms (1) Unregelmäßige Verben: Past Participle

to come, came, **come**	gekommen	to lie, lay, **lain**	gelegen
to drive, drove, **driven**	gefahren	to light, lit, **lit**	angezündet
to fly, flew, **flown**	geflogen	to ride, rode, **ridden**	geritten
to forget, forgot, **forgotten**	vergessen	to take, took, **taken**	genommen
to go, went, **gone**	gegangen	to think, thought, **thought**	gedacht
to leave, left, **left**	verlassen	to write, wrote, **written**	geschrieben

Alle unregelmäßigen Verben findest du auf S. 152–153.

Wörterverzeichnis UNIT 4

T1
gunpowder ['gʌnpaʊdə]	Schießpulver	
plot [plɒt]	Komplott, Verschwörung	
Catholic ['kæθəlɪk]	katholisch; Katholik/in	
soldier ['səʊldʒə]	Soldat, Soldatin	
spring [sprɪŋ]	Frühling, Frühjahr	
plotter ['plɒtə]	Verschwörer/in	
to **dig** [dɪg]	graben	
dug, dug [dʌg, dʌg]		
tunnel ['tʌnl]	Tunnel	
matter ['mætə]	Angelegenheit	
God [gɒd]	Gott	
empty ['empti]	leer	
cellar ['selə]	Keller	
across [ə'krɒs]	über, hinüber	
to drop [drɒp]	fallen lassen, fallen	
barrel ['bærəl]	Fass (aus Holz)	
Lord [lɔ:d]	Lord	
death [deθ]	Tod	

*What's the **matter**?* (Was ist los?)

✗ *full*
› *a room in the ground under a house*
› *from one side to the other*

✗ *life (pl. lives)*

Irregular past participle forms (2)   Unregelmäßige Verben: Past Participle

to buy, bought, **bought**	gekauft	to get, got, **got**	bekommen
to catch, caught, **caught**	gefangen	to make, made, **made**	gemacht
to drink, drank, **drunk**	getrunken	to read, read, **read**	gelesen
to eat, ate, **eaten**	gegessen	to say, said, **said**	gesagt
to fall, fell, **fallen**	gefallen	to see, saw, **seen**	gesehen
to find, found, **found**	gefunden	to wear, wore, **worn**	getragen

Alle unregelmäßigen Verben findest du auf S. 152–153.

Sit3
… **yet?** [jet]	schon (*bei Fragen*)	›› *not … up to now*
not… yet [nɒt 'jet]	noch nicht	
already [ɔ:l'redi]	schon (*bei Aussagen*)	›› *before now*

MERKE: schon / noch nicht

Aussagesätze	I've **already** finished.	schon
Fragesätze	Has she arrived **yet**?	schon
Verneinte Sätze	I have**n't** finished my homework **yet**.	noch nicht

---

just [dʒʌst]   genau, gerade

MERKE: just

It's **just** seven o'clock.	Es ist **genau** sieben Uhr.
Just look at this funny picture.	Schau **nur** dieses lustige Bild an.
We're **just** leaving.	Wir gehen **gerade** weg.

---

to **lay the table** [leɪ ðə 'teɪbl]   den Tisch decken
laid, laid [leɪd, leɪd]

UNIT 4   **Wörterverzeichnis**

Ex11	**enough** [ɪ'nʌf]	genug	*Is Emily old **enough** to drive a car?*
	to **wash up** [ˌwɒʃ 'ʌp]	abspülen	
Sit4	**any** ['eni]	(irgend)eine(r, s)	*Do we need **any** milk? Brauchen wir Milch?*
			⚠ *any* in Fragen bleibt oft unübersetzt.
	comic ['kɒmɪk]	Comic	
	to **lend** [lend]	leihen	*Please **lend** me your walkman for an hour, Ben.*
	lent, lent [lent, lent]		

Irregular past participle forms (3)   Unregelmäßige Verben: Past Participle

to be, was/were, **been**	gewesen	to send, sent, **sent**	geschickt
to do, did, **done**	getan	to sleep, slept, **slept**	geschlafen
to feel, felt, **felt**	gefühlt	to speak, spoke, **spoken**	gesprochen
to hear, heard, **heard**	gehört	to teach, taught, **taught**	unterrichtet
to hurt, hurt, **hurt**	verletzt	to tell, told, **told**	erzählt
to ring, rang, **rung**	angerufen, geklingelt	to win, won, **won**	gewonnen

Alle unregelmäßigen Verben findest du auf S. 152–153.

Ex13	**concert** ['kɒnsət]	Konzert	
T2	**doctor** ['dɒktə]	Arzt, Ärztin	*When you're ill you phone a **doctor**.*
	castle ['kɑ:sl]	Schloss, Burg	
	above [ə'bʌv]	oberhalb, über	*The plane is flying **above** the clouds.*
	to **be glad** [glæd]	froh sein	≫ *to be happy*
	winter ['wɪntə]	Winter	*spring, summer, autumn, **winter***
	soft [sɒft]	weich, zart	✕ *hard*
	tough [tʌf]	robust, hart, zäh	≫ *hard* ✕ *soft*
	sweets [swi:ts]	Süßigkeiten	
	entrance ['entrəns]	Eingang	≫ *way in*
	ahead (of) [ə'hed əv]	voraus, vor	≫ *before*
			*The two boys came back 5 minutes **ahead of** us.*
	to **warn** [wɔ:n]	warnen	
	bang [bæŋ]	peng!	
	to **laugh (at)** [lɑ:f]	lachen (über)	*Don't **laugh at** him. He isn't silly. He's nice.*
	signal ['sɪgnəl]	Signal	
	to **fire** ['faɪə]	feuern, schießen	*The soldiers **fired** their guns.*
	appetite ['æpɪtaɪt]	Appetit	⚠ 'Guten Appetit' existiert im Englischen nicht.
Ex17	to **copy** ['kɒpi]	kopieren, abschreiben	
Ex18	**duck** [dʌk]	Ente	
PYE2	to **load** [ləʊd]	laden, beladen	› *to put things on a car or ship*
PYE4	**encyclopedia** [ɪnˌsaɪklə'pi:diə]	Lexikon, Enzyklopädie	*An **encyclopedia** is a book, CD or DVD. It gives information about very many subjects.*
PYE6	**trip** [trɪp]	Reise	≫ *journey* *to go on / make / take a **trip***
	sightseeing ['saɪtsi:ɪŋ]	Besichtigungen	*a **sightseeing** tour.*

Wörterverzeichnis UNIT 5

> **LERNTIPP: Wie unregelmäßig sind unregelmäßige Verben?**
>
> Wenn du genau vergleichst, wirst du feststellen, dass viele unregelmäßige Verben gar nicht so unregelmäßig sind, wie ihr Name vermuten lässt.
>
> Es lassen sich verschiedene Gruppen bilden:
>
> | Alle Formen gleich: | 1. und 3. Form gleich: | 2. und 3. Form gleich: | alle Formen verschieden: |
> |---|---|---|---|
> | ● put   hurt | ● come   run | ○ leave   meet | ○ go   steal |
> | ● put   hurt | ○ came   ran | ● left   met | ◆ went   stole |
> | ● put   hurt | ● come   run | ● left   met | ■ gone   stolen |
>
> In welche der vier Gruppen passen die unregelmäßigen Verben, die du bereits kennst? Lege dir diese Gruppen in deinem Vokabelheft an und ergänze immer wieder die Verben.

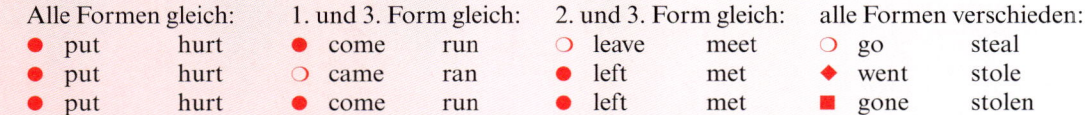

Unit 5

WPA	to **deliver** [dɪˈlɪvə]	(aus)liefern, austragen	❯ to take something to a place where it must go
	so [səʊ]	so	This case is **so** heavy.
	factory [ˈfæktəri]	Fabrik	Mike's dad works in a **factory**. He makes cars.
	jam [dʒæm]	Marmelade, Konfitüre	
	marmalade [ˈmɑːməleɪd]	Marmelade aus Zitrusfrüchten	*marmalade* wird nur aus Orangen und anderen Zitrusfrüchten hergestellt. Andere Marmelade heißt *jam*.
	honey [ˈhʌni]	Honig	
	manager [ˈmænɪdʒə]	Geschäftsführer/in, Manager/in	Her dad is the **manager** of a hotel.
WPB	to **sell** [sel]	verkaufen	✕ to buy
	sold, sold [səʊld, səʊld]		They **sell** books and CDs in this shop.
	clothes [kləʊðz]	Kleidung	⚠ Aussprache
	market [ˈmɑːkɪt]	Markt	
	to **earn** [ɜːn]	verdienen	❯ to get money for work
	extra [ˈekstrə]	zusätzlich	
	dirty [ˈdɜːti]	schmutzig	
	clean [kliːn]	sauber	✕ dirty
	to **get clean** [ˌget ˈkliːn]	sauber machen, sauber bringen	She **got** her bike **clean**. = Sie brachte ihr Rad sauber.
WPC	to **keep** [kiːp]	halten, behalten	Mr Tilbury is a farmer. He **keeps** cows and sheep. (hält)
	kept, kept [kept, kept]		I don't need this magazine. You can **keep** it. (behalten)
	driver [ˈdraɪvə]	Fahrer/in	a bus **driver**, a taxi **driver**
WPD	**office** [ˈɒfɪs]	Büro	
	machine [məˈʃiːn]	Maschine	
	vet [vet]	Tierarzt, Tierärztin	❯ a doctor for animals
Sit1	**future** [ˈfjuːtʃə]	Zukunft	✕ the past
	robot [ˈrəʊbɒt]	Roboter	
	will [wɪl]	werden	My birthday **will** be on a Sunday next year.
Ex2	**puzzle** [ˈpʌzl]	Rätsel, Geduldsspiel	❯ a game where you must find an answer

one hundred and forty-five **145**

UNIT 5   Wörterverzeichnis

	to **take** (time) [teɪk]	dauern, Zeit in
	took, taken [tʊk, 'teɪkən]	Anspruch nehmen
Sit2	to **get ready** [get 'redi]	vorbereiten, (sich) fertig machen
	until [ən'tɪl]	bis
	bean [biːn]	Bohne
	help [help]	Hilfe
	tin [tɪn]	Büchse, Dose
	bread [bred]	Brot
	butter ['bʌtə]	Butter
	purse [pɜːs]	Geldbeutel
	coat [kəʊt]	Mantel
T1	to **arrive** [ə'raɪv]	ankommen
	without [wɪ'ðaʊt]	ohne
	to **save** [seɪv]	sparen
	to **exist** [ɪg'zɪst]	existieren, vorhanden sein
	potato [pə'teɪtəʊ]	Kartoffel
	pl. **potatoes** [pə'teɪtəʊz]	
	soon [suːn]	bald
	to **steal** [stiːl]	stehlen
	stole, stolen [stəʊl, 'stəʊlən]	
	fair [feə]	fair, gerecht
	price [praɪs]	Preis
	damn [dæm]	verflucht, verdammt
Ex6	**present** ['preznt]	Gegenwart
Com	**test** [test]	Test, Schulaufgabe
	to **sponsor** ['spɒnsə]	finanziell unterstützen
	pity, it's a [ɪts ə 'pɪti]	schade
	that's a pity	
Sit4	**ever** ['evə]	jemals
	trampolining ['træmpəliːnɪŋ]	Trampolinspringen
	once [wʌns]	einmal
	twice [twaɪs]	zweimal
Ex12	**etc** [ˌet 'setərə]	usw
Ex13	**simple** ['sɪmpl]	einfach, schlicht
T2	**sale** [seɪl]	Verkauf, Ausverkauf
	cupboard ['kʌbəd]	Schrank
	toy [tɔɪ]	Spielzeug
	piece [piːs]	Stück, Teil
	paper ['peɪpə]	Papier
	to **paint** [peɪnt]	malen, streichen
	lemonade [ˌlemə'neɪd]	Zitronenlimonade
	to **fix** [fɪks]	befestigen
	gate [geɪt]	Tor
	rubbish ['rʌbɪʃ]	Abfall, Müll
	cassette [kə'set]	Cassette
	broken ['brəʊkən]	zerbrochen, kaputt

*How long does it **take** to get from Piccadilly Circus to Trafalgar Square? – It **takes** about 8 minutes.*
*It's half past eight. We must **get ready** for school.*

*My dad is going to work **until** 7 today.*

*You can keep your money in a **purse**.*

✗ to leave
✗ with
▸ to keep money to use later
*Does life **exist** on Mars?*

*Someone **has stolen** my purse.*

*What's the **price** of the tickets? – It's £3.*

*I've got a maths **test** today.*
*Which company **is sponsoring** the game?*
▸ it is sad

▸ 1x   *He watches this programme **once** a week.*
▸ 2x
▸▸ and so on

*a piece of **paper***

▸ a door in a fence or wall outside

*Martin dropped the glass and now it is **broken**.*

Wörterverzeichnis UNIT 5

drink [drɪŋk]   Getränk
to **pay** [peɪ]   zahlen   ein Getränk bezahlen = *to **pay for** a drink*
paid, **paid** [peɪd, peɪd]

> **MERKE: to pay**
> - to pay for (**a thing**) — He **paid for** the trip.
> - to pay (**a person**) — Can I **pay you** next month?
> - to pay (**money**) for (**a thing**) — His dad **paid** £10,000 **for** his car.

Ex17   **label** [ˈleɪbl]   Etikett, Schildchen

LERNTIPP: Wie kann ich Wörter ordnen und gruppieren?

Neue Wörter merkt man sich besonders gut, wenn man sie mit bereits bekannten Wörtern in Verbindung bringt. Es gibt dabei mehrere Möglichkeiten:

Du kannst sie als Vokabelnetz in dein Vokabelheft eintragen. Lernst du später noch weitere Wörter aus dem Sachfeld dazu, so lässt sich das Netz ohne Schwierigkeiten ergänzen. Übrigens, du kannst dabei nichts falsch machen, denn jeder ordnet die Wörter anders an. Dein Vokabelnetz zu einem Begriff kann also ganz anders aussehen als das deines Klassenkameraden.

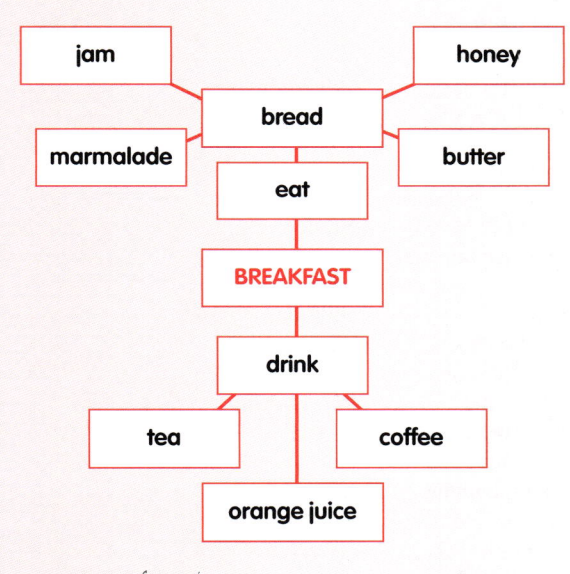

```
    jam                           honey
          \                      /
           bread
    marmalade                     butter
              \                 /
               eat
                |
            BREAKFAST
                |
              drink
              /    \
           tea      coffee
              \    /
          orange juice
```

Du kannst auch Bilder oder Fotos zu einem Sachfeld gruppieren und eventuell später ergänzen.

| flat | house | cottage
in the country
small | palace
king, queen |

Auch eine Gruppierung nach Wortfeldern

| child | kid | boy | girl | baby |

oder nach Wortfamilien ist möglich.

| bus | bus station | bus-stop | to catch a bus |

Wörterverzeichnis

Unit 6

WPA	**programme** ['prəʊgræm]	Sendung		*Did you see that **programme** on elephants last night?*
	soap opera ['səʊp ɒprə]	Seifenoper		*'Lindenstraße' is a German **soap opera**.*
	character ['kærəktə]	Figur, Charakter		⟩ *someone in a book, film etc.*
	twin [twɪn]	Zwilling		
	series ['sɪəri:z]	Serie		⟩ *a group of programmes on TV or on the radio*
	comedy ['kɒmədi]	Komödie		
	teenager ['ti:neɪdʒə]	Teenager		⟩ *a boy or girl between the ages of 13 and 19*
	safari [sə'fɑ:ri]	Safari		⟩ *a journey to see wild animals*
	science ['saɪəns]	(Natur-)Wissenschaft		
	cartoon [kɑ:'tu:n]	Zeichentrickfilm		*Donald Duck and Mickey Mouse are **cartoon** characters.*
	to **test** [test]	testen, ausprobieren		
	ghost [gəʊst]	Geist, Gespenst		
	guest [gest]	Gast		*About 20 **guests** came to our party.*
	to **meet** [mi:t]	treffen		*Can we **meet** after school?*
	met, **met** [met, met]			
WPB	**actor** ['æktə]	Schauspieler		*Sean Connery is a famous **actor**.*
	documentary [ˌdɒkju'mentri]	Dokumentarfilm		
	dinosaur ['daɪnəsɔ:]	Dinosaurier		*'Jurassic Park' is a film about **dinosaurs**.*
WPC	**millionaire** [ˌmɪljə'neə]	Millionär		⟩ *a very rich man*
	to **become** [bɪ'kʌm]	werden		⟩ *to **become** = werden ≠ bekommen = to get*
	become, **became** [bɪ'keɪm]			
	rich [rɪtʃ]	reich		⟩✕ *poor*
	to **invite** [ɪn'vaɪt]	einladen		⟩ *to ask someone to come*
	round [raʊnd]	Runde		
	to **decide** [dɪ'saɪd]	entscheiden		*We **have decided** to go to France on holiday.*
WPD	**visitor** ['vɪzɪtə]	Besucher/in		
Sit1	to **understand** [ˌʌndə'stænd]	verstehen		*I don't **understand** this word. What is it in German?*
	understood, **understood** [ˌʌndə'stʊd, ˌʌndə'stʊd]			
	to **expect** [ɪk'spekt]	erwarten		*I can't go out now. **I'm expecting** visitors.*
Ex2	**dream** [dri:m]	Traum		
	musical instrument [ˌmju:zɪkl 'ɪnstrəmənt]	Musikinstrument		
Ex3	**skirt** [skɜ:t]	Rock		
T1	to **have to** ['hæv tə]	müssen		
	as [əz]	als, während		⟩⟩ *when*
	main [meɪn]	Haupt-		*the **main** road/problem/thing*
	maze [meɪz]	Labyrinth		
	middle ['mɪdl]	Mitte		⟩⟩ *centre*
	inside [ˌɪn'saɪd]	innen, drinnen		⟩✕ *outside*
	to **follow** ['fɒləʊ]	folgen		
	between [bɪ'twi:n]	zwischen		
	hedge [hedʒ]	Hecke		
	turning ['tɜ:nɪŋ]	Abzweigung		
	dead end [ˌded 'end]	Sackgasse		
	to **turn** [tɜ:n]	drehen		
	to **get to** ['get tə]	gehen zu, kommen zu		
	got, **got** [gɒt, gɒt]			*between the hedges a turning a dead end*

Wörterverzeichnis UNIT 6

	probably ['prɒbəbli]	wahrscheinlich	
	to **get lost** [get 'lɒst]	sich verlaufen	
	almost ['ɔːlməʊst]	beinahe	*It's two minutes to seven. It's **almost** seven.*
	to **miss** [mɪs]	verpassen	*I **missed** the bus because I got up late.*
Com	to **describe** [dɪ'skraɪb]	beschreiben	
	tall [tɔːl]	groß	
	eye [aɪ]	Auge	
	jeans [dʒiːnz]	Jeans	
	face [feɪs]	Gesicht	
	ear [ɪə]	Ohr	
	nose [nəʊz]	Nase	
	mouth [maʊθ]	Mund	
Ex8	**paragraph** ['pærəgrɑːf]	Absatz, Abschnitt	
Ex9	**nervous** ['nɜːvəs]	nervös	*I always get **nervous** before a test.*
Sit3	**well** [wel]	gut	*He's a good footballer. He plays **well**.*
T2	**favour** ['feɪvə]	Gefallen	*Can you do me a **favour**?*
	traffic ['træfɪk]	Verkehr	
	fault [fɔːlt]	Fehler	*It's not my **fault** that I'm late.* = Es ist nicht meine Schuld ...
	to **record** [rɪ'kɔːd]	aufnehmen	
	should [ʃʊd, ʃəd]	sollte(n)	
	to **dial** ['daɪəl]	wählen (Telefonnummer)	
	worth [wɜːθ]	wert	*The house is **worth** £95 000.*
	mean [miːn]	gemein, geizig	*It's **mean** of her not to tell us. He's **mean** with his money.*
	channel ['tʃænl]	Programm, Kanal	

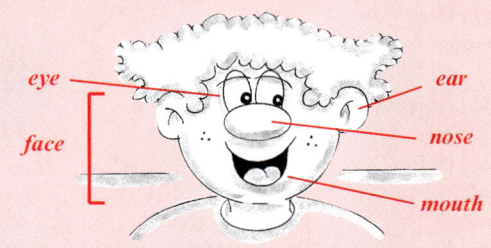

> **MERKE:** channel/programme
>
> *Programm* = **channel** BBC1, MTV, Sky One are television **channels**.
> **programme** = *Sendung* 'Wetten dass … ?' and 'Glücksrad' are German television **programmes**.

	tape [teɪp]	Tonband, Videoband	
Ex14	**rest** [rest]	Rest	

LERNTIPP: Welche Kombinationsmöglichkeiten hat ein Wort?

Wenn du neue Wörter lernst, genügt es oft nicht, nur die deutsche Entsprechung zu kennen. Man muss auch wissen, mit welchen anderen Wörtern das neue Wort kombinierbar ist.

to pay < for something / a person

road — problem — thing
     main

Du solltest dir auch Folgendes notieren:
- Besonderheiten, die leicht zu Fehlern führen
- Aussprachepobleme
- bei unregelmäßigen Verben alle 3 Formen
- einen Beispielsatz aus dem Text

to worry — about

he worr**ies** / he worri**ed** / he is worry**ing**
Don't **worry**. We've got our tickets.

Häufig unterscheiden sich diese Wortkombinationen vom Deutschen. Vergleiche:

deine Hausaufgaben **machen**	eine Party **feiern**	eine Reise **unternehmen**
to **do** your homework	to **have** a party	to **make** a journey

Wörterverzeichnis

Unit 7

	golden ['gəʊldən]	golden, aus Gold
	state [steɪt]	Staat; Zustand
WPA	**surfing** ['sɜːfɪŋ]	Surfen
	movie ['muːvi] *esp AE*	Film
	huge [hjuːdʒ]	riesig
	redwood ['redwʊd]	Redwood
	desert ['dezət]	Wüste
	national ['næʃnəl]	national, National-
	waterfall ['wɔːtəfɔːl]	Wasserfall
	ridge [rɪdʒ]	Bergkamm, Grat
	to **ski** [skiː]	Ski fahren
	resort [rɪˈzɔːt]	Ferienort
	cable car ['keɪbl kɑː]	Straßenbahn (in San Francisco)
	steep [stiːp]	steil
	hill [hɪl]	Hügel
	wine [waɪn]	Wein
	silicon ['sɪlɪkən]	Silikon
	valley ['væli]	Tal
	mission ['mɪʃn]	Mission, Auftrag, Missionsstation
WPB	**ocean** ['əʊʃn]	Meer, Ozean
Song	**land** [lænd]	Land, Boden
	island ['aɪlənd]	Insel
	gulf [gʌlf]	Golf
	highway ['haɪweɪ]	Hauptverkehrsstraße
	endless ['endləs]	endlos
	skyway ['skaɪweɪ]	Himmelsweg
	below [bɪˈləʊ]	unten, unterhalb
Sit1	**vacation** [vəˈkeɪʃn] *AE*	Urlaub, Ferien
	spelling ['spelɪŋ]	Rechtschreibung
Ex1	**petrol** ['petrəl] *BE*	Benzin
	lorry ['lɒri] *BE*	LKW
	to **mail** [meɪl] *AE*	schicken, aufgeben
	french fries [ˌfrentʃ 'fraɪz]	Pommes frites
	gas [gæs] *AE*	Benzin
	truck [trʌk] *AE*	LKW
Sit2	**lots of** ['lɒts əv]	viel
T1	**welcome** ['welkəm]	Willkommen
	barbecue ['bɑːbɪkjuː]	Grillparty; -gericht
	mom [mɒm]	Mama
	camping ['kæmpɪŋ]	Camping, Zelten
	to **sound** [saʊnd]	klingen
	bowling ['bəʊlɪŋ]	Bowling, Kegeln
	meanwhile ['miːnwaɪl]	inzwischen
	cap [kæp]	Mütze
	equipment [ɪˈkwɪpmənt]	Ausrüstung
	jet lag ['dʒet læg]	Jet-lag

California and Texas are US **states**.

≫ *film BE*
≫ *very big*

The Sahara is a **desert** in Africa.

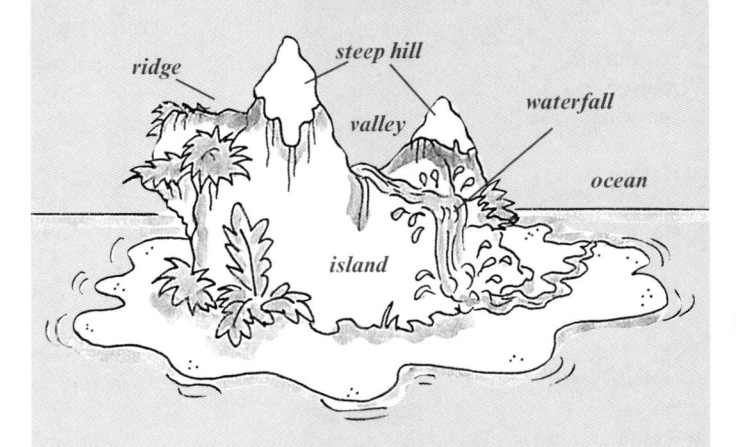

The **Gulf** Stream = der Golfstrom

❌ *above*
≫ *holiday(s)*

≫ *to post BE* to **mail** a letter
≫ *chips BE*

≫ *petrol BE*

≫ *a lot of*

≫ *mother*
Camping isn't fun when it rains.
He told me about the new film – it **sounds** interesting.

› *at the same time*

kein Plural
Entsteht durch Zeitumstellung bei langen Flugreisen, z.B. man ist tagsüber müde, nachts hellwach.

Wörterverzeichnis **UNIT 7**

catcher *hitter* *pitcher*

	player ['pleɪə]	Spieler/in
	catcher ['kætʃə]	Fänger/in (*Baseball*)
	position [pə'zɪʃn]	Stellung, Lage
	burger ['bɜːgə]	Hamburger
Sit3	**pitcher** ['pɪtʃə]	Werfer/in (*Baseball*)
	to **hit** [hɪt]	schlagen, treffen
	hit, hit [hɪt, hɪt]	
	batter ['bætə]	Schlagmann/-frau (*Baseball*)
Sit4	**garbage** *esp AE* ['gɑːbɪdʒ]	Müll, Abfall
	to **recycle** [ˌriː'saɪkl]	wiederaufbereiten, wiederverwerten
T2	**luck** [lʌk]	Glück
	friendly ['frendli]	freundlich
	square [skweə]	Platz
	building ['bɪldɪŋ]	Gebäude
	to **splash** [splæʃ]	bespritzen, platschen
	exact [ɪg'zækt]	genau
	kiss [kɪs]	Kuss
Com	**explanation** [ˌeksplə'neɪʃn]	Erklärung

›› *rubbish BE*

Don't throw away those bottles – **recycle** them.

Good **luck** for your maths test.
›› *nice*

Houses, schools and hotels are **buildings**.

›› *correct*

to give an **explanation**

LERNTIPP: Wie arbeite ich mit einem Wörterbuch?

Wenn du die Bedeutung eines Wortes nicht aus dem Textzusammenhang erkennen kannst, musst du ein Wörterbuch verwenden:

My **study** has got two small windows.

Das Wort **study** ist dir unbekannt. Wenn du in einem Englisch-deutschen Wörterbuch nachschlagst, findest du folgende Informationen:

Das **Stichwort** ist alphabetisch einsortiert.

Die **Lautschrift** sagt dir, wie man das Wort ausspricht.

Die **Ziffern** geben die verschiedene Bedeutungen des Wörterbucheintrags an.

Hochgestellte Ziffern bei Stichwörtern mit gleicher Schreibung aber unterschiedlicher Wortart.

Die **Beispielsätze** helfen dir, das Wort richtig anzuwenden.

Study bedeutet also im Satz oben „Arbeitszimmer".

> **study**[1] /'stʌdi/ *Nomen* (studies) **1.** Lernen, Studieren
> **2. studies** *Plural* Studium **my studies** mein Studium **social studies** Sozialwissenschaft **oriental studies** Orientalistik
> **3.** Studie, Untersuchung **a scientific study** eine wissenschaftliche Untersuchung
> **4.** Arbeitszimmer
>
> **study**[2] /'stʌdi/ *Verb* (**studies, studied, studied**)
> **1.** lernen, studieren **Leslie has been studying hard for his exams.** Leslie hat fleißig für seine Prüfung gelernt.
> **2.** untersuchen, beobachten **They are studying the causes of acid rain.** Sie untersuchen die Ursachen des sauren Regens.
> **3.** + *Obj* studieren, sich ansehen **study a map** eine Karte studieren

Irregular verbs Unregelmäßige Verben

Infinitive	Simple past	Past Particicple	
to be	was/were	been	sein
to become	became	become	werden
to blow	blew	blown	blasen, wehen
to bring	brought	brought	bringen
to build	built	built	bauen
to burn	burnt/burned	burnt/burned	(ver)brennen
to buy	bought	bought	kaufen
to catch	caught	caught	fangen
to come	came	come	kommen
to cost	cost	cost	kosten
to dig	dug	dug	graben
to do	did	done	tun, machen
to draw	drew	drawn	ziehen, zeichnen
to drink	drank	drunk	trinken
to drive	drove	driven	fahren
to eat	ate	eaten	essen
to fall	fell	fallen	fallen
to feed	fed	fed	füttern
to feel	felt	felt	fühlen
to find	found	found	finden
to fly	flew	flown	fliegen
to forget	forgot	forgotten	vergessen
to get	got	got	bekommen
to give	gave	given	geben
to go	went	gone	gehen
to have	had	had	haben
to hear	heard	heard	hören
to hit	hit	hit	treffen, schlagen
to hold	held	held	halten
to hurt	hurt	hurt	verletzen
to keep	kept	kept	halten, behalten
to know	knew	known	wissen, kennen
to lay	laid	laid	legen
to learn	learnt/learned	learnt/learned	lernen
to leave	left	left	verlassen
to lend	lent	lent	leihen, borgen
to let	let	let	lassen, zulassen
to lie	lay	lain	liegen
to light	lit	lit	anzünden
to lose	lost	lost	verlieren
to make	made	made	machen
to mean	meant	meant	bedeuten, meinen
to meet	met	met	treffen, begegnen
to pay	paid	paid	bezahlen
to put	put	put	setzen, stellen
to read	read	read	lesen
to ride	rode	ridden	reiten

Unregelmäßige Verben

Infinitive	Simple past	Past Particicple	
to ring	rang	rung	klingeln, anrufen
to run	ran	run	laufen
to say	said	said	sagen
to see	saw	seen	sehen
to sell	sold	sold	verkaufen
to send	sent	sent	schicken, senden
to show	showed	shown/showed	zeigen
to sing	sang	sung	singen
to sit	sat	sat	sitzen
to sleep	slept	slept	schlafen
to speak	spoke	spoken	sprechen
to stand	stood	stood	stehen
to steal	stole	stolen	stehlen
to swim	swam	swum	schwimmen
to take	took	taken	nehmen
to teach	taught	taught	unterrichten, lehren
to tell	told	told	erzählen
to think	thought	thought	denken, glauben
to throw	threw	thrown	werfen
to understand	understood	understood	verstehen
to wear	wore	worn	tragen
to win	won	won	gewinnen
to write	wrote	written	schreiben

sing – sang – sung und *ring – rang – rung* klingen sehr ähnlich.

Ja, ich merke mir die unregelmäßigen Verben so:

Chicken verbs

put	put	put
hurt	hurt	hurt

Cat verbs

MI-A-U

sing	sang	sung
ring	rang	rung

The echo verbs

win	won	won
sit	sat	sat

Hamburger verbs

come	came	come
run	ran	run

The lost letter verbs

meet	met	met
feed	fed	fed

one hundred and fifty-three

List of names Liste der Eigennamen

Boys/Men

A
Adam [ˈædəm]

B
Ben [ben]

C
Carl [kɑːl]

D
Daniel [ˈdænjəl]

J
James [dʒeɪmz]
Jim [dʒɪm]
Justin [ˈdʒʌstɪn]

L
Luke [luːk]

M
Mark [mɑːk]
Mike [maɪk]

O
Oliver [ˈɒlɪvə]

R
Ravi [ˈrɑːvi]
Richard [ˈrɪtʃəd]
Royston [ˈrɔɪstən]

S
Sam [sæm]
Sanjay [ˈsændʒeɪ]
Simon [ˈsaɪmən]
Steve [stiːv]

T
Thomas [ˈtɒməs]
Tom [tɒm]

Girls/Women

A
Alison [ˈælɪsn]
Anita [əˈniːtə]

C
Charlotte [ˈʃɑːlət]
Cindy [ˈsɪndi]

D
Diana [daɪˈænə]

E
Emily [ˈeməli]
Erisha [ɪˈrɪʃə]

H
Hayley [ˈheɪli]
Holly [ˈhɒli]

J
Jade [dʒeɪd]
Jessica [ˈdʒesɪkə]

K
Kate [keɪt]
Kim [kɪm]
Kirsty [ˈkɜːsti]

L
Laura [ˈlɔːrə]
Lauren [ˈlɒrən]
Lehka [ˈleɪkə]
Libby [ˈlɪbi]

M
Monika [ˈmɒnɪkə]

N
Nicole [nɪˈkəʊl]

S
Sophie [ˈsəʊfi]

T
Tara [ˈtɑːrə]
Tessa [ˈtesə]

U
Usha [ˈʌʃə]

Family names

A
Anderson [ˈændəsn]
Avery [ˈeɪvəri]

B
Batty [ˈbæti]

C
Cassidy [ˈkæsədi]
Coleman [ˈkəʊlmən]

D
Dillon [ˈdɪlən]

F
Foster [ˈfɒstə]

H
Hurst [hɜːst]

J
Jewell [ˈdʒuːəl]

L
Lester [ˈlestə]

M
MacDonald [məkˈdɒnəld]
Mitchell [ˈmɪtʃəl]

P
Parry [ˈpæri]
Patel [pəˈtel]
Preston [ˈprestən]

S
Scott [skɒt]
Sharma [ˈʃɑːmə]

W
Williams [ˈwɪljəmz]

Famous people

B
Mr Bean [ˌmɪstə ˈbiːn] Figur in einer britischen Fernsehkomödie
The Beatles [ˈbiːtlz] brit. Popgruppe von 1962–1970

C
Naomi Campbell [neɪˌəʊmi ˈkæmbl] englisches Model (*1970)
Robert Catesby [ˌrɒbət ˈkeɪtsbi] einer der Mitverschwörer von Guy Fawkes
Sean Connery [ˌʃɔːn ˈkɒnəri] brit. Schauspieler (*1930)

D
Leonardo DiCaprio [ˌliːəˈnɑːdəʊ di ˈkæpriəʊ] am. Schauspieler (*1974)
Dracula [ˈdrækjʊlə] Vampirfigur in Horrorfilmen und im gleichnamigen Roman von Bram Stoker

F
Guy Fawkes [ˌgaɪ ˈfɔːks] berühmtester der Verschwörer, die 1605 das Parlament in die Luft jagen wollten

G
Thomas Gottschalk Fernsehmoderator und Showmaster (*1950)

H
Alfred Hitchcock [ˌælfrəd ˈhɪtʃkɒk] Regisseur (1899–1980)
Buddy Holly [ˌbʌdi ˈhɒli] am. Sänger, der bei einem Flugzeugabsturz ums Leben kam (1936–1959)
Sherlock Holmes [ˌʃɜːlɒk ˈhəʊmz] Detektivfigur in den Büchern von Sir Arthur Conan Doyle

J
Mick Jagger [ˌmɪk ˈdʒægə] Mitglied der Rolling Stones (*1943)

J
King James [ˌkɪŋ ˈdʒeɪmz] König James I (1566–1625)

List of names

K
John F. Kennedy [ˌdʒɒn ef ˈkenədi] 35. amerikanischer Präsident von 1961–63
Jürgen Klinsmann Fußballspieler (*1964)

M
Lord Monteagle [ˌlɔːd mɒntˈiːgl] Parlamentsmitglied zur Zeit des Gunpowder Plot
Marilyn Monroe [ˌmærəlin mənˈrəʊ] am. Schauspielerin (1926-1962)

O
Michael Owen [ˌmaɪkl ˈəʊin] englischer Fußballspieler (*1979)

P
Brad Pitt [ˌbræd ˈpɪt] am. Schauspieler (*1964)
Elvis Presley [ˌelvɪs ˈprezli] am. Sänger und Gitarrist, der den Rock'n'Roll in den 50er Jahren populär machte (1935–1977)

R
The Rolling Stones [ˌrəʊlɪŋ ˈstəʊnz] brit. Popgruppe seit den 60er Jahren

S
Will Smith [ˌwɪl ˈsmɪθ] am. Rap-Sänger und Schauspieler (*1968)
Britney Spears [ˌbrɪtni ˈspɪəz] am. Sängerin (*1981)

W
Kate Winslet [ˌkeɪt ˈwɪnslət] brit. Schauspielerin (*1975)
Tom Winter [ˌtɒm ˈwɪntə] einer der Mitverschwörer von Guy Fawkes

Other names

A
April Fool's Day [ˌeɪprɪl ˈfuːlz deɪ] Erster April
Arsenal [ˈɑːsnəl] englischer Fußballclub

B
Baywatch [ˈbeɪwɒtʃ] am. Fernsehserie
BBC [ˌbiː biː ˈsiː] British Broadcasting Corporation (britische Rundfunk- und Fernsehgesellschaft)
Big Ben [ˌbɪg ˈben] (Glocke im) Glockenturm des Parlamentsgebäudes

C
Conway Street [ˈkɒnweɪ striːt] Name einer Straße

D
Diwali [dɪˈwɑːli] hinduistisches Lichterfest

E
East Enders [ˈiːstendəz] beliebte britische Seifenoper, die im East End von London spielt

H
Home and Away [ˌhəʊm ənd əˈweɪ] Name einer Seifenoper
Houses of Parliament [ˌhaʊzɪz əv ˈpɑːləmənt] britisches Parlamentsgebäude in London, Sitz des Ober- und Unterhauses

L
Lollipop [ˈlɒlipɒp] Name eines Ponys

M
Manchester United [ˌmæntʃestə juˈnaɪtɪd] englischer Fußballverein
MTV [ˌem tiː ˈviː] Name eines Musiksenders

N
Neighbours [ˈneɪbəz] Name einer Seifenoper
New York Yankees [ˌnjuː jɔːk ˈjæŋkiz] Baseballclub in den USA

R
Rusty [ˈrʌsti] Hundename

S
Sainsbury's [ˈseɪnzbəriz] große britische Supermarktkette
San Diego Padres [ˌsæn diˌeɪgəʊ ˈpɑːdreɪz] Name einer Baseballmannschaft
San Francisco Giants [ˌsæn frænˌsɪskəʊ ˈdʒaɪənts] Baseballclub in den USA
Spiceworld [ˈspaɪswɜːld] Name eines Filmes der Spice Girls
Star Trek [ˈstɑː trek] Science-fiction Serie (Raumschiff Enterprise)

T
Texas Rangers [ˌteksəs ˈreɪndʒəz] Baseballclub in den USA

V
Valentine's Day [ˈvæləntaɪnz deɪ] Valentinstag (14. Februar)

W
West End Sports [ˌwest end ˈspɔːts] Name eines Sportgeschäftes

List of place names Liste der Ortsnamen

A
3 Com Park [ˌθriː kɒm ˈpɑːk] Stadion der San Francisco Giants
Africa [ˈafrɪkə] Afrika
America [əˈmerɪkə] Amerika
Atlantic (Ocean) [ətˌlæntɪk ˈəʊʃn] Atlantik, Atlantischer Ozean
Australia [ɒˈstreɪliə] Australien

B
Badger Pass [ˌbædʒə ˈpɑːs] Pass in der Sierra Nevada
Baker Street [ˈbeɪkə striːt] Straße in London
Bakerloo Line [ˌbeɪkəˈluː laɪn] U-Bahnlinie in London
Bank [bæŋk] U-Bahnstation in der City von London
Bavaria [bəˈveəriə] Bayern
Black Forest [ˌblæk ˈfɒrɪst] Schwarzwald
Bond Street [ˈbɒnd striːt] Straße und U-Bahnstation in London
Britain [ˈbrɪtn] Großbritannien
Brookfield [ˈbrʊkfiːld] Name einer Schule
Buckingham Palace [ˌbʌkɪŋəm ˈpæləs] Buckingham-Palast, London

C
California [ˌkæləˈfɔːniə] Bundesstaat der USA an der Pazifikküste
Cannon Street [ˈkænən striːt] U-Bahnstation in der City von London
Central Line [ˈsentrəl laɪn] U-Bahnlinie in London
Chicago [ʃɪˈkɑːgəʊ] Stadt in den USA
Circle Line [ˈsɜːkl laɪn] U-Bahnlinie in London
Covent Garden [ˌkɒvənt ˈgɑːdn] ehemaliger Obst- und Gemüsemarkt Londons

D
Disneyland [ˈdɪznilænd] Vergnügungspark in Kalifornien, USA
Drumnadrochit [ˌdrʌmnəˈdrɒkɪt]

E
Edinburgh [ˈedɪnbərə] Hauptstadt Schottlands
England [ˈɪŋglənd] England
Europe [ˈjʊərəp] Europa
European [ˌjʊərəˈpiːən] Europäer/in, europäisch

F
Fisherman's Wharf [ˌfɪʃəmənz ˈwɔːf] Stadtteil von San Francisco
France [frɑːns] Frankreich

G
Germany [ˈdʒɜːməni] Deutschland
German [ˈdʒɜːmən] Deutsch, Deutsche/r, deutsch
Glasgow [ˈglɑːsgəʊ] Universitätsstadt in Westschottland
Golden Gate Bridge [ˌgəʊldən geɪt ˈbrɪdʒ] Brücke in San Francisco
Great Britain [ˌgreɪt ˈbrɪtn] Großbritannien
Green Park [ˌgriːn ˈpɑːk] Park im Zentrum Londons
Greenwich [ˈgrenɪtʃ] Stadt im Südosten von London

H
Hampton Court [ˌhæmptən ˈkɔːt] königlicher Palast westlich von London
Heathrow [ˌhiːˈθrəʊ] Flughafen im Westen Londons
Highway 101 [ˈhaɪweɪ wʌn ˌhʌndrəd ənd ˈwʌn] Autobahn in Kalifornien
Hollywood [ˈhɒliwʊd] Stadt in den USA
Hyde Park [ˌhaɪd ˈpɑːk] großer Londoner Park

I
India [ˈɪndiə] Indien

J
Japan [dʒəˈpæn] Japan

K
Kew Gardens [kjuː ˈgɑːdnz] Park im Westen Londons
King's Cross [ˌkɪŋz ˈkrɒs] Bahnhof und U-Bahnstation in London

L
Loch Ness [ˌlɒk ˈnes]
London [ˈlʌndən] Hauptstadt von Großbritannien
London Bridge [ˌlʌndən ˈbrɪdʒ] Brücke über die Themse
Los Angeles [lɒs ˈændʒɪliːz] Stadt in den USA

M
Madame Tussaud's [ˌmædəm təˈsɔːdz] Londoner Wachsfigurenkabinett
Manchester [ˈmæntʃestə] Großstadt im Nordwesten Englands
Midway Farm [ˌmɪdweɪ ˈfɑːm] Name eines Bauernhofs
Millennium Dome [mɪˌleniəm ˈdəʊm] riesige Ausstellungshalle in Greenwich, am 1.1. 2000 eröffnet
Munich [ˈmjuːnɪk] München

N
New Forest [ˌnjuː ˈfɒrɪst] Waldgebiet in Südengland, bekannt wegen seiner freilebenden Ponys
New York [njuː ˈjɔːk] größte Stadt in den USA
Nob Hill [ˌnɒb ˈhɪl] Hügel in San Francisco

O
Oxford Street [ˈɒksfəd striːt] bekannte Einkaufsstraße in London

P
Pacific (Ocean) [pəˌsɪfɪk ˈəʊʃn] Pazifik, Pazifischer Ozean
Paddington [ˈpædɪŋtən] Bahnhof und U-Bahnstation in London
Piccadilly Circus [ˌpɪkədɪli ˈsɜːkəs] verkehrsreicher Platz in London, bekannt wegen seiner Erosstatue; U-Bahnstation
Princes Street [ˈprɪnsɪz striːt] Einkaufsstraße in Edinburgh, Schottland

List of place names

Q
Queensway ['kwi:nzweɪ] Einkaufsstraße und U-Bahnstation in London

S
San Diego [ˌsæn diˈeɪgəʊ] Stadt in Kalifornien
San Jose [ˌsæn həʊˈzeɪ] Stadt in Kalifornien
Scotland [ˈskɒtlənd] Schottland
Serpentine [ˈsɜːpəntaɪn] See im Hyde Park, London
Sherlock Holmes Museum [ˌʃɜːlɒk ˈhəʊmz mjuːˈzɪəm] Museum in London
Sierra Nevada [siˌerə nɪˈvɑːdə] Gebirgszug in Kalifornien
Silicon Valley [ˌsɪlɪkən ˈvæli] Gegend in der Nähe von San Francisco, in der sich viele Computer- und Elektronikfirmen niedergelassen haben
Snowdon [ˈsnəʊdn] höchster Berg in Wales (1085 m)
Sonoma [səˈnəʊmə] Stadt in Kalifornien
South Kensington [saʊθ ˈkenzɪŋtən] Stadtteil von London; U-Bahnstation
Spain [speɪn] Spanien

T
Texas [ˈteksəs] Bundesstaat der USA
Thames [temz] Themse, Englands bedeutendster Fluß
The British Museum [ˌbrɪtɪʃ mjuːˈzɪəm] Museum in London; berühmte Kunst- und Antiquitätensammlungen
the Plaza [ˈplɑːzə] Platz in Sonoma
Tower Bridge [ˌtaʊə ˈbrɪdʒ] Klappbrücke in der Nähe des Tower of London
Tower of London [ˌtaʊər əv ˈlʌndən] Befestigungsanlage im Osten der City of London

U
Venus [ˈviːnəs] Venus (Planet)
Victoria Station [vɪkˌtɔːriə ˈsteɪʃn] Bahnhof und U-Bahnstation in London

W
Wales [weɪlz] Wales
Wimbledon [ˈwɪmbldən] Stadtteil von London
York [jɔːk] Stadt in North Yorkshire, England

Y
Yosemite National Park [jəʊˈsemətɪ ˌnæʃnəl ˈpɑːk] Nationalpark in Kalifornien, USA

INDEX

Aa

a, an ein, eine, ein **5-U0**, D
a bit etwas, ein wenig **6-U4**, WPB
a few ein paar **6-U4**, Sit2
a lot of eine Menge, viel **6-U1**, Sit2
about ungefähr **5-U7**, T2
about über **5-U2**, T2
above oberhalb, über **6-U4**, T2
across über, hinüber **6-U4**, T1
act spielen, aufführen **5-U6**, Ex9
action Handlung **5-U6**, Ex6
activity Aktivität, Tätigkeit, Beschäftigung **5-U5**, Sit2
actor Schauspieler **6-U6**, WPB
add hinzufügen **5-U5**, Ex5
address Adresse **6-U3**, T1
advertisement Reklame **6-U1**, Ex14
afraid, be Angst haben **6-U2**, Sit4
after nach, hinter, danach **5-U5**, WPA
afternoon Nachmittag **5-U1**, Sit6
again wieder, noch einmal **5-U5**, T1
against gegen **6-U2**, Ex10
age Alter **5-U1**, PYE6
ago vor **6-U2**, T1
ahead (of) voraus, vor **6-U4**, T2
air Luft **6-U2**, WPB
airport Flughafen **5-U7**, Sit5
all alle **5-U4**, WPB
all right in Ordnung **5-U3**, T2
almost beinahe **6-U6**, T1
along entlang **6-U2**, T1
alphabet Alphabet **5-U7**, Ex5
already schon **6-U4**, Sit3
also auch **5-U4**, Sit5
always immer **5-U1**, T2
am bin **5-U0**, A
ambulance Krankenwagen **6-U2**, T2
American Amerikaner/in; amerikanisch **5-U0**, A
and und **5-U0**, A
and so on und so weiter **6-U3**, T1
angry wütend, verärgert **5-U6**, T2
animal Tier **6-U2**, WPA
another ein(e) andere(r, s), noch ein(e, es) **6-U4**, WPC
answer Antwort **5-U2**, Sit2
any (irgend)eine(r, s) **6-U4**, Sit4
appetite Appetit **6-U4**, T2
apple Apfel **5-U0**, D
April April **5-U4**, Sit5
arcade Spielhalle, Arkade **5-U7**, WPA
are bist, sind, seid **5-U0**, B

argument Streit **6-U1**, T1
arm Arm **5-U5**, T1
around herum, umher **5-U3**, WPA
arrive ankommen **6-U5**, T1
as als, während **5-U6**, T1
as … as so … wie **6-U1**, Sit5
ask fragen; bitten **5-U2**, T2
at an, auf, in **5-U1**, WPB
at last endlich **5-U7**, T1
at (nine o'clock) um (neun Uhr) **5-U1**, Ex10
at school in der Schule **5-U1**, WPB
at the moment im Augenblick **5-U4**, Sit1
August August **5-U4**, Sit5
aunt Tante **6-U1**, Sit1
auntie Tante **5-U1**, Song
autumn Herbst **6-U4**, WPB
away weg, fort **5-U1**, Sit6
awful schrecklich **5-U1**, Sit2

Bb

baby Baby **5-U3**, Sit3
back zurück **5-U3**, T2
back Rücken **6-U2**, T2
back Rückseite **5-U6**, Ex4
bad schlecht **5-U2**, Ex17
badger Dachs **6-U2**, T1
bag Tasche **5-U0**, D
ball Ball **5-U6**, T1
banana Banane **5-U6**, Sit4
band Band, Musikgruppe **5-U2**, T2
bang peng! **6-U4**, T2
bank Bank(haus) **5-U2**, T1
barbecue Grillparty; Grillgericht **6-U7**, T1
barrel Fass **6-U4**, T1
baseball Baseball **5-U6**, Sit3
basket Korb **5-U6**, Ex4
basketball Basketball **5-U2**, Ex12
bathroom Badezimmer **5-U1**, T2
batter Schlagmann **6-U7**, Sit3
be sein **5-U0**, F
beach Strand **5-U7**, WPA
bean Bohne **6-U5**, Sit2
because weil **5-U7**, Sit4
become werden **6-U6**, WPC
bed Bett **5-U1**, Sit6
bedroom Schlafzimmer **5-U2**, WPB
before vor, vorher, bevor **5-U5**, Sit2
behind hinter **5-U2**, WPA
bell Glocke, Klingel **6-U1**, WPA

belong to gehören **5-U5**, T2
below unten, unterhalb **6-U7**, WPSong
best beste(r, s) **5-U3**, PYE3
better besser **6-U1**, Sit4
between zwischen **6-U6**, T1
big groß **5-U5**, T2
bike Rad **5-U2**, Sit3
bird Vogel **6-U2**, WPB
birthday Geburtstag **5-U0**, G
biscuit Keks **5-U4**, WPA
black schwarz **5-U0**, C
blow up in die Luft jagen, explodieren **6-U4**, WPA
blue blau **5-U0**, C
board (Wand-)Tafel **5-U0**, D
boat Boot, Schiff **5-U7**, WPD
bonfire Freudenfeuer, Guy-Fawkes-Feuer **6-U4**, WPA
book Buch **5-U0**, D
bookshop Buchhandlung **5-U6**, WPB
bored gelangweilt **6-U2**, T2
boring langweilig **6-U1**, Sit5
borrow sich ausleihen, borgen **5-U7**, Ex14
both beide **6-U2**, Sit5
bottle Flasche **5-U5**, PYE4
bottom Boden, Fuß (Berg) **5-U7**, T2
bowling Bowling, Kegeln **6-U7**, T1
box Kiste, Schachtel, Kasten **5-U5**, T2
boy Junge **5-U1**, WPA
boyfriend fester Freund **5-U1**, WPC
bread Brot **6-U5**, Sit2
breakfast Frühstück **5-U4**, WPB
brick Ziegelstein **6-U1**, Song
bridge Brücke **6-U1**, WPA
bring bringen **5-U4**, Ex6
broken zerbrochen, kaputt **6-U5**, T2
brother Bruder **5-U0**, I
brown braun **5-U4**, Ex16
budgie Wellensittich **5-U3**, WPB
build bauen **6-U1**, Song
building Gebäude **6-U7**, T2
burger Hamburger **6-U7**, T1
burn verbrennen, brennen **6-U4**, WPA
bus Bus **5-U0**, D
bus station Busbahnhof **5-U6**, WPA
bus-stop Bushaltestelle **5-U3**, Sit3
bush Busch, Strauch **5-U3**, T1
busy beschäftigt, belebt **6-U1**, T1
but aber **5-U1**, Sit2
butter Butter **6-U5**, Sit2

Index

buy kaufen **5-U4**, WPA
by an, bei, neben **6-U1**, WPA
bye Tschüss **5-U0**, B

Cc

cable car Straßenbahn (in San Francisco) **6-U7**, T2
café Imbiss, Café **5-U6**, WPA
cage Käfig **5-U3**, WPA
cake Kuchen **5-U4**, WPC
called, be heißen **5-U3**, WPA
camera Fotoapparat, Kamera **5-U2**, WPC
camp Lager **5-U7**, WPD
camp zelten **5-U7**, Ex14
camp site Campingplatz **5-U7**, WPD
camping Camping, Zelten **6-U7**, T1
can können **5-U0**, F
canal Kanal **5-U6**, Ex16
candle Kerze **6-U4**, WPB
cap Mütze **6-U7**, T1
car Auto **5-U1**, Sit6
car park Parkplatz, Parkhaus **5-U5**, T2
caravan Wohnwagen **5-U7**, WPB
card Karte **6-U3**, Ex4
careful vorsichtig, sorgfältig **5-U5**, T1
carry tragen **6-U2**, T2
cartoon Zeichentrickfilm **6-U6**, WPA
case Koffer **5-U7**, T1
cassette Cassette **6-U5**, T2
castle Schloss, Burg **6-U4**, T2
cat Katze **5-U0**, E
catch fangen **5-U3**, T2
catch a bus einen Bus erreichen **6-U2**, Ex9
catcher Fänger **6-U7**, T1
Catholic katholisch; Katholik/in **6-U4**, T1
CD CD **5-U2**, T2
cellar Keller **6-U4**, T1
central zentral **6-U1**, WPB
centre Zentrum **6-U1**, WPA
chair Stuhl **5-U0**, D
chamber of horrors Gruselkabinett **6-U1**, T1
channel Programm, Kanal **6-U6**, T2
character Figur, Charakter **6-U6**, WPA
cheap billig **6-U1**, Sit2
check überprüfen **5-U5**, Ex17
cheese Käse **5-U4**, WPB
chess Schach **5-U5**, WPB
child Kind **5-U3**, Sit3

chips Pommes frites **5-U4**, WPA
chocolate Schokolade **5-U4**, Song
Christmas Weihnachten **5-U4**, Sit5
cinema Kino **5-U3**, PYE3
circle Kreis **6-U1**, WPB
city Stadt, Großstadt **6-U1**, WPA
class Klasse; Unterrichtsstunde **5-U1**, WPB
classroom Klassenzimmer **5-U0**, D
clay Lehm **6-U1**, Song
clean sauber **6-U5**, WPB
click on anklicken **6-U3**, WPB
close schließen **5-U0**, F
clothes Kleidung **6-U5**, WPB
cloud Wolke **5-U7**, T2
club Club **5-U5**, WPB
coast Küste **6-U2**, T1
coat Mantel **6-U5**, Sit2
coffee Kaffee **5-U4**, WPA
cola Cola **5-U4**, WPC
cold kalt **5-U7**, WPD
colour Farbe **5-U0**, C
come kommen **5-U0**, F
Come. Komm, Kommt **5-U0**, F
Come on Komm!, Komm schon! **5-U4**, Sit1
comedy Komödie **6-U6**, WPA
comic Comic **6-U4**, Sit4
communication Kommunikation, Verständigung **5-U1**, Com
company Firma **5-U2**, T1
complete vervollständigen **5-U5**, Ex1
computer Computer **5-U1**, Sit7
concert Konzert **6-U4**, Ex13
control Kontrolle **5-U7**, Sit5
conversation Gespräch **6-U2**, Ex13
cool kühl **6-U2**, T1
copy kopieren, abschreiben **6-U4**, Ex17
cornflakes Cornflakes **5-U1**, Sit2
correct richtig **5-U5**, Ex15
cost kosten **5-U5**, Sit4
cottage Hütte, kleines Landhaus **6-U2**, WPA
country Land **6-U2**, WPA
cousin Cousin, Cousine **6-U1**, Sit1
cow Kuh **6-U2**, WPA
criminal Verbrecher/in **6-U1**, T2
crisps Kartoffelchips **5-U4**, T2
cross überqueren **6-U1**, Sit3
cup Tasse; Pokal **6-U4**, Sit1
cupboard Schrank **6-U5**, T2

Dd

dad Vati, Papa **5-U1**, WPC
damn verflucht, verdammt **6-U5**, T1
dance tanzen **5-U4**, Ex2
dangerous gefährlich **5-U5**, T1
dark dunkel **6-U2**, T1
date Datum **5-U4**, Ex13
daughter Tochter **6-U1**, Sit1
day Tag **5-U1**, Sit4
day-dream Tagtraum **6-U2**, Sit2
dead end Sackgasse **6-U6**, T1
dear lieber, liebe, liebes **5-U4**, Sit4
death Tod **6-U4**, T1
December Dezember **5-U4**, Sit5
decide entscheiden, beschließen **6-U6**, WPC
deer Reh, Hirsch **6-U2**, WPB
deliver (aus)liefern, austragen **6-U5**, WPA
describe beschreiben **6-U6**, Com
desert Wüste **6-U7**, WPA
desk Schülertisch, Schreibtisch **5-U0**, D
dial wählen (Telefonnummer) **6-U6**, T2
dialogue Dialog **5-U5**, Ex8
diary Tagebuch **6-U2**, Sit2
did tat **6-U2**, Sit3
different verschieden, anders **5-U6**, Ex16
difficult schwierig **5-U7**, T1
dig graben **6-U4**, T1
dining-room Esszimmer **5-U2**, WPB
dinosaur Dinosaurier **6-U6**, WPB
dirty schmutzig **6-U5**, WPB
disc Disk **6-U3**, WPB
disco Disco **5-U1**, Ex16
do tun **5-U1**, Sit6
doctor Arzt, Ärztin **6-U4**, T2
documentary Dokumentarfilm **6-U6**, WPB
dog Hund **5-U1**, WPA
dome Kuppel **6-U1**, WPA
door Tür **5-U0**, D
double doppelt **5-U1**, PYE6
doughnut Berliner, Krapfen **5-U4**, WPA
down unten, nach unten **5-U0**, F
download herunterladen **6-U3**, T1
drama Schauspiel **5-U5**, Sit2
draw zeichnen **5-U4**, Sit2
dream Traum **6-U6**, Ex2
dress Kleid **5-U0**, C
drink trinken **5-U4**, WPB

Index

drink Getränk **6-U5**, T2
drive fahren **5-U1**, Sit7
driver Fahrer/in **6-U5**, WPC
drop fallen lassen, fallen **6-U4**, T1
duck Ente **6-U4**, Ex18
DVD DVD **6-U3**, WPB

Ee

e-mail E-mail **6-U3**, WPC
each jeder, jede, jedes **5-U5**, Ex18
ear Ohr **6-U6**, Com
earn verdienen **6-U5**, WPB
east Osten **6-U1**, WPA
Easter Ostern **5-U4**, Sit5
easy einfach, leicht **5-U6**, T1
eat essen **5-U3**, WPA
eight acht **5-U0**, G
eighteen achtzehn **5-U0**, G
eighty achtzig **5-U4**, WPA
elephant Elefant **6-U3**, WPA
eleven elf **5-U0**, G
empty leer **6-U4**, T1
encyclopedia Lexikon, Enzyklopädie **6-U4**, PYE4
end Ende **5-U1**, Song
end beenden **6-U2**, Ex6
endless endlos **6-U7**, WPB
English englisch; Engländer/in **5-U0**, A
enjoy gern haben, genießen **5-U7**, WPC
enough genug **6-U4**, Ex11
entrance Eingang **6-U4**, T2
equipment Ausrüstung **6-U7**, T1
er äh **5-U2**, Ex4
etc usw **6-U5**, Ex12
evening Abend **5-U1**, Sit6
ever jemals **6-U5**, Sit4
every jeder, jede, jedes **5-U1**, Sit6
everyone jede(r), alle **6-U2**, Sit2
everything alles **6-U3**, WPC
everywhere überall **6-U2**, Song
exact genau **6-U7**, T2
exciting spannend, aufregend **6-U1**, WPA
excuse me Entschuldigung **5-U6**, WPB
exercise Übung **5-U1**, Ex1
exercise book Schulheft **5-U0**, D
exist existieren, vorhanden sein **6-U5**, T1
expect erwarten **6-U6**, Sit1
expensive teuer **5-U7**, WPA
explain erklären **6-U2**, T2
explanation Erklärung **6-U7**, Com

extra zusätzlich **6-U5**, WPB
eye Auge **6-U6**, Com

Ff

face Gesicht **6-U6**, Com
factory Fabrik **6-U5**, WPA
fair fair, gerecht **6-U5**, T1
fair schön, liebreizend **6-U1**, Song
fall fallen **5-U5**, T1
fall off herunterfallen **6-U2**, T2
family Familie **5-U1**
famous berühmt **6-U1**, WPA
fan Anhänger/in, Fan **5-U2**, T2
fancy mögen **6-U3**, T2
fantastic wundervoll **5-U2**, T1
far weit **5-U5**, T1
farm Bauernhof **6-U2**, WPA
farmer Bauer, Bäuerin **5-U3**, Song
fast schnell **5-U5**, WPA
father Vater **5-U2**, Sit4
fault Fehler **6-U6**, T2
favour Gefallen **6-U6**, T2
favourite Lieblings- **5-U1**, Sit2
February Februar **5-U4**, Sit5
feed füttern **5-U3**, WPA
feel (sich) fühlen **6-U2**, T1
fence Zaun **5-U3**, T1
festival Fest, Festival **6-U4**, WPB
fifteen fünfzehn **5-U0**, G
fifty fünfzig **5-U1**, Sit5
film Film **5-U1**, Sit1
find finden **5-U0**, J
find out herausfinden **6-U3**
fine gut, schön **5-U0**, B
finish beenden **5-U4**, WPA
fire Feuer **6-U4**, WPA
fire feuern, schießen **6-U4**, T2
fire-eater Feuerschlucker **6-U1**, WPA
fireworks Feuerwerk **6-U4**, WPA
first erste, erster, erstes **5-U1**, Sit3
first floor erster Stock **5-U2**, WPB
five fünf **5-U0**, G
fix befestigen **6-U5**, T2
flat Wohnung **5-U2**, WPA
flight Flug **5-U7**, Ex2
floor (Fuß)Boden **5-U5**, Sit1
flower Blume **6-U2**, WPB
fly fliegen **5-U1**, Sit8
follow folgen **6-U6**, T1
food Essen, Lebensmittel **5-U4**, WPC
fool Narr, Dummkopf **6-U4**, WPD
foot Fuß **5-U5**, T1

football Fußball **5-U1**, Ex10
footballer Fußballspieler/in **6-U1**, Ex2
for für **5-U1**, WPB
forecast Vorhersage **6-U3**, Sit1
forest Wald, Forst **6-U2**, Sit3
forget vergessen **5-U4**, T2
forgot vergaß **6-U3**, Ex10
form Form **6-U1**, Ex4
Formula One Formel 1 **5-U2**, T1
forty vierzig **5-U1**, Sit5
four vier **5-U0**, G
fourteen vierzehn **5-U0**, G
free kostenlos, frei **5-U7**, Sit1
French Französisch, französisch **5-U1**, Sit3
french fries Pommes frites **6-U7**, Ex1
Friday Freitag **5-U1**, Sit4
friend Freund/in **5-U1**
friendly freundlich **6-U7**, T2
from von, aus **5-U0**, A
front Vorderseite **6-U2**, T1
full voll **5-U7**, T2
fun Spaß **6-U4**, WPD
funny witzig, komisch, seltsam **5-U7**, T2
future Zukunft **6-U5**, Sit1

Gg

game Spiel **5-U1**, Sit7
garage Garage **5-U2**, WPA
garbage Müll, Abfall **6-U7**, Sit4
garden Garten **5-U2**, WPA
gas Benzin **6-U7**, Ex1
gate Tor **6-U5**, T2
German Deutsch; deutsch; Deutsche/r **5-U0**, A
get bekommen, werden **6-U3**, T2
get holen **5-U3**, T1
get clean sauber machen, sauber bringen **6-U5**, WPB
get home heimkommen **5-U2**, T1
get (in) einsteigen (in) **5-U1**, T2
get ready vorbereiten, (sich) fertig machen **6-U5**, Sit2
get to gehen zu, kommen zu **6-U6**, T1
get up aufstehen **5-U1**, Sit6
ghost Geist, Gespenst **6-U6**, WPA
girl Mädchen **5-U1**, WPA
girlfriend Freundin **5-U1**, Song
give geben **5-U3**, Sit1
glad froh **6-U4**, T2
glass Glas **6-U3**, Ex14
go gehen **5-U0**, A

go-kart Go-Kart **5-U7**, Sit4
God Gott **6-U4**, T1
going to, be werden **6-U3**, Sit1
golden golden, aus Gold **6-U7**, WPA
good gut **5-U1**, Sit2
goodbye auf Wiedersehen **5-U0**, B
grandad Opa **5-U5**, Sit3
grandma Oma **6-U3**, Sit1
grandparents Großeltern **6-U2**, WPA
grass Gras **5-U3**, WPA
great großartig **5-U1**, Sit2
green grün **5-U0**, C
grizzly bear Grizzlybär **5-U0**, Song
ground Grund, Boden **6-U2**, WPB
ground floor Erdgeschoss **5-U2**, WPB
group Gruppe **5-U1**, Ex4
guess raten, schätzen **6-U2**, Ex7
guest Gast **6-U6**, WPA
guide Führer/in **6-U2**, T1
guitar Gitarre **5-U0**, E
gulf Golf **6-U7**, WPSong
gun Schusswaffe **5-U3**, Song
gunpowder Schießpulver **6-U4**, T1
guy Typ, Bursche **6-U4**, WPA

Hh

hair Haar **6-U2**, Sit2
half halb **5-U1**, Sit5
half past (ten) halb (elf) **5-U1**, Sit5
half term Schulferien **5-U4**, Sit5
hall Flur **5-U2**, WPB
hamburger Hamburger **5-U4**, WPA
hamster Hamster **5-U3**, WPA
hand Hand **5-U6**, T1
happen passieren, geschehen **6-U2**, Ex3
happy glücklich, froh **5-U0**, G
Happy birthday! Herzlichen Glückwunsch zum Geburtstag! **5-U0**, G
hard hart, schwer, schwierig **5-U6**, T1
hate hassen, gar nicht mögen **5-U5**, Sit2
have got haben, besitzen **5-U0**, E
have to müssen **6-U6**, T1
have you got? hast du, habt ihr, haben Sie? **5-U0**, E
he er **5-U1**, WPA
he, she, it does er, sie es tut **5-U2**, Sit2
he, she, it has got er, sie, es hat, besitzt **5-U1**, WPB
he's fed up er hat die Nase voll **6-U1**, T2

head Kopf, Oberhaupt **6-U2**, Ex7
hear hören **5-U7**, T1
hedge Hecke **6-U6**, T1
hello Hallo **5-U0**, A
help helfen **5-U3**, Com
help Hilfe **6-U5**, Sit2
hen Henne, Huhn **6-U2**, WPA
her ihr, ihre, ihr **5-U1**, T1
her sie, ihr **5-U2**, Sit5
here hier; hierher **5-U0**, F
hers ihr(e, s) **6-U3**, Sit2
hey Hey! **5-U7**, T1
hi Hallo **5-U0**, A
high hoch **5-U7**, T2
high school Oberschule **6-U3**, T2
highway Hauptverkehrsstraße **6-U7**, WPSong
hill Hügel **6-U7**, WPA
him ihn, ihm **5-U2**, Sit5
Hindu Hindu **6-U4**, WPB
his sein, seine, sein **5-U1**, WPB
history Geschichte **6-U3**, WPE
hit schlagen, treffen **6-U7**, Sit3
hockey Hockey **5-U5**, Sit2
hold halten **5-U4**, T1
hole Loch **5-U3**, T1
holiday Ferien, Urlaub **5-U4**, Sit5
home Heim, Zuhause **5-U1**, Sit6
homework Hausaufgaben **5-U1**, Sit6
honey Honig **6-U5**, WPA
hope hoffen **5-U2**, T2
hopeless hoffnungslos **6-U1**, T1
horrible fürchterlich, schrecklich **6-U1**, T2
horse Pferd **6-U2**, WPA
hospital Krankenhaus **5-U6**, WPA
hot heiß **5-U7**, WPD
hotel Hotel **5-U7**, WPD
hour Stunde **5-U5**, Sit3
house Haus **5-U0**, G
how wie **5-U0**, B
How many … ? Wie viele … ? **5-U0**, H
how much … ? Wie viel … ? **5-U6**, Sit3
huge riesig **6-U7**, WPA
hundred hundert **5-U4**, WPA
hungry hungrig **5-U4**, WPA
hurry eilen, sich beeilen **5-U1**, Sit6
hurry (up) sich beeilen **5-U1**, T2
hurt schmerzen, weh tun **5-U6**, T1
husband Ehemann **6-U1**, Sit1
hutch Kaninchenstall **5-U3**, WPA

Ii

I ich **5-U0**, A
I haven't got a brother. Ich habe keinen Bruder. **5-U0**, I
I'm ich bin **5-U0**, A
I'm fine Mir geht's gut. **5-U0**, B
I've got Ich habe, ich besitze **5-U0**, E
ice-cream (Speise)Eis **5-U4**, WPA
idea Idee **5-U4**, T2
idiot Dummkopf, Idiot **5-U6**, T2
if wenn, falls **6-U1**, Sit2
ill krank **6-U2**, Ex1
imagine sich vorstellen **5-U7**, WPD
in in **5-U0**, A
in front of vor **5-U2**, WPA
in-line skates Inline Skates, Rollerblades **5-U5**, WPA
information Information(en) **5-U7**, Ex3
inside innen, drinnen **6-U6**, T1
interested in, be interessiert sein (an) **6-U3**, T2
interesting interessant **6-U1**, WPA
internet Internet **6-U3**, WPC
interview interviewen **6-U2**, Ex9
into hinein, in **6-U2**, T1
introduction Einführung **5-U1** Intro
invite einladen **6-U6**, WPC
is ist **5-U0**, A
island Insel **6-U7**, WPSong
it es **5-U0**, B
it's es ist **5-U0**, B
it's fun es macht Spaß **6-U4**, WPD
It's my turn. Ich bin dran. Ich bin an der Reihe. **5-U1**, T2
It's your turn. Du bist dran. **5-U4**, Sit2
its sein, seine, sein, ihr, ihre, ihr **5-U3**, Sit1

Jj

jacket Jacke, Jackett **5-U4**, Ex16
jam Marmelade, Konfitüre **6-U5**, WPA
January Januar **5-U4**, Sit5
jeans Jeans **6-U6**, Com
jet lag Jet-lag **6-U7**, T1
job Job, Arbeitsplatz **5-U2**, T1
joke Witz, Scherz **6-U1**, Sit4
journey Reise **5-U7**, WPC
judo Judo **5-U5**, WPB
juggler Jongleur/in **6-U1**, WPA
July Juli **5-U4**, Sit5

Index

jump springen **5-U5**, WPA
June Juni **5-U4**, Sit5
just genau, gerade **6-U4**, Sit3
just nur, bloß **5-U4**, T1

Kk

keep halten, behalten **6-U5**, WPC
keep back zurückbleiben, zurückhalten **6-U2**, T2
kid Kind **5-U5**, WPB
king König **6-U1**, T2
kiss Kuss **6-U7**, T2
kitchen Küche **5-U1**, T2
know wissen, kennen **5-U2**, Sit2

Ll

label Etikett, Schildchen **6-U5**, Ex17
lady Dame **6-U1**, Song
lake See **5-U7**, T2
land Land, Boden **6-U7**, WPSong
land landen **6-U2**, T2
large groß **5-U4**, Sit4
last letzte(r, s) **6-U2**, Sit2
late spät **5-U1**, Sit1
later später **5-U7**, T1
laugh (at) lachen (über) **6-U4**, T2
lay the table den Tisch decken **6-U4**, Sit3
league Bündnis, Liga **6-U3**, T1
learn lernen, erfahren **5-U1**, Sit8
leave verlassen, weggehen, abfahren **5-U1**, Sit6
leave lassen, liegenlassen **5-U5**, Sit1
left links **5-U6**, WPB
left (ver)ließ **6-U3**, Ex10
leg Bein **5-U5**, T1
lemonade Zitronenlimonade **6-U5**, T2
lend leihen **6-U4**, Sit4
lesson Unterrichtsstunde **5-U1**, Ex4
let out hinauslassen, herauslassen **5-U3**, WPA
let's Lass(t) uns **5-U0**, A
letter Brief **5-U6**, Sit1
letter Buchstabe **6-U1**, Ex19
library Bibliothek, Bücherei **5-U3**, T2
lie liegen **6-U2**, WPB
life Leben **5-U6**, T1
lift hochheben **6-U2**, T2
light Licht **6-U2**, T1
light anzünden **6-U4**, WPA
like mögen **5-U1**, Sit7
like wie **5-U7**, WPD
line Linie, Zeile **6-U1**, WPB
list Liste **5-U5**, PYE6
listen (to) zuhören **5-U1**, Sit8
little klein **5-U0**, Song
live leben, wohnen **5-U0**, A
lively lebendig, rege, lebhaft **6-U1**, WPA
living-room Wohnzimmer **5-U2**, WPB
load laden, beladen **6-U4**, PYE2
long lang **5-U1**, T2
look aussehen **6-U1**, T2
look schauen **5-U2**, Sit5
look after sich kümmern um **6-U1**, T1
look for suchen **5-U6**, WPB
look forward to sich freuen auf **6-U1**, Ex5
Look out! Pass auf! **5-U5**, T1
look round sich umschauen **6-U3**, Sit1
Lord Lord **6-U4**, T1
Lorry LKW **6-U7**, Ex1
lose verlieren **6-U4**, Sit1
lost, get sich verlaufen **6-U6**, T1
lots of viel **6-U7**, Sit2
love herzliche Grüße **5-U4**, T2
love Liebe **5-U5**, PYE4
love lieben **6-U2**, T1
lovely schön, hübsch **6-U2**, WPB
luck Glück **6-U7**, T2
lucky glücklich **5-U1**, T1
lunch Mittagessen **5-U3**, WPA
lunch-time Mittagsstunde **5-U3**, WPA

Mm

machine Maschine **6-U5**, WPD
madam Meine Dame, Gnädige Frau **5-U7**, Sit5
magazine Zeitschrift **5-U5**, WPB
mail schicken, aufgeben **6-U7**, Ex1
main Haupt-, hauptsächlich **6-U6**, T1
major größer, bedeutend **6-U3**, T1
make machen **5-U4**, Sit1
man Mann **5-U3**, Sit3
manager Geschäftsführer, Manager, Filialleiter/in **6-U5**, WPA
many viele **5-U7**, Sit4
map Landkarte **5-U7**, T1
March März **5-U4**, Sit5
market Markt **6-U5**, WPB
marmalade Marmelade aus Zitrusfrüchten **6-U5**, WPA
maths Mathematik **5-U1**, Ex4
matter Angelegenheit **6-U4**, T1
May Mai **5-U4**, Sit5
may I? darf ich? **5-U7**, Sit5
maybe vielleicht **5-U7**, T2
maze Labyrinth **6-U6**, T1
me mich, mir **5-U2**, Sit5
meal Mahlzeit **5-U4**, WPB
mean meinen, sagen wollen **5-U6**, T2
mean gemein, geizig **6-U6**, T2
meanwhile inzwischen **6-U7**, T1
medium mittelgroß **5-U4**, Sit4
meet treffen **6-U6**, WPA
member Mitglied **6-U3**, T1
menu Speisekarte **5-U4**, WPA
message Mitteilung, Nachricht, Botschaft **6-U3**, WPC
metre Meter **5-U7**, T2
middle Mitte **6-U6**, T1
mile Meile **5-U1**, Sit6
milk Milch **5-U4**, WPA
millennium Jahrtausend, Millennium **6-U1**, WPA
million Million **6-U3**, WPC
millionaire Millionär **6-U6**, WPC
mine meine(r, s) **6-U3**, Sit2
mini-golf Minigolf **5-U2**, Sit1
minute Minute **5-U1**, Sit1
miss verpassen **6-U6**, T1
missing fehlend, nicht vorhanden **6-U1**, Ex8
mission Mission, Auftrag, Missionsstation **6-U7**, WPA
mobile (phone) tragbares Telefon, Handy **6-U2**, T2
model Modell, Fotomodell **6-U1**, Ex20
mom Mama **6-U7**, T1
moment Moment **6-U2**, T1
Monday Montag **5-U1**, Sit4
money Geld **5-U4**, Sit3
month Monat **5-U4**, Sit5
more mehr **6-U1**, Com
morning Morgen **5-U1**, Sit6
most meiste (r,s) **5-U6**, T1
mother Mutter **5-U2**, Sit2
mountain Berg **5-U2**, Song
mouse Maus **5-U3**, WPB
mouth Mund **6-U6**, Com
move (sich) bewegen, umziehen **5-U5**, T2
movie Film **6-U7**, WPA
Mr Herr **5-U0**, F

Index

Mrs Frau **5-U0**, B
much viel **5-U5**, Sit3
mum Mutti, Mama **5-U1**, WPC
museum Museum **6-U1**, Sit2
music Musik **5-U1**, Sit3
musical instrument Musikinstrument **6-U6**, Ex2
must müssen **5-U6**, Sit1
my mein, meine, mein **5-U0**, A
My name is Mein Name ist, ich heiße **5-U0**, A

Nn

name Name **5-U0**, A
national national, National- **6-U7**, WPA
near nah **5-U1**, Sit6
need brauchen **5-U4**, Sit1
neighbour Nachbar/in **5-U3**, Sit1
nervous nervös **6-U6**, Ex9
never niemals **5-U5**, Sit2
never mind macht nichts, vergiss es **6-U1**, T2
new neu **5-U0**, E
news Neuigkeit(en), Nachricht(en) **6-U3**, WPC
newspaper Tageszeitung **6-U3**, WPD
next nächster, nächste, nächstes **5-U3**, T1
nice nett, schön, hübsch **5-U1**, Sit2
night Nacht **5-U7**, Sit1
nine neun **5-U0**, G
nineteen neunzehn **5-U0**, G
ninety neunzig **5-U4**, WPA
no nein **5-U0**, B
no kein(e) **6-U1**, T1
noise Lärm **6-U2**, T1
north Norden **5-U7**, T1
nose Nase **6-U6**, Com
not nicht **5-U0**, B
nothing nichts **6-U2**, T2
November November **5-U4**, Sit5
now jetzt **5-U0**, F
number Zahl **5-U0**, G

Oo

o'clock Uhr **5-U1**, Sit5
ocean Meer, Ozean **6-U7**, WPB
October Oktober **5-U4**, Sit5
odd word out Wort, das anders ist **6-U2**, Ex16
of von **5-U1**, Sit2
of course natürlich **5-U1**, Sit8

off von … herunter, weg **6-U2**, T2
officer Beamte, Beamtin **5-U7**, Sit5
office Büro **6-U5**, WPD
often häufig, oft **5-U3**, PYE3
oh Oh **5-U0**, G
Oh, dear! Ach du meine Güte! **5-U4**, Sit4
OK OK **5-U0**, B
old alt **5-U0**, G
on auf **5-U1**, T2
on (Monday) am (Montag) **5-U1**, Sit4
on time pünktlich **5-U1**, Sit6
on your own (ganz) allein **6-U1**, T2
once einmal **6-U5**, Sit4
one eins **5-U0**, G
only nur, bloß **5-U5**, Sit3
onto auf … (hinauf) **6-U3**, Ex7
open öffnen **5-U0**, F
opposite Gegenteil **5-U5**, Ex16
or oder **5-U0**, I
orange Orange, Apfelsine **5-U6**, Sit4
orange juice Orangensaft **5-U4**, WPA
order Reihenfolge **5-U7**, Ex9
other andere(r, s) **5-U4**, Ex6
our unser, unsere, unser **5-U3**, Sit1
ours unsere(r, s) **6-U3**, Sit3
out (of) hinaus **5-U1**, Sit7
outside draußen **6-U1**, Sit4
over über **5-U3**, T1
over there dort drüben **6-U1**, T2
ow Au, Aua **5-U5**, T1
own eigen **5-U2**, WPB

Pp

packet Paket **5-U5**, PYE4
page Seite **5-U1**, Ex1
paint malen, streichen **6-U5**, T2
pair Paar **6-U4**, Ex1
palace Palast **6-U1**, WPA
paper Papier **6-U5**, T2
paragraph Absatz, Abschnitt **6-U6**, Ex8
paramedic Rettungsassistent/in **6-U2**, T2
parents Eltern **5-U2**, T1
park Park **5-U2**, Sit3
parliament Parlament **6-U1**, WPA
part Teil **6-U1**, T1
partner Partner/in **5-U5**, WPB
party Party, Feier **5-U4**, WPC
passport Reisepass **5-U7**, Sit3

past Vergangenheit **6-U2**, Sit3
past nach **5-U1**, Sit5
path Fußweg, Pfad **5-U5**, T1
pay zahlen **6-U5**, T2
pen Füllfederhalter, Füller **5-U0**, D
pencil Bleistift **5-U0**, D
penny Penny **5-U4**, WPA
people Leute **5-U3**, Sit3
person Person **5-U1**, T1
pet Haustier **5-U3**, WPA
pet shop Tierhandlung **5-U6**, WPB
petrol Benzin **6-U7**, Ex1
petrol station Tankstelle **5-U2**, T1
phone telefonieren **5-U5**, PYE4
photo Foto **5-U1**, Sit2
phrase Ausdruck, Phrase, Satzglied **6-U3**, WPC
piano Klavier **5-U1**, Sit8
picture Bild **5-U1**, WP
piece Stück, Teil **6-U5**, T2
pig Schwein **6-U1**, Ex19
pitcher Werfer **6-U7**, Sit3
pity, it's a schade **6-U5**, Com
pizza Pizza **5-U4**, WPA
place Ort, Platz **5-U6**, WPA
plan Plan **5-U2**, WPB
plane Flugzeug **5-U7**, WPC
plate Teller **5-U4**, WPA
play spielen **5-U1**, Sit7
player Spieler/in **6-U7**, T1
playground Spielplatz **5-U6**, Sit2
please bitte **5-U0**, F
plot Komplott, Verschwörung **6-U4**, T1
plotter Verschwörer/in **6-U4**, T1
pocket Tasche **6-U1**, T1
policeman Polizist **5-U5**, T1
polite höflich **6-U1**, Com
pony Pony **6-U2**, WPA
poor arm **5-U3**, T1
pop (music) Popmusik **5-U1**, Sit7
popular beliebt **6-U1**, Sit2
position Stellung, Lage **6-U7**, T1
post zur Post bringen, aufgeben **5-U6**, Sit1
post office Postamt **5-U6**, WPA
postcard Postkarte **5-U7**, WPD
poster Poster **5-U0**, D
postman Postbote **5-U2**, T1
potato Kartoffel **6-U5**, T1
pound Pfund **5-U4**, WPA
practise üben **5-U1**, PYE
present Geschenk **5-U3**, Sit5

Index

present Gegenwart **6-U5**, Ex6
presenter Moderator/in **6-U1**, T2
president Präsident/in **6-U1**, T2
price Preis **6-U5**, T1
princess Prinzessin **6-U1**, T2
print (out) (aus)drucken **6-U3**, WPB
prison Gefängnis **6-U1**, WPA
prize Preis, Gewinn **6-U4**, Ex3
probably wahrscheinlich **6-U6**, T1
problem Problem **5-U1**, T2
programme Sendung **6-U6**, WPA
project Projekt **6-U2**, Sit2
public öffentlich **5-U5**, T1
pupil Schüler/in **5-U1**, WPB
purse Geldbeutel **6-U5**, Sit2
push schieben, anrempeln **5-U6**, T1
put setzen, stellen, legen **5-U3**, T1
puzzle Rätsel, Geduldsspiel **6-U5**, Ex2

Qq

quarter Viertel **5-U1**, Sit5
queen Königin **6-U1**, WPA
question Frage **5-U2**, Sit2
queue Warteschlange **6-U1**, Sit2
quick schnell **5-U3**, T1
quiet ruhig, still **5-U1**, T2
quiz Quiz **5-U5**, Sit3

Rr

rabbit Kaninchen **5-U3**, WPA
race Rennen **5-U5**, T2
racket Tennisschläger **5-U2**, WPC
radio Radio **5-U1**, T2
rain regnen **5-U4**, Sit1
rain Regen **6-U1**, Ex13
read lesen **5-U1**, Sit7
ready fertig, bereit **5-U1**, T1
real echt **5-U3**, Sit4
really wirklich **5-U5**, Sit3
record aufnehmen **6-U6**, T2
recycle wiederaufbereiten, wiederverwerten **6-U7**, Sit4
red rot **5-U0**, C
redwood Redwood **6-U7**, WPA
relative Verwandte/r **5-U7**, WPC
remember sich erinnern **5-U6**, Ex6
repeat wiederholen **5-U5**, Ex17
report Bericht **6-U3**, T1
resolution Vorsatz, Beschluss **6-U3**, Ex2
resort Ferienort **6-U7**, WPA
rest Rest **6-U6**, Ex14
result Ergebnis **6-U3**, WPC
rich reich **6-U6**, WPC
ride Karussell, Fahrt **5-U7**, Sit4
ride fahren **5-U2**, Sit3
ridge Bergkamm, Grat **6-U7**, WPA
riding accident Reitunfall **5-U6**, T1
right rechts **5-U6**, WPB
right richtig **5-U1**, T1
ring anrufen **6-U2**, T2
river Fluss, Strom **6-U1**, WPA
road Straße **5-U1**, Sit6
robot Roboter **6-U5**, Sit1
room Zimmer **5-U1**, Ex4
rough uneben, rau **5-U5**, T2
round Runde **6-U6**, WPC
round umher, um … herum **5-U2**, Song
royal königlich **6-U1**, T2
rubbish Abfall, Müll **5-U5**, T2
rule Regel **6-U1**, Ex10
ruler Lineal **5-U0**, D
run laufen **5-U3**, WPA

Ss

sad traurig **6-U2**, T2
safari Safari **6-U6**, WPA
salad Salat **5-U4**, WPA
sale Verkauf, Ausverkauf **6-U5**, T2
same gleich **5-U1**, Sit6
sandwich Sandwich, belegtes Brot **5-U1**, T2
Saturday Samstag, Sonnabend **5-U1**, Sit4
sausage Wurst **5-U4**, WPA
save sparen **6-U5**, T1
say sagen **5-U2**, Sit2
scene Szene **6-U1**, T2
school Schule **5-U1**, WPB
science (Natur-)Wissenschaft **6-U6**, WPA
screen Bildschirm, Leinwand **6-U3**, WPB
sea Meer, die See **6-U2**, Sit3
search (for) suchen (nach) **6-U3**, WPC
seaside Meeresküste **5-U7**, WPA
seat Sitz, Sitzplatz **5-U7**, T2
see sehen **5-U0**, B
see you bis dann!, tschüss! **5-U0**, B
sell verkaufen **6-U5**, WPB
send schicken **6-U3**, WPC
sentence Satz **5-U5**, Ex1
September September **5-U4**, Sit5
series Serie **6-U6**, WPA
serious ernst **6-U3**, T2
seven sieben **5-U0**, G
seventeen siebzehn **5-U0**, G
seventy siebzig **5-U4**, WPA
sh Psst **5-U1**, Sit3
she sie **5-U1**, Sit2
shed Schuppen, Stall **5-U3**, T2
sheep Schaf **6-U2**, WPA
shelf Regal, Ablage **5-U5**, Sit1
shirt Hemd **5-U0**, C
shock Schock **6-U2**, T2
shoe Schuh **5-U3**, Sit2
shop Geschäft **5-U4**, Sit1
shopping centre Einkaufszentrum **5-U6**, WPB
short kurz **6-U1**, Ex3
should sollte(n) **6-U6**, T2
shout schreien, rufen **5-U6**, T2
show Sendung **5-U5**, Sit3
show zeigen **6-U1**, Ex21
side Seite **6-U2**, T1
sights Sehenswürdigkeiten **6-U1**, WPA
sightseeing Besichtigungen **6-U4**, PYE6
sign Schild, Zeichen **5-U7**, T1
signal Signal **6-U4**, T2
silicon Silikon **6-U7**, WPA
silly albern **5-U1**, T1
simple einfach, schlicht **6-U5**, Ex13
sing singen **5-U1**, Ex13
singer Sänger/in **6-U1**, T2
sir mein Herr **5-U1**, Ex7
sister Schwester **5-U0**, I
sit sitzen; sich hinsetzen **5-U0**, F
Sit down. Setz dich hin. Setzt euch hin. **5-U0**, F
site Stelle, Platz **5-U7**, WPD
situation Situation **5-U1**, Sit1
six sechs **5-U0**, G
sixteen sechzehn **5-U0**, G
sixty sechzig **5-U4**, WPA
size Größe **5-U4**, Sit4
skate Rollschuh laufen **5-U5**, WPA
skate park Skatinggelände **5-U5**, T1
ski Ski fahren **6-U7**, WPA
skirt Rock **6-U6**, Ex3
sky Himmel **5-U7**, T2
skyway Himmelsweg **6-U7**, WP Song
sleep schlafen **6-U2**, Sit4
slogan Slogan, Parole, Wahlspruch **6-U1**, Ex14
slow langsam **5-U5**, Ex1

Index

small klein **5-U2**, WPA
smell riechen **5-U3**, WPB
smile lächeln **6-U1**, T2
snack Imbiss **5-U5**, PYE5
so so **5-U7**, Sit4
soap opera Seifenoper **6-U6**, WPA
soft weich, zart **6-U4**, T2
softball Softball **6-U3**, T2
soldier Soldat, Soldatin **6-U4**, T1
some etwas, ein wenig; einige, ein paar **5-U4**, Sit1
someone jemand **6-U2**, Sit2
something etwas **5-U4**, Sit3
sometimes manchmal **5-U1**, T1
son Sohn **6-U1**, Sit1
song Lied **5-U0**, J
soon bald **6-U5**, T1
sorry tut mir Leid **5-U1**, Sit1
sound Klang, Laut **5-U5**, Ex17
sound klingen **6-U7**, T1
south Süden **6-U1**, WPA
space Lücke, Raum, Platz **5-U5**, Ex18
spare time Freizeit **5-U5**, WPA
speak sprechen **5-U1**, Sit8
special spezial, besonder(e,er) **6-U4**
spell buchstabieren **5-U0**, J
spelling Rechtschreibung **6-U7**, Sit1
spider Spinne **6-U4**, WPD
splash besprize, platschen **6-U7**, T2
sponsor finanziell unterstützen **6-U5**, Com
sport Sport **5-U2**, Sit1
spot Fleck(en) **5-U7**, Ex13
spring Frühling, Frühjahr **6-U4**, T1
square Platz **6-U7**, T2
stamp Briefmarke **5-U6**, Sit1
stand stehen; sich hinstellen **5-U0**, F
Stand up! Steh auf!, Steht auf! **5-U0**, F
star (Film)star **5-U1**, Sit2
start anfangen **5-U4**, WPA
state Staat; Zustand **6-U7**
station Bahnhof, Station **5-U7**, T2
stay bleiben, wohnen **5-U7**, Sit1
steal stehlen **6-U5**, T1
steep steil **6-U7**, WPA
stereo Stereogerät **5-U2**, WPC
stew Eintopf **5-U3**, Song
still ruhig **6-U2**, T2
stone Stein **6-U1**, Song
stop anhalten, aufhören **6-U2**, Sit2
story Geschichte **6-U2**, T1
straight ahead geradeaus **5-U6**, WPB

strange merkwürdig **6-U2**, T2
stream Bach **6-U2**, WPB
street Straße **6-U1**, WPB
stretcher Tragbahre **6-U2**, T2
stupid dumm, blöd **5-U3**, T2
subject Schulfach **5-U6**, T1
suddenly plötzlich **6-U2**, T2
sugar Zucker **5-U4**, Sit1
suggestion Vorschlag **5-U5**, Ex18
summer Sommer **5-U4**, Sit5
sun Sonne **6-U2**, Sit3
Sunday Sonntag **5-U1**, Sit4
supermarket Supermarkt **5-U2**, Sit4
support unterstützen **5-U2**, T1
sure sicher **5-U1**, Sit3
surfing Surfen **6-U7**, WPA
swallow Schwalbe **6-U2**, WPB
swap tauschen **5-U2**, Ex1
sweater Pullover **5-U0**, C
sweets Süßigkeiten **6-U4**, T2
swim schwimmen **5-U1**, Sit8
swimming-pool Schwimmbad **5-U6**, WPA
swing Schaukel **5-U3**, T1
switch on anschalten, einschalten **6-U3**, T2

Tt

T-shirt T-shirt **5-U4**, Sit3
table Tisch **5-U1**, T2
take nehmen **5-U4**, WPA
take dauern, Zeit in Anspruch nehmen **6-U5**, Ex2
take a photo ein Foto machen **5-U5**, WPB
talk reden **5-U2**, T2
tall groß **6-U6**, Com
tape Tonband, Videoband **6-U6**, T2
taxi Taxi **5-U7**, Ex6
tea Abendessen **5-U3**, Sit1
tea Tee, Schwarzer Tee **5-U4**, WPA
teach unterrichten **6-U3**, T1
teacher Lehrer/in **5-U0**, D
team Team, Mannschaft **5-U1**, Ex17
technology Technik **6-U3**, T1
teenager Teenager **6-U6**, WPA
telephone Telefon **5-U1**, PYE6
television Fernsehen **5-U1**, Sit6
tell erzählen, mitteilen **5-U5**, WPB
temple Tempel, Kultstätte **6-U4**, WPB
ten zehn **5-U0**, G

tennis Tennis **5-U2**, WPC
term Semester, Trimester **5-U4**, Sit5
terrible schrecklich **5-U6**, T2
test testen, ausprobieren **6-U6**, WPA
test Test, Schulaufgabe **6-U5**, Com
text Text **5-U1**, T1
textbook Lehrbuch **5-U3**, Ex11
than als **6-U1**, Sit3
thank you danke **5-U0**, B
thanks danke **5-U0**, B
that der, die, das (dort) **5-U0**, D
the der, die, das **5-U0**, D
their ihr, ihre, ihr **5-U1**, WPB
theirs ihre(r, s) **6-U3**, Sit3
them sie, ihnen **5-U2**, Sit5
then dann **5-U1**, Sit7
then also, nun **5-U3**, Sit1
there dort **5-U1**, Ex4
there are es gibt, es sind vorhanden **5-U1**, WPA
there is es gibt, es ist vorhanden **5-U1**, WPA
these diese **5-U3**, Sit2
they sie **5-U1**, WPB
thing Sache, Gegenstand **5-U4**, T2
think denken, meinen **5-U1**, T2
thirteen dreizehn **5-U0**, G
thirty dreißig **5-U1**, Sit5
this dieser, diese, dieses, dies **5-U0**, D
those jene **5-U3**, Sit2
thousand tausend **5-U7**, T2
three drei **5-U0**, G
through durch **6-U2**, T1
throw werfen **5-U6**, Ex4
Thursday Donnerstag **5-U1**, Sit4
ticket Fahrkarte; Eintrittskarte **6-U1**, T1
tidy aufräumen **5-U5**, Sit1
tiger Tiger **6-U3**, Ex3
time Zeit **5-U0**, B
timetable Stundenplan **5-U1**, PYE1
tin Büchse, Dose **6-U5**, Sit2
tired müde **5-U6**, T1
to zu **5-U0**, B
toast Toast **5-U4**, WPB
today heute **5-U0**, G
together zusammen **5-U5**, Ex6
tomorrow morgen **6-U2**, Sit2
tonight heute abend **6-U4**, Ex2
too auch **5-U0**, G
too zu **5-U5**, Ex1
top Spitze, Gipfel **5-U7**, T2

one hundred and sixty-five **165**

Index

torture Folter, Qual **6-U1**, T2
tough robust, hart, zäh **6-U4**, T2
tour Rundfahrt, Führung **6-U1**, WPA
tourist Tourist/in **6-U1**, Sit2
tower Turm **6-U1**, WPA
town Stadt **5-U6**, WPA
toy Spielzeug **6-U5**, T2
traffic Verkehr **6-U6**, T2
train Zug **5-U7**, WPA
trampolining Trampolinspringen **6-U5**, Sit4
travel reisen **5-U7**, WPA
tree Baum **5-U3**, PYE2
trip Reise **6-U4**, PYE6
truck LKW **6-U7**, Ex1
try versuchen **5-U5**, T1
tube U-Bahn **6-U1**, WPB
Tuesday Dienstag **5-U1**, Sit4
tunnel Tunnel **6-U4**, T1
turn einbiegen **5-U6**, WPB
turn drehen **6-U6**, T1
turning Abzweigung **6-U6**, T1
tutor Betreuungslehrer/in, Klassenlehrer/in **5-U1**, WPB
TV Fernsehen **5-U6**, Ex9
twelve zwölf **5-U0**, G
twenty zwanzig **5-U0**, G
twice zweimal **6-U5**, Sit4
twin Zwilling **6-U6**, WPA
two zwei **5-U0**, G
type (in) (ein)tippen **6-U3**, WPC

Uu

umbrella Regenschirm **5-U0**, D
uncle Onkel **5-U1**, Song
under unter **5-U3**, T1
underground U-Bahn **6-U1**, WPB
understand verstehen **6-U6**, Sit1
uniform Uniform **5-U1**, WPB
unit Unit, Lektion **5-U1**
until bis **6-U5**, Sit2
up hinauf, herauf, nach oben **5-U0**, F
up-to-date aktuell, modern **6-U3**, WPD
us uns **5-U2**, Sit5
use gebrauchen, verwenden **5-U5**, WPB
usually gewöhnlich **5-U5**, WPB

Vv

vacation Ferien **6-U7**, Sit1
valley Tal **6-U7**, WPA
verb Verb, Tunwort **5-U5**, Ex1
very sehr **5-U1**, Sit1

vet Tierarzt, Tierärztin **6-U5**, WPD
video (cassette) Videocassette **5-U4**, T2
view Ausblick **5-U7**, T2
village Dorf **6-U2**, Sit3
visit besuchen, besichtigen **5-U3**, Ex16
visitor Besucher/in **6-U6**, WPD
voice Stimme **6-U2**, T2

Ww

wait warten **5-U5**, T2
walk gehen, wandern **5-U2**, Sit3
walkman Walkman **5-U4**, T1
wall Mauer, Wand **5-U2**, T2
want wollen **5-U2**, T2
wardrobe (Kleider)Schrank **5-U2**, WPC
warm warm **6-U3**, Sit1
warn warnen **6-U4**, T2
was war **5-U6**, T1
wash (sich) waschen **6-U2**, Sit2
wash away wegspülen **6-U1**, Song
wash up abspülen **6-U4**, Ex11
watch Uhr **5-U1**, T2
watch sehen, beobachten **5-U1**, Sit6
water Wasser **5-U4**, WPA
waterfall Wasserfall **6-U7**, WPA
waxwork Wachsfigur **6-U1**, Sit2
way Art und Weise **6-U1**, Ex4
way Weg **5-U1**, Sit7
we wir **5-U1**, Sit1
wear tragen **5-U4**, Sit3
weather Wetter **5-U7**, WPD
website Website **6-U3**, WPC
Wednesday Mittwoch **5-U1**, Sit4
week Woche **5-U1**, Sit3
weekend Wochenende **5-U1**, Sit4
welcome Willkommen **6-U7**, T1
well gut **6-U6**, Sit3
well nun **5-U1**, Sit8
Welsh walisisch **5-U7**, T1
west Westen **6-U1**, Sit1
what was **5-U0**, A
what about? wie wär's mit … ? **5-U2**, WPA
What colour is … ? Welche Farbe hat … ? **5-U0**, C
what's was ist **5-U0**, A
wheel Rad **5-U3**, WPA
wheelchair Rollstuhl **5-U6**, T1
when wann **5-U4**, Ex14
when als **5-U6**, T1
when (immer) wenn **5-U7**, Sit4
where wo **5-U0**, J

which welche(r, s) **6-U1**, WPB
white weiß **5-U0**, C
who wer **5-U1**, T2
whose wessen **5-U6**, Sit3
why warum **5-U4**, T1
wife Ehefrau **6-U1**, Sit1
wild wild, ungezügelt **6-U2**, T1
will werden **6-U5**, Sit1
win gewinnen **5-U4**, Sit1
window Fenster **5-U0**, D
wine Wein **6-U7**, WPA
winter Winter **6-U4**, T2
with mit **5-U1**, Sit2
without ohne **6-U5**, T1
woman Frau **5-U3**, Sit3
wonderful wunderbar **5-U7**, WPD
wood Holz **6-U1**, Song
woof Wauwau **5-U7**, T1
word Wort **5-U0**, J
work arbeiten **5-U2**, Sit4
work Arbeit **5-U1**, Sit7
world Welt **6-U1**, T1
worry sich sorgen **6-U1**, T1
worse schlechter **6-U1**, Sit4
worst am schlechtesten **6-U1**, Sit4
worth wert **6-U6**, T2
would like möchte gern **5-U4**, WPA
wow Mann!, Wahnsinn! **6-U3**, T2
write schreiben **5-U3**, Com
wrong falsch **5-U2**, Ex5
wrote schrieb **6-U3**, T2

Yy

year Jahr **5-U1**, Sit3
yellow gelb **5-U0**, C
yes ja **5-U0**, B
yesterday gestern **6-U2**, Sit1
yet: not … yet noch nicht **6-U4**, Sit3
yet: … yet? schon **6-U4**, Sit3
yoghurt Joghurt **5-U4**, WPA
you du, ihr, Sie **5-U0**, A
you were du warst, ihr wart, Sie waren **6-U2**, Sit1
You're lucky. Du hast Glück. Du bist gut dran. **5-U1**, T1
young jung **6-U2**, WPB
your dein, deine, dein, ihr, ihre, ihr **5-U0**, A
yours deine(r, s) **6-U3**, Sit2

Zz

zoo Zoo, Tierpark **5-U3**, Ex16

Umschlag	David Graham
Illustrationen	Kim Lane, Angus Montrose
Cartoons	Wendy Sinclair (*Raben*), David Banks, Peter Muggleston
Fotos	David Graham, Picturefile
zusätzliche Fotos	Kate Anderson *(S. 22)*, Attic Futura (UK) Ltd. *(S. 79)*, Australian Tourist Commission *(S. 47)*, BBC Worldwide Ltd. (Walking with Dinosaurs) *(S. 79)*, www.Britney.com *(S. 35)*, Allan Cash Photolibrary *(S. 4, 10/x2, 15, 22, 47/x3, 50, 58, 60, 82/x2, 94, 102, 105, 110/x4)*, Celador Ltd. *(S. 79)*, Paul.Dixon@albermarle-london.com *(S. 17)*, Harrods Ltd. *(S. 10)*, Helga Holtkamp *(S. 46, 63)*, Hulton Getty Images *(S. 100)*, ICN Co-ordination Bureau *(S. 70)*, Independent on Sunday *(S. 49)*, London Transport Museum *(S. 5, 10)*, Madame Tussaud's London *(S. 7, 14/x4)*, Mindscape *(S. 34)*, PWE Kinoarchiv, Hamburg *(S. 73)*, Qdos Entertainment *(S. 17)*, The Rock Circus, London *(S. 10)*, Safeway Supermarkets *(S. 64)*, Tony Stone Images *(S. 4, 7, 10, 18, 19, 22 48, 58, 66, 70, 78, 94/x3, 100, 102/x2)*, Elke Zahn *(S. 61)*
Textquellen	*A Gorilla* from SILLY RHYMES, Mik Brown (ed.) © Mik Brown 1987 *(S. 109)* *Eletelephony* from SILLY RHYMES, Mik Brown (ed.) © Laura E. Richards 1932, this collection © Mik Brown 1987 *(S. 24)* *Everyday* Words & Music by Norman Petty, Buddy Holly © PEER INTERNATIONAL NEW YORK, für Deutschland PEERMUSIC (GERMANY) GMBH *(S. 17)* *Grizzly Bear* from THE CHILDREN SING IN THE FAR WEST by Mary Austin. Copyright 1928 by Mary Austin, © renewed 1956 by Kenneth M. Chapman and Mary C. Wheelwright. Reprinted by permission of Houghton Mifflin CO *(S. 100)* *Octopus* from SILLY RHYMES, Mik Brown (ed.) © Mik Brown 1987 *(S. 108)* *Rudolph the Red-Nosed Reindeer* Words & Music by Johnny Marks © 1949 by SAINT NICHOLAS MUSIC PUBL./CHAPPEL & CO INC./WARNER CHAPPELL INTERN. MUSIC PUBL. LTD, für Deutschland, GUS und osteuropäische Länder CHAPPEL & CO GMBH, Hamburg *(S. 46)* *San Francisco (Be Sure To Wear Some Flowers in Your Hair)* Words & Music by John Phillips © 1967, 1970 MCA Music USA. MCA Music Limited, 77 Fulham Palace Road, London W6 for the world (excluding North, Central & South America, Japan, Australasia and the Philippines). Used by permission of Music Sales Limited. All Rights Reserved. International Copyright Secured. *(S. 101)* *Yellow Submarine* Words & Music by John Lennon und Paul McCartney © SONY/ATV MUSIC PUBLISHING LLC alle Rechte für Deutschland, Österreich, Schweiz und Osteuropa SONY/ATV MUSIC PUBLISHING (GERMANY) GMBH *(S. 61)* *This land is your land…*, Words & Music by Woody Guthrie © LUDLOW MUSIC INC. Rechte für Deutschland, Österreich, Schweiz und Osteuropa: ESSEX MUSIC VERTRIEB GMBH, Hamburg *(S. 95)*
	Nicht alle Copyrightinhaber konnten ermittelt werden; deren Urheberrechte werden hiermit vorsorglich und ausdrücklich anerkannt.
Acknowledgements	*The publishers wish to thank the staff, pupils, parents and friends of Alleyn's School, Dulwich, London and Carl-von-Linde-Realschule, Staatliche Realschule, Kulmbach for their continued help and assistance. The publishers also wish to thank G.B. Walker & Son for permission to use their farm location and Hartley-Chivers Plc. for use of their warehousing premises.*
Danksagung	Wir danken den Lehrern und Lehrerinnen, den Schülern und Schülerinnen, ihren Eltern und den Freunden der Alleyn's School, Dulwich, London und der Carl-von-Linde-Realschule, Staatliche Realschule, Kulmbach für ihre Hilfe und Unterstützung. Wir danken außerdem G.B. Walker & Son, die ihre Farm und Hartley-Chivers Plc., die ihre Fabrikhallen für Fotoaufnahmen zur Verfügung stellten.

The UNITE

ALASKA

WASHINGTON

OREGON

IDAHO

MONTANA

NEVADA

WYOMING

CALIFORNIA

UTAH

COLORADO

ARIZONA

NEW MEXICO

HAWAII

MEXICO